KU-531-342

AN INTRODUCTION TO CRITICAL MANAGEMENT RESEARCH

MIHAELA KELEMEN AND NICK RUMENS

SAGE

Los Angeles • London • New Delhi • Singapore

© Mihaela Kelemen and Nick Rumens 2008

First published 2008

Apart from any fair dealing for the purposes of research or private study, or criticism or review, as permitted under the Copyright, Designs and Patents Act, 1988, this publication may be reproduced, stored or transmitted in any form, or by any means, only with the prior permission in writing of the publishers, or in the case of reprographic reproduction, in accordance with the terms of licences issued by the Copyright Licensing Agency. Enquiries concerning reproduction outside those terms should be sent to the publishers.

SAGE Publications Ltd
1 Oliver's Yard
55 City Road
London EC1Y 1SP

SAGE Publications Inc.
2455 Teller Road
Thousand Oaks, California 91320

SAGE Publications India Pvt Ltd
B 1/I 1 Mohan Cooperative Industrial Area
Mathura Road
New Delhi 110 044

SAGE Publications Asia-Pacific Pte Ltd
33 Pekin Street #02-01
Far East Square
Singapore 048763

Library of Congress Control Number: 2007940379

British Library Cataloguing in Publication data

A catalogue record for this book is available from the British Library

ISBN 978-1-4129-0186-4
ISBN 978-1-4129-0187-1 (pbk)

Typeset by C&M Digitals (P) Ltd., Chennai, India
Printed in India at Replika Press Pvt. Ltd
Printed on paper from sustainable resources

SOUTHAMPTON SOLENT
UNIVERSITY LIBRARY
SUPPLIER Dawson L
ORDER No
DATE 3-10-08

543143

658.072 KEL
IWL

ONE WEEK LOAN

AN INTRODUCTION TO CRITICAL MANAGEMENT RESEARCH

Southampton
SOLENT
University

MOUNTBATTEN LIBRARY
Tel: 023 8031 9249

Please return this book no later than the date stamped.
Loans may usually be renewed - in person, by phone,
or via the web OPAC. Failure to renew or return on time
may result in an accumulation of penalty points.

ONE WEEK LOAN		
28 NOV 2008		
03 FEB 2009		
25 FEB 2009		
-2 MAR 2009		
23 MAR 2009		

0095906 9Z

Contents

Acknowledgements

A number of people are owed thanks for their support, without which this book would not have reached completion.

Mihaela I would like to thank colleagues and friends at Keele University for their intellectual stimulation, moral support and great sense of humour, in particular Paul Willis, Dirk Bunzel, Matthias Klaes, Gordon Pearson and Rolland Munro. Many thanks to my PhD students, Beverley Hawkins, Teresa Oultram and Lindsay Hamilton, for aving such bright minds and keeping me always alert to what is happening in other fields of research. I owe special thanks to my work collaborators and friends, Martin Kilduff, Tuomo Peltonen, Tima Bansal and John Hassard for sharing so generously with me their erudite knowledge. Martin Parker's careful and critical commentary and genuine belief in the potential of this book have meant a great deal. Thank you!

Last but not least, my gratefulness goes to my family, in particular to my husband, Csabi, and my son, Michael, who have been more than understanding while I was writing the book. Without them, nothing would be worthwhile in my world!

Nick I would also like to thank colleagues at Keele University for their support and words of wisdom – they have given me plenty to think about. Colleagues and friends at Southampton Solent University have also been kind and generous in their words of encouragement and providing other resources that allowed this project to reach fruition. Of these individuals, Matthew Cannon is singled out for his unflagging support, faith and his stature as a friend in whom I could always confide whenever my confidence failed me. Similarly, my closest friends have performed a magnificent role of helping me in so many ways that, for reasons of keeping my acknowledgements concise, I could not hope to document here. However, I wish to name the following individuals, all of whom deserve special thanks: Trish Buckley, Beverley Hawkins, Su Holmes, Danny Macdonald, Chris Stevens, Cathie Turner-Jones and Sam Warren. Heartfelt thanks also to my parents, Susan and Gerald Rumens, and to my brother Adam. Finally, and most of all, I thank my partner Peter for his endless patience, warmth and generosity of spirit that has enabled me to work tirelessly on this project for some time. This book is for Peter as much as it is for Susan and Gerald.

Finally, we would like to thank Delia Alfonso from Sage Publications for her enthusiasm, kindness, patience and practical help in getting this book over various publishing hurdles. Additional thanks also go to the production team at Sage for their patience and commitment.

We also need to acknowledge the use of material in this book that has appeared elsewhere, although it has been expanded upon and revised. This is as follows:

Hassard, J. and Kelemen, M. L. (2002) 'Production and consumption in organizational knowledge: the case of the "paradigms debate"', *Organization*, 9 (2): 331–355.

Kelemen, M. and Bansal, P. (2002) 'The conventions of management research and their relevance to management practice', *British Journal of Management* 13 (2): 97–108.

Kelemen, M. and Peltonen, T. (2001) 'Ethics, morality and the subject: the contribution of Zygmunt Bauman and Michel Foucault to "postmodern" business ethics', *Scandinavian Journal of Management*, 17 (2): 151–166.

Kelemen, M. (2000) 'Too much or too little ambiguity: the language of total quality management', *Journal of Management Studies*, 37 (4): 483–498.

Kelemen, M. (2003) *Managing Quality: Managerial and Critical Perspectives*. London: Sage.

Kilduff, M. and Kelemen, M. (2004) Deconstructing discourse. In D. Grant, C. Hardy, C. Oswick, N. Phillips, and L. Putnam (eds), *The SAGE Handbook of Organizational Discourse*, pp. 259–272. London: Sage.

Mihaela L. Kelemen and Nick Rumens
November 2007

Introduction

This book explores the relationship between critical theory and management research. One of the main motivations for writing this text is because we strongly feel that critical theory matters not only to academics within university business schools, but also to all those individuals involved in management research. The debates contained within the book are set against and in synch with the main intellectual currents that form the contemporary field of Critical Management Studies (CMS). Over the last decade or so there has been considerable growth in the interest shown by business school academics in the potential of CMS to generate anti-oppressive and emancipatory forms of research. We would also include ourselves in the swelling numbers of scholars who are committed to the spirit of CMS. For it is our belief that CMS is a very fertile site for crafting critical management research that challenges management knowledge by questioning the purposes it may serve and the sort of practices and taken-for-granted conventions/norms it helps to (re)produce. As such, critical theory has a vital role to play in that endeavour and is, therefore, of great value to management researchers.

In that regard, we follow a number of scholars before us who have written about the importance of doing critical management research (Alvesson and Deetz, 2000; Alvesson and Wilmott, 1992, 1996). Our contribution to the critical wing of management research builds upon the foundations already established by the works cited above. For example, we similarly understand critical theory in two broad ways: first, as a label to denote a specific branch or school of academic thought; second, as a process of critique that has an emancipatory quality. Regarding the latter, the anti-oppressive/emancipatory goal of critical theory derives from embracing any one (or all) of the three concerns described by Fournier and Grey (2000). First, an attempt to question the performative intent of managerial practices that regard management as a wholly desirable and unproblematic phenomenon; second, the denaturalisation of management by deconstructing management rhetoric in order to discover what certain taken-for-granted management discourses conceal or erase; third, an emphasis on reflexivity in methodological and philosophical terms. All of this foreshadows the discussion that will be developed later in this book.

While much excellent work has already been done in pointing up the need for critical perspectives that overturn well-established ways of thinking about the world of management, there is further scope for expanding the range of critical theories available to management researchers for developing forms of emancipatory critical management research. With this in mind, the book makes three claims to distinctiveness in how it approaches the task of (re)introducing critical perspectives on management research.

First, while we acknowledge and commend the previous efforts of those who have committed themselves to providing theoretical and practical guidance to doing critical management research (Alvesson and Deetz, 2000), we include examples of theory that have largely been overlooked or sidelined within mainstream and critical management theory: American pragmatism, postmodernism, deconstructionism, poststructuralist feminism and queer theory. Our principal motivation for assembling these specific theories in the book is because we have, at various times in our teaching and research activities, been frustrated with the subject of critical management research. To our minds, texts in this area tend to concentrate on critical theory within well established, albeit limited, parameters. For instance, critical theory has a close association with the work of academics belonging to 'the Frankfurt School'. As we acknowledge in Chapter 1, the influence of the Frankfurt School scholars (e.g., Theodor Adorno, Max Horkheimer, Herbert Marcuse and Jürgen Habermas) on developing a specific form of emancipatory critique has been far-reaching. Previous texts on critical management research acknowledge the legacy of the Frankfurt School for providing us with a rich intellectual heritage that has informed later developments within critical theory such as the emergence of postmodern theories.

Books such as Alvesson and Deetz's *Doing Critical Management Research* (2000) are widely acknowledged as making a good job of covering the development of critical theory in management research, from Marx to the Frankfurt School to postmodernism. It is not our intention to rehash and regurgitate these discussions here. Readers of this book wanting a comprehensive history of these theoretical contributions to the realm of organisation theory are advised to go to texts such as that of Alvesson and Deetz (2000). In reading them, however, they may also note that these books often present an analysis of critical theory within a well-ploughed Marx-Frankfurt School-Postmodernism furrow. As Alvesson and Deetz comment:

> **Critical management research may, of course, be conducted in a multitude of ways. There are many sources of theoretical inspiration – of which we have only addressed Frankfurt School critical theory and some versions of postmodernism – and many ways of engaging in research practices.** (2000: 208)

Since Alvesson and Deetz's contribution other books have been published that convey the diversity of theoretical perspectives that have emerged in the wake of the postmodern turn within the social sciences. For instance, Steven Linstead's *Organization Theory and Postmodern Thought* (2004) provides a stimulating collection of edited essays that explore the relevance of critical theory perspectives deriving from the work of the grand theorists associated with the postmodern tradition: Foucault, Lyotard, Derrida,

Baudrillard, to mention but a few. As insightful as such publications are, theoretical explorations of this kind do not seem to run deeply in current texts that explore how these theories have informed the process of doing critical management research.

It is with this observation in mind that we have constructed this text in order to incorporate a range of theories that seldom (if at all) rub shoulders together in one place. The assemblage of theories which form the spinal column of this book is a representation of those theories already afforded a generous degree of accommodation within the canon of critical management theory (postmodernism) and theories that require (greater) inclusion (American pragmatism, deconstructionism, poststructuralist feminism, and queer theory). In regard to the latter group of theories it is worth noting that some have barely made an impression on critical management research – American pragmatism most particularly. As such, our aim is to introduce these theories as new sources of theoretical inspiration for management researchers.

Undeniably, the choice of theories within this book is entirely a product of our combined subjectivity. What is presented here is a selection influenced by our own preferences, political affiliations and identity claims, so we acknowledge that the book might fall short in the eyes of others who view critical theory differently. It is clear that we favour those theories that exhibit connections to and are largely (and potentially) sympathetic towards the theoretical positions within postmodernism. It is inevitable that by putting forward our medley of critical theories, alternative theories are excluded. This does not mean, however, those theoretical perspectives that did not make it into the final line up are therefore deemed by us to be intellectually redundant (we will return to this point in the book's Concluding Reflections). Ideally, students would read other (management) theory texts that explore specific critical theories that fall outside our selection (such as critical realism, Marxism, the theoretical work of the Frankfurt School, postcolonial theories, and so on), so as to further their exploration of critical theory and complement the reading of this text.

The second way in which this book claims distinctiveness is that we have developed it by drawing upon a wide range of scholarly materials that employ different research methodologies and methods. We have marshalled together seminal studies in management alongside informed empirical analyses of organisations so as to enable the reader to make their own assessments of the (potential) value of each critical theory. Bringing together such a wide array of academic sources into one text is, in our view, of much value to those readers wanting explicit signposting to help them to develop deeper insights into the theories that make up the backbone of the book. What is more, since this is a book that holds critical theory as one of its main concerns, we try whenever possible to make the theoretical content accessible to most readers. This is an important aim because some theoretical perspectives and approaches – like deconstruction and queer theory – have often been criticised for being wrapped up in dense conceptual language. It is our intention to provide a readable and illustrative account of some aspects of these theories, supplying the stimuli for readers to at least consider the empirical possibilities of some theories they might not ordinarily favour.

Lastly, the book is distinct is the particular way in which it taps into debates about the (in)commensurability of paradigms. While many existing texts on management theory underscore the importance of the notion of paradigm for conceptually framing empirical analysis, not all advocate multi-paradigm research. This is not to say that organisational scholars are not interested in multi-paradigm research. Far from it. Academic debates on the (in)commensurability of paradigms have raged on for the past few decades. These arguments are pertinent to the critical study of management because whether one is an adherent or opponent of the (in)commensurability paradigm thesis will dramatically shape a researcher's approach to doing critical management research. Rather, acknowledging the growth in interest and application of multi-paradigm approaches to research we wish to point up (but not impose) the benefits of this approach for critical management researchers. The line of reasoning this book follows is that borderlines between paradigms are pliable and that connections may be formed between the theoretical components of certain paradigms. Making these sorts of inter-paradigm connections does not amount to an 'anything goes' approach; moreover, multi-paradigm research is always constrained by the theoretical contours of any given paradigm. Yet, as the book goes on to show, multi-paradigm research can open up exciting possibilities for generating theoretically sophisticated and innovative empirical analysis.

Purpose and outline of the book

With the above in mind, we have developed the book for final year undergraduate and graduate students wishing to develop critical forms of management research. Our aim is to provide students as well as business school academics with a stimulating, postmodern-slanted introduction on critical theory within the field of management research.

Part I: Theory and paradigms

The book is broadly, though not equally, divided into four parts. Part I contains two chapters. The first chapter, 'Critical Theory: an introduction', aims to make clear to the reader the crucial role theory has to play within critical management research. This chapter will introduce some of the complex but lively academic perspectives on the notion of 'critical theory', most particularly how critical theory has been variously understood and the idea that the 'non-critical' can be separated from the 'critical'. This chapter is largely informed by current debates on critical theory within the field of CMS, an intellectual project aimed at generating anti-oppressive/emancipatory forms of research. Chapter 2, entitled 'Organisational paradigms and management research', then explores the importance of organisational paradigms in doing critical management research. The chapter reviews Burrell and Morgan's (1979) and Guba and Lincoln's (1994) well-known paradigm typologies. The former is credited to have sparked the so-called 'paradigm incommensurability' thesis, a position which suggests that 'a synthesis between paradigms is not possible, since in their pure form (paradigms) are contradictory, being based on at least one set of meta-theoretical assumptions' (Burrell and Morgan, 1979: 25).

As the paradigm incommensurability debate rages on, management studies appears increasingly fragmented and reflexive. Many researchers, despite their differing theoretical stances, recognise that adopting a single paradigm is limiting, as each paradigm exposes certain facets of organisations while obscuring others (Burrell, 1996; Weick, 1999). This chapter puts forward the view that multi-paradigm research may be of great benefit for critical management researchers. In summary, Part I of the book establishes a foundation for exploring how the world of management can be viewed and understood from different critical theoretical perspectives.

Part II: Theoretical perspectives on management

Part II contains five chapters that, taken together, form the core of the book's theoretical content. Across these chapters we provide examples of critical perspectives that may be used to promote and advance forms of critical management research. In this vein, Chapter 3, 'American Pragmatism', explores the potential contribution of early American pragmatist theory. The chapter argues that American pragmatist theories represent a largely untapped theoretical resource for management researchers. The chapter offers a short history of American pragmatism and underlines its distinct emphasis on the value of crafting social and political practice over abstract theory. Referring to the work of one of its founding figures, John Dewey, the chapter provides details of pragmatism's theoretical building blocks, its rise to popularity and its relative obscurity within the field of management. Here, our efforts to introduce American pragmatism to a new audience form part of a renewed interest in the key ideas of pragmatist philosophy among a wide range of scholars including feminists (Mottier, 2007; Seigfried, 1996). After advancing a rationale for using pragmatism in management research, we sketch out some of the challenges involved in mobilising some of pragmatism's most useful conceptual resources.

Chapter 4, 'Postmodernism', reviews the contribution of postmodernist theorising, arguing that postmodernism is a viable and useful set of theoretical approaches for doing critical management research. The chapter outlines what is central to the postmodern movement of ideas in management science and what are simply damaging, unsubstantiated myths. In doing so, we argue that postmodernism is a critical stance as opposed to a nihilistic one. At this stage, readers may also find points of connection between the central tenets of American pragmatism and postmodernism. To enhance the pragmatic value of management research and at the same time ensure that postmodern theories of management are rigorous, ethical and emancipatory, we argue that researchers have to scrutinise the practical relevance of their ideas for the larger community and the extent to which they make a difference to existing social and cultural practices. This is not an easy task for it requires the researcher to shift mental gears continuously and be prepared to explore unorthodox paths of research. One such unorthodox research path within the postmodern tradition is deconstruction.

Chapter 5, 'Deconstruction', provides an overview of deconstructive analysis. The chapter aims to draw out the spirit of deconstruction: its desire to displace the taken-for-granted meanings of a text through a restless search for alternative meanings while accounting for the impossibility of a final interpretation. Put simply, deconstruction is interested in what is absent from the text as much as what is present. After summarising Jacques Derrida's views (the philosopher most heavily associated with deconstruction), the chapter provides examples of deconstructive analysis in the field of management. We appraise the value of deconstruction positively insomuch that it can, vociferations to the contrary, shed light on those aspects of evidence in management texts (e.g., seminal academic books, organisational documents, texts) used to substantiate a point of view and discard others. To illustrate the power of deconstruction, we refer to a deconstructive analysis by Kilduff and Kelemen (2004) of Chester Barnard's seminal book *The Functions of the Executive* (1938).

Chapter 6, 'Poststructuralist Feminism', focuses on this specific branch of feminist theorising that, over the past decade or so, has gained in popularity among management researchers. We briefly outline poststructuralist feminism's philosophical heritage before moving to review its key conceptual resources. The chapter aims to show how this collection of feminist perspectives may allow researchers to accentuate certain facets of managers' lives in terms of resistance, identity and subjectivity; notably, issues that are largely obscured in traditional management theory. In that regard, examples are provided to illustrate the value of adopting poststructuralist feminist perspectives to inform discursive empirical analyses of management. The focus on gender is a key concern in these studies and, therefore, carries on the feminist tradition of maintaining gender as an illuminating epistemic category of analysis.

Chapter 7, 'Queer Theory', examines the potential of queer theory as a source of theoretical inspiration for management researchers. We note that queer theory is more closely associated with the body of work belonging to scholars within the field of cultural studies than it is with business school academics. But, as a relatively new academic discipline, management has made connections with other intellectual fields such as sociology, psychology and cultural studies. There is no reason why management researchers cannot look to cultural studies for queer theory perspectives that can be pressed into the service of generating a self-critical and destabilising form of critique on management. Following a similar structure in the previous chapters, we outline some of queer theory's most salient conceptual features, most especially its impulse to destabilise and resist normative discourses, dualisms and ideas. At the same time, we debunk some of the myths surrounding queer theory – e.g., that only gay men, lesbians, bisexuals and other non-heterosexuals can engage with and find relevance in queer theory. What is more, the idea that queer theory merely focuses attention on sexuality is a far too narrow reading of queer theory's potential. We then review the small number of scholarly contributions that have introduced queer theorising into organisational studies. In summary, Part II of the book provides a theoretical platform from which the book can then explore the impact of these critical theories on the traditions of quantitative and qualitative research.

Part III: Methodologies of management research

Part III of the book contains two chapters that explore the methodological choices facing management researchers within and between the traditions of qualitative and quantitative research. Our overarching aim in these two chapters is to point out the ways in which the theories reviewed in Part I of the book have variously influenced the field of qualitative and quantitative research. Chapter 8, 'Critical Perspectives on Quantitative Research', makes clear the point that critical management researchers do not have to dispense with quantitative forms of research. In other words, we do have to throw away numbers in favour of qualitative methodologies that appear to promise better approaches for developing anti-oppressive/emancipatory research. On the basis of this idea, Chapter 8 outlines how critical perspectives have permeated debates on quantitative research. We provide two examples: ethnostatistics and feminist engagements with quantitative forms of research. Our argument is that some critical theories can reformulate approaches to generating quantitative data that are of considerable value for examining the social, cultural, political and economic factors that surround organisational quantification processes.

In a similar vein, Chapter 9, 'Critical Perspectives on Qualitative Research', examines the impact of critical theory on the qualitative research tradition. Using a wider selection of examples taken from the theories presented in Part I, this chapter considers how certain theories have carved out distinct approaches to the generation of qualitative data. The aim here is to signpost some of the more challenging and adventurous, as well as the more frequently trodden, qualitative approaches for doing critical management research. In summary, Part III of the book builds upon existing, well-established arguments that research methodologies and methods are not intrinsically quantitative or qualitative.

Part IV: Consequences of management research

Part IV of the book is comprised of one chapter and the book's Concluding Reflections. Chapter 10, 'Ethics and Reflexivity', introduces the concepts of ethics and reflexivity and outlines the impact of postmodernist, feminist, pragmatist and queer theory approaches to debates on ethics in management research. Though we cannot hope to provide a detailed overview of the complex debates on ethics and reflexivity within the limitations of a single chapter, we seek to underline a crucial point: management researchers encounter a range of ethical/moral questions associated with the design and implementation of research interventions. As this chapter shows, a researcher's ethical positioning reflects not just their own moral viewpoints, but also their location theoretically. This chapter, however, does not offer up neat and tidy answers to resolving the ethical and moral dilemmas that arise in the practice of doing ethically comfortable and reflexive critical management research. Moreover, we highlight the potential offerings of critical theory to help management researchers appreciate and address the complexities of researching aspects of organisational life. Finally, in the book's Concluding Reflections we briefly explicate the major themes that run throughout the text, presenting them as a possible manifesto of ideas and skills for doing critical management research.

How to use this book

While the book is designed in such a way as to permit readers some flexibility in how they approach the theoretical core of the book (here you can read any chapter that appeals), we recommend reading beforehand the two chapters contained in Part I of the book. These chapters establish a wider and informative context on the definition and role of theory and paradigms in critical management research against which the book's later chapters on theory and methodologies are introduced. We would also point out that the theoretical hub of the book is not arranged haphazardly. For those readers wishing to gain a sense of how the theories in Part II interlink, they are advised to read these parts of the book in the order they are presented. This will not only allow the reader to be guided in a largely chronological fashion through the theoretical material, but also to gain a sense of where each theory has points of connection with some of the others. For this purpose we have indicated some of these overlaps. Having read Part I, followed by all or a selection of Part II, readers can then choose to read the chapters in Part III in the order they wish, no doubt influenced by their personal proclivities towards quantitative or qualitative forms of research. Part IV of the book can be read independent of Part III. The book's Concluding Reflections provide a succinct account of the text's main themes that, ideally, should be read last of all, in order to leave the book with a strong impression of our thoughts on critical management research in the present and for the future.

Since this book is an introduction, for reasons of economy we cannot comprehensively cover all the issues we explore. However, it is our intention here to create an appetite for further reading. For example, some book-length projects on the critical theories covered here are a richer source of detail that cannot be captured in a single chapter. As such, at the end of each chapter we provide a number of suggestions for further reading.

Part I

Theory and Paradigms

1

Critical Theory: An Introduction

Introduction

Knowledge of alternative ways of theoretically underpinning critical management research requires an understanding of the role of theory and what makes theory critical. Indeed, since we have already placed much emphasis on the importance of critical theory for generating anti-oppressive, emancipatory and self-critical forms of management research, it seems fitting to begin this book by exploring in a little more detail what theory is, why it matters and to whom. Different conceptions and typologies of theory abound within organisational studies and it is not always easy to detect a general consensus among academics about, for example, what constitutes 'critical theory'. In shedding light on some of these issues, this chapter (the first of two chapters in Part I) performs a crucial role in establishing the background against which the discussion developed in later chapters is set.

The chapter begins by outlining the role of theory in management research. We then briefly discuss the types of theory commonly found in organisation studies: predictive and interpretive theories. Since it is critical theory that concerns us most here, the rest of the chapter unpacks the notion of critical theory. We start by providing a short history of critical theory by pointing out its association with the Frankfurt School and subsequent developments that paved the way to postmodern critical theories. We also provide an illustration of critical theory applied in a management context, before sketching out in more detail how we understand critical theory. Next, we examine some of the conceptual features of critical management research. We do this in three ways. First, we discuss the influence of CMS for furthering critical forms of management research. Second, we examine how scholars have made distinctions between 'non-critical' and 'critical' theories. Third, we argue that being a critical management researcher does not equate to someone who is anti-management. Here we elaborate a nuanced version of what critical management research entails. We then summarise the chapter's main themes and draw out the implications for thinking about paradigmatic approaches to management research.

The role of theory

Popular perceptions suggest theory to be abstract and detached from the 'real life' everyday concerns of people. This conception of theory has often led to criticisms that academics, paid to theorise for a living, have little knowledge of the world around them. *At worst*, common perception suggests that academics occupy ivory towers in which they produce theory that has little relevance for practitioners. It is worth commenting upon this in more detail (see also Kelemen and Bansal, 2002). Numerous commentators have argued that management researchers' interests are different from practitioners' and that is why some researchers pursue 'knowledge for knowledge's sake' (Huff, 2000). These researchers are less interested in how knowledge is used and more concerned with pursuing a line of enquiry. In most cases, such pursuits do not match the concerns and real problems of the practitioners and are perceived as esoteric and irrelevant (Astley and Zammuto, 1992). Other researchers, for example 'critical researchers', make a deliberate choice not to contribute to improving the efficiency of managerial practice in terms defined by current management orthodoxies. Instead, they redefine what counts as best managerial practice in line with the concerns of multiple stakeholders and the society at large (Alvesson and Willmott, 1992, 1996). In so doing, they challenge the 'technical neutrality' of management practice, shifting the research focus on its social and political aspects (Grey and Mitev, 1995), in particular on the moral preferences and commitments inherent in what managers say and do.

From another perspective, academic theorising may not permeate the world of management due to poor dissemination channels (Willmott, 1994), and the lack of communication between researchers and practitioners, particularly once research findings are in the public domain. We do not doubt that many researchers engage successfully in communicating with both managers and other organisational actors during the research process. Many researchers are also very successful in relaying the essence of very complex social science research in the classroom to practitioner audiences of middle and junior managers. However, given that researchers are expected to publish their findings mainly in academic journals, they have no choice but to follow academic writing conventions. These may prevent the practitioner from fully grasping the essence and practical implications of their theoretical insights. This is not to say that practitioners are to be treated as an undifferentiated mass; they vary tremendously, not least in their willingness and ability to handle social science abstractions and management theoretical jargon.

Without needing to develop the argument any further, it is already clear that the relationship between theory and practice is vexed. The crucial point we wish to draw out is that we do not see theory as having little or no relevance for practitioners. After all, any managerial act is influenced by past events or expectations about the future. These serve as theoretical anchors that make individuals (be they managers or workers) think and behave in a certain way. While the tensions arising out of the relationship between theory and practice are very complex and require extensive analysis, we do wish to outline a framework for the role of theory that may inform our readers about the value of theory for management practice.

Here, we draw upon Alvesson and Deetz's careful (2000) assessment of the function of theory. Accepting the idea that theory is better viewed as a way of seeing and thinking about the world around us rather than as an opaque abstract representation of it, theory may have certain roles to play. Alvesson and Deetz contemplate the function of theory in a threefold manner. First, theory is good at 'directing attention'. By that, they mean that theory has a guiding characteristic for it draws our attention to details that are important. Theory helps us to note key differences that assist us in making sense of the world. The problem here is that some differences are presumed to be 'natural' and unproblematic, obscuring other ways of seeing. For example, the interrelationship between sex, gender and sexuality has often been explained and analysed along the lines of human biology. But, noting differences and ascribing them importance is a perceptual matter. Theory can help us to recognise this, prompting us to ask what comes into view and what we can think about if, for example, we could re-consider the linkages between sex, gender and sexuality as culturally constructed.

Second, theory is good at 'organising experience'. In other words, theory helps us to present our observations of the world around us to others. We can then locate our observations as being part of a wider pattern of how humans structure and make sense of the world. The importance attributed to the identification of certain patterns will vary historically, culturally and across time. But the impulse to identify patterns that can help us to specify what things are and how they might be related to other things is a key driver of much social science theorising.

Third, theory 'enables useful responses'. In making this assertion Alvesson and Deetz pinpoint a pragmatic motive behind theory. Theory can be extremely useful for certain individuals or groups of people in helping them to satisfy their needs, as well as designing and building future organisational worlds. Nevertheless, how the pragmatic motive of any given theoretical response is weighed up and decided upon will vary enormously. Issues of importance, as they might pertain to managers, for example, are likely to diverge from those issues considered important by their subordinates. For instance, the useful theoretical responses to management dilemmas of engendering employee motivation, leadership and commitment may well have different features and implications than those orientated towards an employee's point of view.

Just as theory may be conceived of as having different functions, so different types of theory will give different emphasis to the functions of theory outlined above. Before outlining how critical theorists might envisage the role of theory, it is worth discussing the most popular types of logic (deductive and inductive) commonly found in management theory; namely, predictive and interpretive theory.

Deductive logic and predictive theories

Deduction presupposes the testing of theories through the observation of the empirical world. The deductive approach argues that what is important in social science is not the sources of theories or hypotheses that researchers start out with. Rather, it is the process by which those ideas are tested and justified. For example, one may read previous work in the field of leadership and hypothesise that charismatic leadership is positively correlated with organisational commitment. Also, one may gain a similar insight by observing day-to-day organisational practices. In addition, one may simply speculate that this is the case based on past experience and immediate expectations. Indeed, human behaviour rests upon assumptions about what has happened and conjectures about what will happen. In other words, it rests on some sort of theory.

Deductive methodologies were initially employed in the natural sciences, but the social sciences were quick to follow suit. Deductive theories take the shape of hypotheses or propositions that link together two or more concepts in an explanatory/causal fashion (Gill and Johnson, 2002). Concepts are abstract ideas that are used to classify together things sharing one or more properties. Deductive logic entails the development of a conceptual and theoretical structure prior to its testing through empirical observation. Gill and Johnson (2002) discuss four stages of the deductive process that the reader may regard as a useful summary:

1 The researcher decides upon the concepts that represent important aspects of the theory or problem under investigation. These concepts are abstract and cannot be observed empirically.
2 The operationalisation of a concept: the researcher creates rules for making observations so that he/she can determine where an instance of a concept has empirically occurred.
3 The creation of standardised procedures for undertaking observations that can be followed by any other researchers.
4 The comparison of assertions put forward by the theory with the facts collected by observation.

In deductive logic, theory is ta[illegible]sentational of experience. Often associated with a positivistic philosophy [illegible]ductive logic has informed countless studies undertaken by scholars within mainstream management theory. For example, research carried out by Bansal and Clelland (2004) which tests propositions regarding organisations' environmental legitimacy exemplifies poignantly the logical process by which theory is tested in the deductive tradition.

Inductive logic and interpretive theory

Induction is the process of moving from the realm of observation of the empirical world to the construction of explanations (namely, theories) of what has been observed. According to this approach, explanations about the world are relatively worthless unless they are grounded in experience. Human behaviour cannot follow a causal model simply because human actions are infused with values, intentions, attitudes and beliefs. Human action has an internal logic of its own which must be understood in order to make action intelligible. As such, the imposition of an external logic upon human action is inappropriate. The starting point of inductive theorising is the immediate reality; observing, reflecting upon it and constructing explanations about what has been observed are the main methodological steps. Interpretive theorising has no concern for classifying objects, whether they are human or otherwise.

This is a rather unstructured approach for it allows the researcher to get inside situations and reflect upon the way in which individuals and groups construct, negotiate, enact and challenge meaning. Resulting theories may be developed in propositional or story-like form. In the former case, theories provide causal explanations of what has been observed and can be subsequently tested via processes of deduction. In the latter case, theories take a story-like shape and serve as meaning-making devices rather than predictive ones. Two inductive strategies popular in management studies include grounded theory (Glaser and Strauss, 1967) and theory from case study research (Eisenhardt, 1989).

Critical theory

As we have already stated, this book is positioned within the realm of critical theory. Critical theory, however, is a contested term. As we outline in some detail over the remainder of this chapter, how critical theory is understood to be critical among academics varies considerably. First of all, we mentioned in the introduction to this book that critical theory is often deployed as a label denoting a particular school of thought. More specifically, the term 'critical theory' has been heavily associated with the collective works of those scholars affiliated at various times during the twentieth century with the Institute of Social Research at Frankfurt University. These scholars (Theodor

Adorno, Max Horkheimer, Herbert Marcuse and Jurgen Habermas, to name but a few) have been gathered together under the banner of 'The Frankfurt School'. The scholarly works produced by the Frankfurt School scholars is characterised by its Neo-Marxist flavour: the academics within this school of thought sought to develop the ideas and theoretical insights derived from Karl Marx. The theories emerging from the Frankfurt School do not feature in Part II of the book, so it is not our intention to repeat previous detailed accounts provided by organisational scholars on the impact of the Frankfurt School on organisation theory. Readers are directed to Alvesson and Deetz (2000) for a solid overview of the relationship between the Frankfurt School and organisational research. Nonetheless, it is vital to acknowledge the importance of the Frankfurt School for promulgating a type of critique that has become familiar within critical management research.

As a process of emancipatory and self-critical critique, critical theory has an important point of origin in the Frankfurt School. As Carr (2005) points out in an incisive overview of the contributions of the Frankfurt School to organisation theory, Max Horkheimer is credited as the first to use the term 'critical theory' in this way. Running counter to positivism as a scientific methodology and as a philosophy, Horkheimer (1976, cited in Carr, 2005) argued that the social world could not be studied in the same way as the natural world. For Horkheimer the notion of the researcher as an all-knowing subject was very troubling indeed. As Carr (2005) duly notes, Horkheimer's insistence on tackling the epistemological questions surrounding the researcher's claims to knowledge, especially claims to know the 'truth', was pivotal in generating a major turn in critical theorising. From this turning to address epistemological questions, critical theory could be seen as a catalyst to change reality through enlightenment and emancipation. This conception of theory as 'critical' radically departed from what Horkheimer and other members of the Frankfurt School saw as 'traditional theory': theory that claimed to accurately mirror reality. Bearing more than a faint resemblance to orthodox Marxist ambitions to emancipate those enslaved by ideology, the idea of critical theory as an emancipatory and enlightened form of knowledge was central to a great deal of the scholarship to emerge from the Frankfurt School. Notably, the concept of critical theory advanced by Horkheimer and others within the Frankfurt School found resonance with other theories such as those developed by Freud, as well as with later (postmodern/poststructuralist) theorists such as Michel Foucault (1983a: 200), who once praised the work of the Frankfurt School in enthusiastic terms.

While the form of critical theory developed by the Frankfurt School fuelled a critique of ideology and consciousness, the idea of critical theory as an emancipatory project has found fertile ground in which to take root within organisation theory. Needless to say, the targets of critique are not confined to matters of ideology or consciousness, as many postmodern and poststructuralist theorists would point out. Discourse, knowledge and language, for instance, have become prominent targets of critique ever since the postmodern turn within the social sciences.

With the above in mind, we see critical theory as providing a wide umbrella for an array of theoretical perspectives including those drawn from the Frankfurt School, American pragmatism, critical realism, postmodernism and feminism, to name but a few. What is more, these theories might be located within broader frameworks – namely, paradigms (see Chapter 2). We can take two examples to illustrate the point. First, our gathering of critical theories may fall under Guba and Lincoln's (1994) 'critical theories and related positions' paradigm. In broad terms, theoretical perspectives within this paradigm assert that reality is constructed by social, political and cultural factors, solidified into structures that, although not 'real', have material effects on individuals. Second, many of the same theories may find accommodation within Burrell and Morgan's (1979) 'radical humanist' paradigm. Generally speaking, theoretical perspectives within this paradigm take the view that science is a social and political process influenced by ideology and related cultural practices. Both paradigmatic positions are explained in much more detail in Chapter 2, but it is useful to show at this stage how theories may be framed by academics in order to articulate the ontological, epistemological and methodological assumptions upon which specific theories rest. These underpinning assumptions help us to determine in what way theories might be considered critical.

Since critical theory is seen to consist of a broad range of perspectives, it goes without saying that certain theoretical perspectives will conflict with some others. Tensions arise partly due to the variation in both the framing and focal point of critique. For example, the Frankfurt School operates within the Marxist tradition in which its claim to criticality derives from its critique of the hegemony and oppressive effects of ideology. In contrast, postmodernist and poststructuralist theories propose that we live within a linguistic universe. Within this frame, the hegemony of ideology is rejected given its deterministic tendencies. Instead, theoretical positions that draw upon postmodernism and poststructuralism focus on the complex ways in which power is exercised within a network of discursive relations used by individuals to construct identities and subjectivities. Although different in their theoretical frame and focus, we argue that such critical theories are broadly united in their concern to explore material inequalities and in their desire to link critique to action. Seen as such, critical theory can generate arresting analyses, challenge orthodox understandings about management and open up new avenues for thought and advancing management knowledge.

It is useful to provide an example to illustrate this train of thought. One of the co-author's empirical explorations (Kelemen, 2000) of the ambiguity of Total Quality Management (TQM) language sought to narrativise organisational life and build critical theory in the area of TQM. The study was based on ethnographic data collected in four UK service organisations, all of which claimed to have embarked on successful TQM programmes. By focusing on the role of language in the 'production' and 'consumption' of TQM, the study embraced postmodern perspectives that were able to point up the limitations of the prescriptive and interpretive perspectives on TQM that have dominated the literature for at least the last three decades.

The study argued that the language of TQM is a powerful device in the hands of top managers, aimed at producing organisational practices and employees of a certain sort. While managers may have a certain amount of discretion over the use of TQM language, the consequences of using language cannot be predicted or, indeed, known beforehand. In the organisations studied, language was used in semantic and poetic fashions: the former attempted to suppress ambiguity by instilling clarity and specificity, while the latter tapped into ambiguity by inviting multiple interpretations from below. For example, quality related labels were used semantically. By labelling certain practices 'quality improvement projects' (in the mail carrier company) or 'our contribution counts circles' (the logistics company), labels made transparent those behaviours that were valued by the organisation and were to be included in the province of quality. Also, by labelling individuals as 'quality champions' (in the mail carrier and logistics companies) or 'missionaries' (in the logistics' case), or 'dinosaurs' (in the case of mail carrier companies), labels made a clear distinction between those who were in favour and those who opposed TQM. Consequently, quality champions and missionaries reflected a type of employee to be emulated by the rest of the organisation, while the dinosaurs were seen as irresponsible and, therefore, to be disregarded, ignored or punished until their eventual extinction.

Quality related metaphors were used poetically. For example, in the logistics company, top managers used the metaphor of the market (with its associated paraphernalia) to enforce the dominant quality message. Talk about 'internal customers', 'the chain of quality' and 'the customer is king' dominated managerial talk, expressing the commodification of internal organisational relationships. Because of their ability to convey different and multiple meanings, metaphors produced order, coherence and a sense of organisational identity. This may sound counter-intuitive, as the conventional view is that people acquire and share meaning before order is established. However, controversial issues, among which quality was one example, were settled by being specified in a form requiring subsequent interpretation, thus permitting disparate groups and individuals to redefine issues in ways that were relevant to their immediate interests or circumstances.

The concluding theory was that there could never be too much or too little ambiguity that managers could not turn to their advantage in the attempt to construct organisational practices and employees aligned to the managerial logic. This is not to say that ambiguity could be entirely instrumental in its usage by managers (even though they might set out to do just that). Employees' responses to such ambiguity stand firmly in the way. Employees may choose to respond to ambiguity with ambiguity, so that top managers will find themselves in a position of having to decipher the meanings coming from below. Ambiguity may also act as the social glue that binds people together. For example, when employees did not understand what was going on at the top level, they banded together in an attempt to find comforting meanings around ideas of survival.

Thus while top managers attempt to produce employees whose identities are inscribed in the TQM language, their achievements can never be complete. Through a process of interest translation (Latour, 1987), which may suppress or elevate ambiguity, employees are seduced, forced or rationally convinced that TQM is a viable and profitable option for all of them. However, the discursive responses of the employees to the language in use (discourses riddled with ambiguity) cannot be fully controlled or managed from the top. In the companies studied, the discursive strategies ranged from resistance and compliance to the internalisation of managerial language.

In summary, what this illustration shows is the concern critical theory holds for questioning what lies behind TQM rhetoric and the managerial practices that draw from mainstream TQM discourses. In that respect, Kelemen (2000) is an empirical example of a form of critique that embodies a critical epistemology that reveals the ambiguities, contradictions and tensions that arise from acknowledging the multiplicity of reality. The next move in our explication of critical theory concerns what we mean by critical management research.

What is critical management research?

As we stated in the introduction to this book, confidence in CMS as a wellspring of critical forms of work on management has grown considerably (if somewhat unevenly) over the last decade and more. Since we are sympathetic to CMS and would posit a relationship between CMS and the theoretical oeuvre of the book, we must say a bit more about what CMS has to offer researchers aiming to undertake management research. In what follows we draw upon a number of key writings on CMS that have emerged in recent times. Among the most informative and inspired (listed here in no particular order of influence and illumination) are Hotho and Pollard (2007), Hancock and Taylor (2004), Parker (2002a), and Fournier and Grey (2000), as well as Sotirin and Tyrell (1998). Of these, Fournier and Grey's (2000) work serves as a guiding framework for the discussion in this section, since we regard it as the most enlightening and accessible overview of CMS in the UK published to date.

On critical management studies (CMS)

As Martin Parker explains in *Against Management* (2002a), CMS is a child of the 1990s and still in a period of infancy. Although well into its second decade, CMS remains something of a puzzle. What we mean here is that despite attempts to the contrary, there is no simple way in which CMS can be neatly summed up. As a body of work its outline is amorphous and its contents extremely varied and nascent. The intellectual endeavours that constitute CMS have explored the phenomenon of management in a number of directions. For instance, Smith et al. (2001) explore management through the tool of science fiction, Parker (2002b) advocates a queering of management, Grey and Sturdy (2007) urge us to consider friendship as a folk concept to explore forms of management and organising, while Brewis et al. (2006) contemplate the dark side of motivation by investigating the roles of addiction, sex and death in organisation. The list of such vibrant forms of critical management inquiry is long, and too long to fully detail here. What this small selection shows, however, is that CMS is a wildly eclectic intellectual project.

Thus as a number of management scholars note of CMS (Fournier and Grey, 2000; Parker, 2002a), it resists the simplicities of classification. Therein lies, perhaps, part of its appeal to those who wish to join its ever-expanding membership. CMS affords spacious accommodation for those academics mobilising ideas and cultural resources in ways that they believe are distinguishable from mainstream managerial studies of business (Parker, 2002a). But even as CMS has started to develop a sense of coherence about its identity, so there are some who now resist assuming the CMS label. Some academics are now in the business of being critical about CMS (Parker, 2002a), perhaps with good reason. So, what then do we make of this creature called CMS?

For us, CMS represents an opportunity to explore resonances with other academic perspectives on management that aim to question the prescriptive/descriptive management literature that finds ample bookshelf space in business school libraries the world over. To our minds, there is much to be concerned about within traditional management theory. As has been amply shown in many ways by different scholars, conventional management wisdom of the type that is issued from mainstream texts has often resulted in oppressive forms of organising and management. A quick review of the myriad of management practices reveals illuminating evidence of a welter of managerial misdemeanours. For instance, within the field of human resource management (HRM), a number of critical writers have lampooned the prescriptions of HRM textbooks and their associated practices in organisations. The insider stories of those at the blunt end of the tools in the HRM kitbag are the object of interrogation in Mabey et al's brilliant (1998) edited collection of essays. The book's aim is to 'give voice to the other players in HRM strategies – i.e., those on the receiving end' (p. 95). This aim turns on the idea that those with a vested interest in perpetuating the rhetoric of HRM are not necessarily the 'best' people to consult in the matter of whether HRM has actually delivered on its promises, as well as naming those advantaged by HRM techniques. One message is elegantly articulated throughout the book: employees have invariably suffered at the hands of those who endeavour to manage and organise labour along the principles of HRM. Elsewhere, similar stories are being told in relation to the gender blind and patriarchal nature of management theory (Collinson and Hearn, 1996;

Hearn et al., 1989) and the inimical effects of the organisation of labour within capitalistic societies, as evidenced in call centre work environments (Taylor and Bain, 1999).

What is clear from all of this research is that management, in some of the forms it finds expression, is problematic. Worryingly, threatening and violent values may characterise some managerial regimes that seek to optimise the human contribution within organisations. One of the most pertinent examples is Business Process Re-engineering (BPR). In his original article, Hammer (1990) defines BPR as the fundamental rethinking and radical redesign of business processes to achieve dramatic improvements in critical contemporary measures of performance such as cost, quality, service and speed. Hammer suggests that BPR inverts much of the logic of the Industrial Revolution, by breaking free from the long established principle of the division of labour. BPR is heralded as a radical departure from conventional change management programmes. Its central idea is that rather than trying to evolve business operations gradually over time, the organisational designer takes a fresh piece of paper to design a radically new system. Hammer and Champy's (1993) bestseller talks about axes, machine guns, lobotomy and shooting as devices to facilitate change in the organisation, while the empirical studies on BPR suggest that reengineering leads to work intensification and is no more than another form of managerial control (Grey and Mitev, 1995; Willmott, 1995). Other critics (Knights and McCabe, 1998) suggest that employees who remain in employment after reengineering experience more stressful and intensive working conditions. Moreover, according to Horsted and Doherty (1994), whether individuals stay with or leave a reengineered organisation, they generally experience feelings of psychological 'trauma' rather than empowerment.

With this in mind and following Hotho and Pollard (2007), one crucial aim of the CMS project is to critique the oppressive regimes of management and organisation and, at the same time, advocate more benevolent forms of management and organising in the workplace. Expressed in a slightly different way, as Fournier and Grey (2000) put it, CMS is a project that 'aims to unmask the power relations around which social and organizational life are woven' (p. 19). We embrace both articulations of the political dimensions to CMS. Indeed, we put our hope in those readers who will be galvanised by what they find in this book's chapters to generate management research that questions forms of domination and asymmetrical power relations. At the same time, we are minded to sound a cautionary note. To simply view CMS as being organised around a central political goal is misleading. The entire CMS project is criss-crossed by political currents that are varied and inseparable from the theories CMS scholars mobilise. Whatever the degree of variation in how these political goals are constructed, CMS pays direct attention to the moral and ethical issues of management. As we note below, the matter of sifting the 'critical' from the 'non-critical' perspectives within CMS in order to attend to the interrogation of these dimensions to management is equally discordant.

On the critical from the non-critical

The distinction between what may be termed as 'critical' and 'non-critical' management research is arbitrary. For one thing, there is cultural variation in what theories academics have badged as being critical. For another, differences among scholars about distinguishing the critical from the non-critical are drawn out according to academics' personal preferences, the reputations of certain university business schools as intellectual powerhouses loyal to a particular body of theory, as well as cultural and political shifts that influence how certain theories wax and wane in terms of their popularity and intellectual currency. It is worth unpacking some of these points in detail.

Arguably, the starkest contrast in academic discourses regarding what counts as critical management research is found in the scholarly outputs from university business schools in the USA and the UK. The USA has long been regarded as a comfortable home for traditional, positivistic management research. As Fournier and Grey (2000) suggest, certain cultural and political climates (e.g., the impact of the Cold War and McCarthyism) in the USA have influenced the availability of access routes to critical resources that scholars in the UK and Europe appear to have been able to draw from more readily. This is not to say that scholars in the UK have enjoyed an unfettered ability to avail themselves of the cultural and material resources to pursue their own brand of non-positivistic, critical management research. This is too suggestive of a strict dichotomy between the USA and UK, especially as numerous scholars can be found in both countries that conform to and rebel against management school orthodoxy. This notwithstanding, business schools in the UK have been subjected to the mean and lean, cost-cutting, efficiency-orientated principles of what has been dubbed 'new managerialism'. One result of this is that certain forms of research (those with the potential to deliver financial pay-offs) are more likely to be prioritised and funded by research councils and committees. Not surprisingly, positivistic research designs and proposals lend themselves well to the quantification processes that abound in UK universities.

Interestingly, Fournier and Grey (2000) also take stock, historically, of the development of US business schools. Established much earlier than those in the UK that first opened their doors to students in the 1960s, the tradition of studying management has a longer pedigree. Efforts to improve the bloodline of US business schools came about in the period following World War II when moves were made to boost the scientific status of these institutions by attaching a high premium to scientific (positivistic) research. As Fournier and Grey highlight, while UK business schools ought not to be seen as 'seething hotbeds of revolutionary fervour' (p. 15), since many can be characterised by their managerialist agendas, the dominance of American positivistic research is keenly felt by many academics on this side of the Atlantic. None, perhaps, capture the dilemma so vividly and neatly as Karen Legge, writing on the status and activities of 'critical writers' in the field of human resource management. It is worth quoting Legge at length on this matter:

> **If British researchers aspire to publish in these top-ranked journals, with all the benefits this confers, they must inevitably engage with the debates and paradigmatic positions that these journals support. Even if they prefer the easier (?) route of publishing in British or other European journals, the influence of the American journals is such that any academic that aspires to an international reputation has to engage with the 'American' debates unless they locate themselves firmly within the non-empiricist, critical, European tradition of the gang of three and eschew the American Academy of Management conference scene, except in the role of guerrilla fighters or lepers. (2001: 34)**

These essays by Legge (2001) and Fournier and Grey (2000) illustrate well the point that critical management research conjures up a number of different meanings for individuals and institutions in different cultural contexts. Admittedly, we have been partial in our account of such debates here, leaving aside the variation in meaning that occurs across parts of Europe, Asia and Australasia. Nonetheless, since one of the anchors for this book is within the British CMS community, it is necessary to provide some insight into the forces that have shaped the debates about critical management research on British shores.

Another factor responsible for the lack of scholarly consensus about what counts as critical management research is the variation that exists in the criteria used to evaluate whether a theory might be eligible enough to be termed 'critical'. The eligibility criteria to determine what theories might be classified as critical vary considerably among academics. Scholars have their own emotional investments in such criteria since it may be that some academic identities pivot on an individual's research or orientation within a certain theoretical vein. Sometimes these preferences and views are put forward with great vitriol.

One reason for all this apparent mayhem over what counts as critical is partly a result of allegiances and orientations scholars might have towards a particular body of theory. For example, as Parker (2002a) points out, tensions within CMS may be witnessed in the bitter quarrels between (post-) Marxists and followers of the poststructuralist theorist Michel Foucault. Here, critical theory has often been used as a term to describe a raft of Neo-Marxist theories that carry on articulating the concerns around the structure and effects of capitalistic societies. Adherents to this rigid conception of critical theory have often lambasted poststructuralism (and postmodernism) for its lack of attention towards social structure and providing an adequate account of power. From the most intractable Neo-Marxist positions, poststructuralists and postmodernists (sometimes referred to pejoratively as 'pomos') are said to have collapsed the social into the literary. In other words, their mobilisation of discursive devices and conceptual resources gives much credence to the notion of a 'linguistic universe' in which individuals are reduced to subjects and the positions, subjectivities and identities they construct and perform. For opponents of the linguistic turn in the social sciences, poststructuralist and postmodernist perspectives eschew analysis of social structures, institutions and the materiality of everyday life. Such intellectual sparring is often characterised by its finer-grained analysis of theory. Unfortunately, it does not mean to say these debates are always conducted in a convivial manner. Academic points of view regarding what is considered critical and, therefore, what really counts in the quest to destabilise the dominance of orthodox management research are worth defending aggressively, so it seems. Indeed, certain academic conferences have achieved notoriety as bastions for followers of specific theoretical perspectives to muster, with 'outsiders' espousing competing theoretical sensibilities venturing within at their peril.

Ontologically, much is at stake in the academic world when it comes to being called a critical theorist or not. Laying claim to such academic identities can confer rewards such as peer admiration and 'celebrity' status. Rather in the manner that chaff is sorted from wheat, so these intellectual manoeuvrings (and associated posturings) can separate the 'hard-boiled theorists' from the 'soft-centred non-critical empiricists'. Disturbingly, such dualisms not only create the separation of theory from empiricism, but they also retrench the very types of behaviours and stances among CMS academics that many within the CMS community would seek to contest. As Fournier and Grey (2000) note, the dissent among academics as to who is 'inside' and who is 'outside' of the circles of critical theory reveals very little about where the boundaries between critical and non-critical actually lie. Indeed, their assertion that 'the theoretical pluralism of CMS and the fact that there is no unitary "critical" position mean that there is no single way of demarcating the critical from the non-critical' (2000: 16) might be a dead hand on our ambition to be 'critical'.

Fournier and Grey offer a way out of this impasse, noting how (non)critical boundary-making within CMS turns upon the three issues of performativity, denaturalisation and reflexivity. As we stated in the introduction to this book, these issues act as the cornerstones of our vision of critical management research. We will briefly describe each one in turn. The performative intent in non-critical work, as it may be found in much mainstream management theory, is concerned with maximising organisational efficiency. Management is taken-for-granted in the sense that it is naturally assumed to be beneficial for all those directing and on the receiving end of its practices. From this perspective, to be 'against management', as some scholars like Parker (2002a) are, is undesirable if not inconceivable. As Fournier and Grey remark, management is only interrogated 'except in so far as this will contribute to its improved effectiveness' (2000: 17).

The second issue, denaturalisation, involves exposing the gaps and absences in mainstream managerial theory. Much in the manner of how organisational gender theorists have unveiled the gendered nature of management (Collinson and Hearn, 1996), so CMS aims to underline similar glaring omissions and erasures, as well as proposing alternative ways of (re)constituting management without replicating the unquestionable 'naturalness' it sometimes betokens (see Parker, 2002b). Lastly, CMS is seen, albeit in different ways and to varying measures, to be reflexive philosophically and methodologically. Indeed, this is a point we are at pains to emphasise throughout this book, since much (though by no means all) orthodox management theory does not question its own methodological underpinnings. As Fournier and Grey (2000) aver, positivistic research is often presented as matter-of-fact, which is to say that research of this kind is often unbothered with justifying the use of positivism – a fault most obvious in American positivistic business research.

In summary, our claim to be critical rests upon the three concepts established above. It might be wise here to anticipate the criticisms that in being critical about management we (and others like us) are, therefore, steadfastly opposed to the strenuous efforts of organisations to improve efficiency. As we have already said, our business across the pages of this book is to showcase a number of the theories that could be employed to question and reformulate those ideas and practices that are often discursively tagged as 'commonsense' ways of going about management. This might lead to efficiency gains, but, then again, it might not. Hopefully, it will lead to an enlightened manner of thinking about management. What this does not amount to, as we discuss below, is an unyielding stance that is 'anti-management'.

On not being anti-management

We have already declared certain forms of management problematic. One perspective might be that we are therefore anti-management, that it is our intention to demolish management practice, to discredit all the mainstream management texts that stand against the theoretical orientation of ours. It is not our intention to throw out the past; arguably, mainstream management is not all bad. It is not a simple case of positioning critical theory in opposition to mainstream management theory – the latter may contain critical components or serve as a source of theoretical inspiration. It is more productive to argue for viewing critical theory as a relational and dialogical concept, but not one that is tethered to mainstream management theory within an artificial dualism.

This careful framing is crucially important, as a recent spate of academic argumentation about whether CMS and specific academics are anti-, against or for management illustrates. Singling out Parker's *Against Management* (2002a) as an object for pillory, Clegg et al. (2006) in an article entitled 'For Management?' voiced their fears about the likes of Parker and CMS more widely for offering up management as a totalitarian phenomenon worthy only of negative criticism. Their slanted (and unjust) reading of Parker and of CMS appears to turn on the notion of 'against management' equating to a reductionist interpretation of management (as a set of practices, as a social group) being rotten to the core.

Like Parker (2006) and Willmott (2006), both of whom responded to Clegg et al. (2006) in the journal *Management Learning*, we do not assume that management (as a form of organising) is all bad. Neither are all managers demons nor all managerial practices nefarious. It is important here to rebuff the assertion that just because we (and many others) lay claim to be critical of management, we must therefore be opposed to management. If, by anti-management, it is taken that we are for the wholesale demonisation of management and managers, then our aim here has been misread. One can be critical and for management in the manner of Parker and others of the same opinion. As Parker (2006) points out, the idea espoused by Clegg et al. (2006) of being both critical and *for* management is one that clearly accords with the polyphonic understanding of management in *Against Management* (2002a); or, as Willmott (2006) pithily puts it, Clegg et al. just seem to be 'pushing clumsily at an open door' (p. 37).

Viewed as a sympathetic form of art, doing critical research on management is not necessarily about tearing down the pillars upon which traditional management theory rests – although some critical theorists might well advocate this for good reasons. There has to be some element of concern in order for critique to be *generative*. Otherwise, we might lapse into a mode of analysis that is ultimately destructive – it is all too easy to bulldoze an idea or argument into rubble and walk away. Generative critique, however, cannot be left there. Even if one is passionately interrogating managerial practices that are clearly beyond the pale in their harmful effects on employees, any critique should be deployed productively. This might involve gutting traditional and other forms of critical management theory (critical theories are not exempt from this endeavour), inspecting their contents, exposing their deficiencies and then, perhaps, reconstituting the form.

In another way, being critical of management is also about recognising the possibilities for individuals to resist management where it is experienced as an oppressive force in organisations. By individuals, we would include managers as well as their subordinates. CMS has been accused by Wray-Bliss (2003) of (re)constructing managers as omnipotently powerful and employees/workers as helpless, thus needing to be liberated by the interventions of critical management researchers. This dichotomous line of thought is problematic in the sense that it assumes all managers are homogeneous, not only in their capacity to exercise power over their subordinates but also in their needs, interests, desires and abilities. Returning to Willmott (2006), managers are a heterogeneous body of people, despite their repeated constructions (often in mainstream management texts) as a uniform group of employees/workers. For instance, the role of management is undertaken by a large number of individuals formally employed as 'managers', but many are not managers. Numerous (non-manager) employees now undertake the work of junior and middle managers. Parker makes a similar observation in the introductory chapter of *Against Management* (2002a). Whichever way we might wish to illustrate the sentiment, being critical of management is not to view management as a monolith.

Summary

In this chapter we have argued that, in order to generate critical forms of management research, researchers need to have an understanding of the potential role theory can perform, why theory matters and to whom. For our purposes, critical theory is a powerful way of (re)thinking and (re)envisioning the world of management. Clearly, theory matters to many business school scholars (theorising keeps some of us in employment), but it should also be of prime concern to critical management researchers. As this chapter has discussed, critical theory can help researchers of management to develop emancipatory forms of research. Indeed, we sponsor the notions of performativity, denaturalisation and reflexivity that, according to Fournier and Grey (2000), underpin much of the critical management research within CMS. But, it is important to note that mobilising these conceptual tools does not equate to arming oneself with a weapon 'against' management. What debates on being anti-, against or for management reveal is that, in order for a critique on management to be effective, it is vital to view management sensitively.

In light of all this, this chapter provides a key building block in the foundations for going about critical management research. Knowledge of what makes theory critical (as arbitrary as it is because it is contingent upon prevailing scholarly views about what criticality should stand for and achieve) is useful for management researchers. Decisions can be made about what types of critical theories are most appealing and suitable for providing the conceptual support that undergirds informed critical empirical analysis. Extending debates about the importance of critical theory in research, we turn in the next chapter to exploring the significance of thinking about paradigms in critical management research. As we have already mentioned in this chapter, theories may be thought of as frameworks – or paradigms – in which researchers operate. The conceptual contours of any given paradigm will influence the decisions made about, for example, what kind of data to gather and how these will be analysed and presented. As we discuss in the next chapter, while paradigms are useful for paving an approach to thinking about research methodology, they can become prisons within which some scholars confine themselves, discounting ideas and evidence that does not accord with their chosen paradigm. We will therefore demonstrate the benefits of multi-paradigm research for generating critical forms of analysis.

Further reading

For more detail on the critical theories inspired by the works of Karl Marx, including those that emerged from the Frankfurt School, and how they have impacted on management research, we would suggest you read Alvesson and Deetz (2000) *Doing Critical Management Research* (London: Sage) (especially Chapter 4, 'The critical tradition: critical theory and postmodernism'). Another informative commentary on the contribution of the Frankfurt School within organisation theory is: Carr (2005) 'The challenge of critical theory for those in organization theory and behavior: an overview', *International Journal of Organization Theory and Behavior*, 8 (4): 466–494.

The edited collection by Grey and Willmott (2005) *Critical Management Studies: A Reader* (Oxford: Oxford University Press) is an excellent collection of papers produced by scholars associated with the CMS project. Also, for more detail about the debates on whether some CMS scholars are anti-, against or for management, a very good place to start is Parker (2002a) *Against Management: Organization in the Age of Managerialism* (Cambridge: Polity). The highly charged journal article aimed at Parker's *Against Management* thesis is Clegg et al's, (2006) 'For Management?', in *Management Learning*, 37 (1): 7–27. The responses by Martin Parker and Hugh Willmott (in the same journal volume) are also essential reading: see Parker (2006) 'Stockholm Syndrome', in *Management Learning*, 37 (1): 39–41; and Willmott (2006) 'Pushing at an open door: mystifying the CMS manifesto', in *Management Learning*, 37 (1): 33–37.

2

Organisational Paradigms and Management Research

Introduction

In the previous chapter we provided a broad outline of the relevance of critical theory for management researchers. Accepting that critical theory is a key to critical management research, we must now consider how theories can operate as paradigms. This chapter, therefore, explores the importance of paradigms within management research. Without a doubt, the dominant way for understanding research methodology is through paradigm thinking. The importance of the concept of paradigm, introduced into the philosophy of science by Thomas Kuhn in 1962, is clearly signalled today in the assertion that the most effective route to a reflexive understanding of research practice lies in exploring the nature of researchers' assumptions, and the consequences they bring to bear on the particular modes of inquiry. Assumptions are helpful in making organisational phenomena researchable and therefore knowable.

However, knowledge is sometimes achieved at the cost of great oversimplifications. Whether we like it or not, researchers tend to favour one set of assumptions at the expense of others and this will be reflected in the research process as well as its outcome. These assumptions constitute the researcher's so-called research paradigm and may refer to how researchers see the world around them, and their views about what constitutes facts, evidence, truth or science. The term 'paradigm' first appeared in English in the fifteenth century, meaning 'an example or pattern', and it still bears this meaning today. However, in the wake of the work of Thomas Kuhn in the 1960s, the concept of paradigm has been used in science to refer to a theoretical framework. More loosely, the term may also refer to 'the prevailing view of things'.

In light of the above, this chapter aims to explore some of the key themes around the term 'paradigm' and its usage within management theory. The chapter starts by reviewing two well-known paradigm typologies: Burrell and Morgan (1979) and Guba and Lincoln (1994). Examples of organisational research carried out within particular paradigms are provided as well as an introduction to multi-paradigm research: its

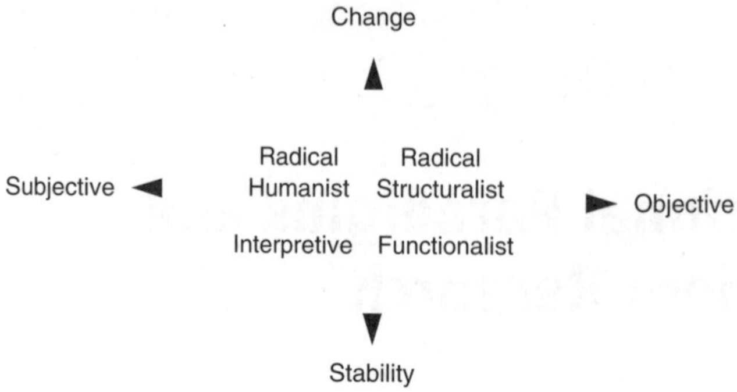

Figure 2.1 Typology of Sociological Paradigms

Source: Burrell and Morgan, 1979

advantages, disadvantages and some important exemplars. The chapter concludes with a number of research dilemmas arising from scholarly debates on paradigms that need careful consideration prior to engaging in management and organisational research.

Paradigm typologies

In organisational studies, the debate on paradigms and their role in the research process was pushed to the forefront by the publication in 1979 of Burrell and Morgan's *Sociological Paradigms and Organizational Analysis*. These authors argue that there are a number of possibilities whereby researchers can look at and understand the social world, but such possibilities are mutually exclusive. Burrell and Morgan's two-by-two matrix maps out four research paradigms that represent the major 'belief systems' of academics and others who practise management and organisational research. Depending on the nature of science (objective/subjective) and the nature of society (stability/change), there can be four views (paradigms) of the social world (see Figure 2.1).

With the above model in mind, if a researcher believes that social science is an objective enterprise, in other words that knowledge is 'true' and the result of the rigorous application of methodology, h/she will situate him/herself either in the functionalist or the radical structuralist paradigm. Alternatively, if science is seen to be a social and political process whose outcomes reflect the interests and agendas of powerful intellectual elites, h/she will be either an interpretivist or a radical humanist. To differentiate his/her position further, h/she will have to ask questions about the nature of society. Is society (or the ideal of a society) a stable, orderly and coherent entity (an output)? Or is it always in a state of flux and transformation (a process), on its way to be constituted but not quite there? If the answer to the former question is yes, then the researcher will be either an interpretivist or a functionalist. If the answer to the latter question is positive, the researcher will be either a radical humanist or a radical structuralist.

Each paradigm has something to offer regarding our engagement with and understanding of the world of management. Morgan (1983) highlights the contributions of each paradigm to management research and practice, while Hassard (1991) applies them individually to research carried out on work behaviour in the British Fire Service.

Morgan (1983) suggests that *functionalism* has provided a language for the control and management of organisations. Indeed, most management theories purport to capture the social world as 'it is' and to provide ways in which it can be known and controlled better. Functionalist theories make claims of generalisability across time and space. The resultant management models are packaged and marketed universally. Business Process Re-engineering, an American management theory that became extremely popular in the 1990s, was exported to the rest of the world with a high degree of success, according to Hammer and Champy (1993), its original proponents. The purported success of this functionalist theory reinforces the idea that models that work in the context in which they have been developed will work in most other contexts, providing that they are correctly implemented and monitored by the interested parties. Functionalist theories have, for years, equipped management with their day-to-day expert language. As such, they provide the benchmark by which managerial activity is judged, assessed and rewarded in today's organisations.

Hassard's (1991) research on work behaviour in the British Fire Service focuses on work motivation. The starting point for his functionalist study was Hackman and Oldham's (1976) Job Characteristics Theory and its associated model. The main objective of the research was to assess how full-time firemen evaluate job characteristics in terms of motivational potential, applying statistical methods for analysing the data. Hassard's evidence suggests that although a fireman's job has low levels of motivation potential, this is not an issue because employees' needs for psychological growth at work are also quite low. He also found no major correlational differences between core job characteristics and their corresponding psychological states, thus backing up the original research by Hackman and Oldham.

The *interpretivist paradigm* takes the view that management theories are the result of a social and political process which we term 'research'. Organisations are seen to be cultures rather than 'black boxes' whose inputs and outputs can be controlled with the help of scientific methods. As such, a researcher needs to get involved in the day-to-day flow of activity in order to decipher the social meaning of a particular situation. He or she becomes part of the research setting, rather than a mere mirror which accurately reflects what is out there. Order and stability are surface phenomena that rest on a precarious web of social interaction: individuals construct a shared reality as they talk and interact with each other. What may appear coherent and stable is in fact the result of power struggles as different individuals and groups compete for a voice in the cacophony of reality making. Researchers belonging to this paradigm embrace a plurality of research methods to give voice to the many interests, concerns and accounts that contribute to the social construction of organisational life.

Hassard's interpretivist study involved an ethnomethodological analysis of the Fire Service's work routines. The aim was to understanding the recipes firemen employ to make sense of their world at work (Schutz, 1967). The main finding was that behaviour was influenced by, and itself influences, the collective understandings of what needs to be done in order to be promoted within the organisation. As such, personal action was indexed by a contextual system of meaning that was constantly enacted by the firemen.

Radical humanism is a paradigm that searches for the ideological blinders that make individuals feel powerless and for ways in which they can regain a sense of agency. Researchers adopting a radical change perspective hold the view that emancipation is only possible if a whole ideology regime is overthrown. Research in this paradigm stresses the political nature of organisational life and the consequences that one's words and deeds have upon others. Aside from an ethical concern there is also engagement with subconscious processes: emotions and irrationality are seen to be powerful devices in day-to-day organisational life. Researchers in this paradigm take the view that science is a social and political process influenced by the dominant ideology and related cultural practices.

The starting point in Hassard's (1991) study is that the role of management functionalist science is central in reproducing organisational 'common sense'. As such, he analysed training practices relating to courses for firemen looking to be promoted to first line supervisors. The study findings reveal the ways in which the dominant culture of the organisation is reproduced with the help of 'acceptable' theories of management.

Radical structuralism stresses the importance of viewing chance as a natural and imminent state of organisational life, the result of conflict between opposing binaries. Understanding the deep structure of particular social phenomena allows a researcher to understand and map out its behaviour. This paradigm offers a useful lens for understanding organisations in crisis and the role organisations play in enacting their environment. Researchers belonging to this paradigm take an objective view on science; hence, theories are valid as long as they are based on objective facts and rigorous methodologies.

Hassard's study also takes a Marxist stance, highlighting crisis points in the fire fighting labour process. More specifically, it analyses the strategic relations between capital and labour as regards the development of the employment contract. Given that firemen's working hours have been reduced in line with other manual occupations, measures have been introduced to control work practices more tightly in order to improve productivity levels. The radical structuralist study illustrates the concrete actions of labour, capital and the state aimed at resolving the various crises within the fire fighting sector.

Despite criticisms, Burrell and Morgan's (1979) framework remains extremely influential for contemporary organisational analysis. Guba and Lincoln (1994) advanced an equally useful paradigmatic framework. They assert that there are

> **... four paradigms that are currently competing, or have until recently competed, for acceptance as the paradigm of choice in informing and guiding inquiry, especially qualitative inquiry: positivism, postpositivism, critical theory and related ideological positions, and constructivism. (1994: 105)**

Unpacking the above quote, Guba and Lincoln suggest that such paradigms rest on three different types of assumptions: ontological, epistemological and methodological. Ontology, or the theory of being, asks questions about the nature of reality. Is social reality a given – or is it, as Berger and Luckmann (1966) suggest, constructed through people's interactions and meanings? Epistemology asks questions about the nature of science: in other words, what constitutes 'valid' knowledge? Objectivist knowledge is the outcome of a mode of research that views the scientist as being removed from the social world under study. He or she acts as a mirror that accurately reflects reality and expresses it within a neutral language. Subjectivist knowledge is the outcome of a process of research deeply embedded in the social, political and cultural milieu in which it is produced. Any researcher is part of the research setting and his/her research language is by no means neutral but intertwined with power relations and cultural conventions. Finally, methodology refers to the actual process by which we can go about finding out what we believe to be 'true'. Quantitative methodologies facilitate the measurement of social phenomena and their subsequent control and prediction. The resultant theory comes in the form of hypotheses that must be tested in order for them to be validated or refuted. At the other end of the spectrum, qualitative methodologies are concerned with interpretation and social meaning. The resultant theory acknowledges the cultural, political and social values and interests that shape what is regarded as 'truth' within management science. Qualitative methodologies throw doubt onto the claims made by researchers who state they have discovered a 'truth'.

A short synopsis of each of the four paradigms follows.

1 Positivism

At its outset, positivism supplied the grounds for the formation of sociology, the science of society. In other words, positivism argued that sociology could share the same logical form as the other sciences, as it was cut free from the residues of metaphysics (understood here as philosophy, magic, religion, tradition and any other non-scientific endeavour). It is for this reason that we should avoid the tendency (now commonplace within management studies) to deride positivism. Rather we should regard it as an important and necessary step in the development of social sciences.

Table 2.1 Basic beliefs of alternative enquiry paradigms

Item	Positivism	Postpositivism	Critical Theory and related positions	Constructivism
Ontology	Out there, apprehendable reality	Out there but only probabilistically apprehendable reality	Virtual reality shaped by power	Local and specific constructed realities
Epistemology	Objectivist findings are true	Objectivist findings probably true	Subjectivist value-mediated findings	Subjectivist created findings
Methodology	Verification of hypotheses, numbers support the truth	Falsification of hypotheses	Dialogue emancipatory	Hermeneutics dialogue

Source: adapted from Guba and Lincoln, 1994

Positivism emerged in the first half of the nineteenth century and its central idea was that the methodology of natural science could be applied to understanding and improving human life. Its main point was that science is the only vehicle for investigating human phenomena, since all the other approaches to acquiring knowledge were unreliable and outmoded (Simon, 1962). Auguste Comte, inventor of the term 'positivism' and author of a treatise that outlines a positivist system, advocates the superiority of the positive or scientific mode of knowledge acquisition over what he regards as philosophising modes. Three features are central in Comte's work, as follows:

- **The idea of a historical progression from fallacious modes of thoughts to scientific thought.**
- **The idea of a hierarchy of science with a new science of society named sociology at the pinnacle.**
- **A specific programme for social betterment.**

Returning to the assumptions underlying paradigmatic stances:

- **Positivism assumes an objective social reality that exists independent of our interpretations (ontological assumptions).**

- **Positivism holds the investigator and the investigated object as independent entities (epistemological assumptions).**
- **Positivism states hypotheses in a propositional form and then subjects them to empirical testing, also perhaps developing new propositions grounded in the data (methodological assumptions).**

Positivist management research remains the dominant form of engagement, particularly in North America where leading journals and academic careers are built on contributions to the positivist body of knowledge. However, critics would argue that positivism simplifies organisational reality to produce distinct variables that can be observed and measured in order to assess what relationships may exist between them. Because of that, positivism is supposedly unable to grapple with and explain satisfactorily the complexities and ambiguities inherent in organisational realities. Despite these and other scathing criticisms, organisation theory and management studies in general have been built around the concept of system theory and its associated view that organisations are made of subparts which interrelate in order to form a coherent whole (see for example, Scientific Management, the Human Relations theories of work motivation, and Contingency Theory).

2 Postpositivism

Postpositivism is a position that assumes reality to exist but to be only probabilistically apprehendable because of the limitations of human cognition. A researcher is no longer seen to be independent from the object of study, but objectivity remains an ideal to be attained in research, either via recourse to external traditions and theories or via the intellectual community (editors, referees and other professionals). As such, methodology plays a significant role in gathering data not only about specific organisational variables but also, and more importantly, about their context. Quantitative data become a useful instrument in this endeavour. The ultimate purpose of researchers is to falsify a theory rather than verify it. If one instance is found not to match the postulated hypothesis the theory is refuted and considered unscientific. Critics argue that falsification is a long and arduous process and that by simply recognising the limits of human cognition one does not acknowledge the power-laden nature of social relations and its impact on what scientific knowledge is all about.

3 Critical theory and related positions

Guba and Lincoln use the critical label as an umbrella term to account for Neo-Marxism, feminism, poststructuralism, and postmodernism. While recognising that there are many tensions between such positions, it is suggested that their commonality lies in the acknowledgement that research outcomes are not value free. Equally and relatedly, the processes of scientific inquiry are not value free. Reality is argued to be a construction shaped by social, political and cultural factors, solidified into structures that, although not 'real', have material and usually limiting consequences upon actors. What can be known is inextricably dependent on the relationship between the knower and the object under study; as such, the distinction between ontology and epistemology is called into question. The preferred methodology of research is one that encourages a dialogue between researchers and the subjects to be studied. Such a dialogue has to be emancipatory and informative. Participant observation, interviewing and other similar methods of research that facilitate a participatory relationship between researchers and the subjects of research are to be embraced.

Management and organisation studies have accorded critical theory a home. As we stated in the introduction to this book, the so-called CMS movement has gathered supporters both in Europe and North America. Even the leading North American journal, *Academy of Management Review*, is now 'receptive to a variety of perspectives, including those seeking to improve the effectiveness of, as well as those critical of, management and organizations' ('Aims of the Journal') and, at the time of writing, has appointed Martin Kilduff as Chief Editor (a scholar whose contributions to CMS, postmodernism and organisational deconstruction are notable). Chapters 3 to 7 will provide examples of critical theory and related positions in more detail, illustrating their impact on management theory by referring to empirical research carried out within these theoretical paradigms. The main criticism brought to critical theory (and related approaches) is its inability to engage managers and practitioners both cognitively and pragmatically. Critical theory, it is argued, is an ivory tower phenomenon that is preventing academics from connecting to the organisational problems facing real people in real organisations (Parker, 2002a).

4 Social constructivism

The perspective known as social constructivism is well established, having been stimulated by the works of Schutz (1967), Berger and Luckmann (1966) and Mannheim (1936). The view was developed that social objects are not given 'in the world' but are constructed, negotiated, managed, reformed, exchanged and organised by human beings in their attempts to make sense of what is happening around them. More recently, social constructivism has been inspired by infusions of the lively postmodern debate (Sarbin and Kitsuse, 1994).

At the core of constructivism lies the idea that in order to understand the social world one must interpret it from the points of view of those who live in it. Thus the researcher is concerned with how meanings are constructed and how meanings are embodied in the language and actions of social actors. Expressed differently, a constructivist account

- **assumes that realities are knowable in the form of multiple constructions that are socially and experientially based (ontological assumptions);**
- **considers the investigator and the object of investigation to be intertwined (epistemological assumptions);**
- **constructs narrative theory that is informed by the individual accounts of the people under study (methodological assumptions).**

If individual accounts are individual attempts to make sense of the world, depending on the information available to the constructor and his or her ability to handle it, then they influence and are influenced by social constructions. Social constructions are collective and systematic attempts to come to agreement about a certain phenomenon. They are a reflection of social and power relationships between individuals and change over time as a result of new information available to the constructor, and as a result of changes in social and power relationships. The task of the researcher is to open up a dialogue between him/herself and the subjects of the research and to employ hermeneutical techniques (namely, interpretative techniques such as deconstruction: see Chapter 5) for deciphering the meaning from within. Findings are usually created as the research investigation proceeds.

In summary, social constructivist research aims to both present the accounts held by individuals and also document the processes by which individuals arrive at consensus on a daily basis. Such consensus may be fragile and provisional: it may be challenged, resisted and manipulated in all sorts of ways but it is taken to be the 'truth', at least temporarily, by suppressing individual accounts that do not align themselves with the dominant line. Karl Weick introduced social constructivism to organisation studies in 1969 in his book entitled *The Social Psychology of Organising*. His theory of enactment argues that individuals at work construct their own surroundings and, in so doing, they also construct their own constraints. Critics argue that social constructivism fails to recognise the materiality of the social world and the ways in which it constrains and influences social meaning and its conditions of possibility.

The relationship between individual paradigms has been debated at great length in the organisational studies literature. Some of the most heated discussions have centred on the notion of whether paradigms can be bridged. Much ink has been spilt by organisational scholars in arguing for and against the idea of paradigm (in)commensurability. These debates, reaching their height in the 1980s and 1990s, have been dubbed the 'paradigm wars', the effects of which can still be felt today. We outline the main argument of the paradigm (in)commensurability thesis below.

Paradigm incommensurability

The so-called paradigm incommensurability thesis posits that individual paradigms cannot be arenas for open, scholarly debate across the field, because they represent hermetically-sealed intellectual compartments. In this vein, Burrell and Morgan advanced a particularly strong version of the paradigm incommensurability thesis:

> ... a synthesis (between paradigms) is not possible, since in their pure form (paradigms) are contradictory, being based on at least one set of meta-theoretical assumptions. They represent alternatives, in the sense that one can operate in different paradigms sequentially over time, but mutually exclusive, in the sense that one cannot operate in more than one paradigm at any given point in time, since in accepting the assumptions of one, we defy the assumptions of all the others. (1979: 25)

As these four incommensurable paradigms – functionalism, interpretivism, radical humanism and radical structuralism – are found to co-exist at one time, it has been argued that bench-marking between paradigms is impossible, as proponents live in different life-worlds and speak different technical languages. Therefore, scientific communication is not so much difficult as logically impossible (Burrell and Morgan, 1979).

During the 1990s the debate had been (re)vitalised by views expressed by the influential American administrative scientist Jeffrey Pfeffer (1993, 1997). Notable, here, is his suggestion that in order to achieve academic respectability, organisation studies should concern itself with producing a discrete paradigm of clearly articulated practices and standards. Pfeffer offers the example of political science as a sub-discipline of social science that has achieved this aim. The 'Pfefferdigm debate', as it became known, is predicated on the view that theoretical variety will lead ultimately to management and organisation studies committing professional suicide.

Hassard and Kelemen (2002) took issue with Pfeffer's position, one that apparently wishes to achieve consensus over standardised research practices to be followed by all management researchers. They argued that research practices are not stable and coherent, but continuously in the making, being shaped by (and shaping) power relations and cultural expectations. Management knowledge is yet another set of cultural practices situated in and inextricably linked with the material and social circumstances in which it is produced and consumed. As social practice, knowledge is processual and provisional: its production relies on resources disembodied from their original content and made available through their transformation, legitimisation and institutionalisation (also see Gherardi and Nicolini, 2000), while its consumption is ensured through processes of social participation in a community of practice. Other commentators also suggest that a single paradigm is necessarily limiting because it helps expose certain facets of organisations while obscuring others (Burrell, 1996; Weick, 1999). This recognition has fostered a growing interest in a provocative alternative, that of multi-paradigm research.

The case for multi-paradigm research

Despite arguments that paradigm purity is a sign of scientific maturity within a particular field of study (Pfeffer, 1993, 1997), we are currently witnessing a shift towards paradigm plurality in numerous management disciplines such as: organisation theory (Hassard, 1993; Schultz and Hatch, 1996), international business (Earley and Singh, 1995; Parkhe, 1993), strategic management (McKinley, 1995; Scherer, 1998), operational research (Mingers, 1997) and technology management (Lewis and Grimes, 1999).

Multi-paradigm research arose out of early attempts to differentiate between modern paradigms and their worldviews (for examples, see Alvesson, 1987; Smircich, 1983). Over time, however, multi-paradigm strategies have become more varied, also seeking to employ and link divergent paradigm perspectives (see Lewis and Grimes, 1999). This provocative alternative seeks to explore contrasting representations, which may offer 'insights into the characteristic contradictions and tensions embodied in contemporary organizations' (Reed, 1985: 201). In sum, the primary goals of a multi-paradigm approach are two-fold:

1 to encourage greater awareness of theoretical alternatives and thereby facilitate discourse and/or inquiry across paradigms;
2 to foster greater understandings of organisational plurality and paradox (Lewis and Kelemen, 2002).

Multi-paradigm research promotes a *stratified* ontology, assuming multiple dimensions of reality. Reality is at once 'made' and 'in the making', as advocates examine entities *and* processes rather than collapsing these dimensions. Social entities (for example, structure, culture) denote contextualised understandings, co-existing with the processes through which actors use, reproduce and transform these understandings (Spender, 1998). According to Reed, entities and processes 'operate at different levels of abstraction that tie into each other within a stratified, multilevel, and relational model of society' (1997: 31). From this ontological foundation, organisations appear as social spaces torn in multiple directions (Bouchihki, 1998), for despite the rise in (often subtle) entities for control, organisational actors increasingly pursue numerous, diverse, even contradictory goals.

In multi-paradigm research a *pluralist* epistemology 'rejects the notion of a single reference system in which we can establish truth', as bounded rationality binds us within our own learning processes while allowing us to explore alternatives (Spender, 1998: 235). Advocates assume that paradigm lenses help construct alternative representations, exposing different dimensions of organisational life. As each lens offers a selective focus, researchers seek multiple perspectives of particularly complex and ambiguous phenomena. Contrasting modern representations may enable more insightful understandings: for example, by revealing forces pulling toward compliance *and* resistance, empowerment *and* discipline. Yet researchers may also tap into postmodern sensibilities to critique socially constructed paradigm boundaries and encourage self-reflection on the research process (for example, Hassard, 1993; Martin, 1992). Hence, researchers use multiple perspectives to highlight the plurality and paradoxes of organisational life, as well as the uncertainties of knowledge.

Multi-paradigm researchers apply an accommodating methodology, valuing diverse methodologies for their potential to inform each other toward more encompassing theories. All methodologies expose certain facets of organisational life by ignoring others:

> **The (postmodern) philosophers ignore everyone; the functionalists ignore workers; critical theorists ignore managers (even oppressed managers because, in the view of many of these theorists, there is no such thing). Even ethnographers distance themselves ... ignoring the power structures that created not only the subject but also themselves. (Clegg and Hardy, 1996: 693: parentheses in original)**

Multi-paradigm research strives to respect opposing methodologies and juxtapose the partial understandings they inspire.

Multi-paradigm research values the prescriptions offered by modern paradigms (for example, positivism, functionalism) and yet, simultaneously, disavows the claim to a singular truth. This does not imply some idyllic, 'best-of-both-worlds' approach. On the contrary, multi-paradigm researchers live in a glasshouse that is open to attack from modernists and postmodernists alike. Some positivists would strongly refute the notion that paradigms are sense-making rather than 'truth bearing' exercises (Donaldson, 1998); others would critique their use as fostering fictitious research (Parker and McHugh, 1991). Meanwhile, postmodernists stress that applying paradigmatic conventions may reify their hegemony and oversimplify, or worse homogenise, their disparate understandings (Burrell, 1996).

In our view, the pursuit of multi-paradigm research ensures the preservation and legitimisation of points of view that may otherwise be perceived as being marginal or suppressed by the dominant orthodoxy. Thus, those theories that try to articulate the perspectives of those who are silenced or ignored (in particular, feminism, postmodernism and queer theory as reviewed in this book) construct a place from which to voice these perspectives and concerns. If management and organisation studies are indeed to be 'ethical' they have to encourage a plurality of rather diverse voices, some of which will stand in total opposition to the interests promulgated by conventional positivist social science.

Therefore, the potential contributions of multi-paradigm research accrue on varied levels (Lewis and Kelemen, 2002). On a *pragmatic* level, this approach facilitates the development of understandings more in tune with the diversity, complexity and ambiguity of organisational life. On a *philosophical* level, multi-paradigm research encourages greater reflexivity in research. Use of a single modern paradigm produces a potentially valuable but narrow view, that is in turn incapable of exposing the multi-faceted nature of organisational reality. In contrast, multi-paradigm inquiry may foster 'more comprehensive portraits of complex organizational phenomena' (Gioia and Pitre, 1990: 587) by helping researchers confront and explore contradictions.

However, there are disadvantages. Committing oneself to more than one paradigm brings with it cognitive and emotional personal costs: leaving behind or pushing away (temporarily) a particular paradigm in order to engage with a new one can be a painful operation. Knowing and acting effectively in a new paradigm makes substantial demands upon the individual, demands which can only be satisfied through active bodily involvement, experience and practice (Brocklesby, 1997). Moreover, operating across paradigms makes it more difficult to engage in acts of 'scientific certification'. Researchers will pursue certification of their knowledge as much as they will pursue knowledge itself, because knowledge without an audience may be deemed useless (McCloskey, 1994). In so doing, they rely on multiple rhetorical devices, some of which may stand in opposition to others. Thus, a positivist may make use of statistical data in order to convey a particular point of view, while a pragmatist may ground his/her argument in rich ethnographic data. Since there are no universal benchmarks to judge the products of one's research, the measure of intellectual achievement can be judged in terms of the effectiveness of one's contribution to the conversation with the rest of the world.

Additionally, while we set out our position for multi-paradigm research we do not foreclose alternative routes into doing critical management research. As Carl Rhodes (2000) valuably points out, paradigm thinking is the dominant approach to understanding research methodology in organisational studies. In his assessment of the paradigm war debates, Rhodes concludes that the emergent victor (paradigm diversity) may well be at risk of becoming a new hegemony:

> **In organizational studies, we may have overturned the hegemony of structural-functionalism in favour of a situation of 'paradigm heterodoxy' ... and even perhaps regaled ourselves in postmodern pluri-paradigmaticism only to find that the notion of paradigms is itself becoming hegemonic ... paradigms leave no opportunities to study organizations in a way that is not framed by the scientific and sociological approach on which paradigm-informed meta-theoretical analysis is based. (2000: 10)**

Rhodes's cautionary note is not without merit. As we have discussed above, by supporting multi-paradigm research we do not see this position as either a dictate for paradigm diversity or akin to opening a floodgate for the integration of a bewildering array of paradigms. As Rhodes observes, there are other ways of researching organisations (he puts forward the use of reading and writing as one example) that go beyond the paradigmatic approach. However, given the benefits we have espoused above for mobilising multiple paradigms, it is also worth reiterating in the concluding stage of this chapter the challenges confronting researchers who wish to pursue multi-paradigm research.

The challenges of multi-paradigm research

Why should we care about our paradigm? The response here is that the paradigm inhabited by the researcher will shape the way in which various research dilemmas are to be resolved (Denzin, 1997). Also, at the risk of repeating ourselves, choosing to engage in multi-paradigm research is not an idyllic 'best of both worlds' approach. One that requires serious thinking about the theoretical antagonisms invoked by varied paradigms and the ways in which such antagonisms could be resolved or transcended. However, in considering these matters one must be careful of not becoming irrevocably lost (or bewildered) within the maelstrom of debate that rages on the matter of whether one is 'for' or 'against' the (in)commensurability thesis. As Czarniawska explains:

> **... there are much more serious dangers in life than dissonance in organization theory. Crossing the street every day is one such instance. We may as well abandon this self-centred rhetoric and concentrate on more practical issues: it seems that we would like to be able to talk to one another, and from time to time have an illusion of understanding what the Other is saying. (1998a: 274)**

While it is true that the research dilemmas facing multi-paradigm researchers are even more complex, requiring a heightened degree of reflexivity and personal scrutiny, this should not stop researchers from actually getting out there and doing critical management research. In the interest of aiding both a philosophical and practical take on multi-paradigm research, we conclude this chapter by offering some insight into some of the key issues researchers face in pursuing multi-paradigm research:

The sense-making dilemma Sense-making is defined as a process by which a researcher decides what to write about, what to exclude and how to represent the data (see the work of Karl Weick). Traditionally, data as reported by positivists and postpositivists tend to flow along nicely: there is no contradiction that is seen to impinge on the quality of the findings and no mention of what was excluded. Social constructivists and critical theorists meanwhile would acknowledge that data are contradictory, problematic and often quite messy.

The representation dilemma Representation is concerned with how a researcher represents and orchestrates various voices including their own. As a positivist (and, to a large extent, as a postpositivist), after finishing collecting the data, one's voice simply vanishes, for respectable positivist theory demands the complete absence of an author from their text. Only facts speak. In critical management research, one's presence as a researcher reverberates throughout the text, being one of the many voices contributing to the construction of theory.

The legitimisation dilemma This is concerned with how a text legitimates itself, or makes claims for its own authority. Positivists and postpositivists will make appeals to absolutist justifications (such as validity, reliability and generalisability criteria), whereas critical theorists will rely on rather more pragmatic and contextually-driven justifications. If the text is perceived as 'authentic' by an audience, and is written with honesty and in a reflexive style, this is usually sufficient enough justification for its quality and value.

The ethical dilemma Ethics (see Chapter 10) represent a set of social norms that cannot be dictated from above but are deeply intertwined with the social, cultural, and political context of the research. One possibility of attaining ethics in management research is the pursuit of reflexivity. For a positivist, this may be about questioning the methods employed and demonstrating that the limitations of a particular piece of work are not seriously compromising any results. For a critical theorist, reflexivity goes beyond the questioning of one's methods. A researcher may scrutinise their ontological, epistemological and methodological assumptions in order to demonstrate that their account is 'valid' and useful to an audience. A multi-paradigm researcher would attempt to transcend the differences between varied theoretical assumptions and methodological approaches, while recognising that his/her account constructs and is constructed by the network of research ideologies and languages and conventions in use.

Summary

Recognising that the mobilisation of a paradigm approach has significant effects upon the research process, this chapter has outlined some of the heated debates that have dogged the paradigmatic approach to research methodology for some time now. The chapter has advocated a multi-paradigm approach – not as a way of imposing a new hegemony within the field of organisation research but rather as a possibility for generating critical dialogues with others. Not wishing to see researchers 'trapped' in one paradigm, blind to viewing the world of management in alternative ways because they are reluctant or unable to step outside their chosen paradigm, we have proposed multi-paradigm research as a way of helping researchers to interrogate management differently. This may entail researchers positioning themselves within certain paradigms that may conflict with their personal proclivities to certain theoretical frameworks. Such a scenario is indicative of the challenge of engaging in multi-paradigm research.

As this chapter has shown, multi-paradigm research is not an easy pursuit for critical management researchers; nonetheless, it can be a rewarding approach because it encourages researchers to constantly question and reflect upon the methodological, epistemological and ontological assumptions that underpin their chosen research process. In Part II of this book we put forward a number of theories that can help researchers to develop critical forms of management research. Some of these, either because of their postmodernist parentage or their potential resonance with various aspects of postmodern thought, may be mobilised together in forms of multi-paradigm research. The first choice on our small menu of critical theory, American pragmatism, is discussed in Chapter 3.

Further reading

Two classics on the paradigm (in)commensurability thesis that we regard as essential reading are Burrell and Morgan (1979) *Sociological Paradigms and Organizational Analysis: Elements of the Analysis of Corporate Life* (London: Heinemann) and Guba and Lincoln (1994) 'Competing paradigms in qualitative research', in N.K. Denzin and Y.S. Lincoln's *Handbook of Qualitative Research* (see pp. 105–117) (Thousand Oaks, CA). For a positive evaluation on multi-paradigm strategies try Lewis and Kelemen (2002) 'Multiparadigm inquiry: exploring organizational pluralism and paradox', in *Human Relations*, 55 (2): 251–275. An important empirical study of multi-paradigm research (referred to above) is Hassard (1991) 'Multiple paradigms and organizational analysis: a case study', in *Organizational Studies*, 12 (2): 275–299. For a different approach to thinking about alternative strategies for conducting research on organisation read Rhodes (2000) 'Reading and writing organizational lives', in *Organization*, 7 (1): 7–29.

Part II

Theoretical Perspectives on Management

3

American Pragmatism

Introduction

This chapter is the first of five chapters in Part II of this book that outline and review the existing contributions and future potential of certain critical theories available to management researchers. As we have stated in the introduction to this book, some of these theories are not well known within the field of management research. American pragmatism, the subject of discussion in this chapter and also the 'oldest' theory that we present in this part of the book, is one example of a critical theory that has yet to make a deep impression within CMS and organisation studies more broadly. In that respect, we hope to offer a number of insights into its potential as a paradigm for developing critical forms of management research.

In this chapter we outline what we believe to be the most important features of American pragmatism and its possible contributions to doing critical management research. Although a largely unfamiliar theory within organisation studies, many organisational theorists owe an intellectual debt to pragmatism – a debt often unacknowledged. The neglect of pragmatism within organisational studies strikes us as a rather curious state of affairs because American pragmatism, or at least the version of it presented below, seems highly capable of helping organisational scholars to explore and interrogate the interrelationship between rationality, knowledge and everyday practices/experiences. What is more, as we indicate below, American pragmatism may find points of reference in postmodern thought, especially regarding its anti-foundational view of knowledge. There are also possible points of connection with feminist theorising (Seigfried, 1996) and even queer theory (Seidman, 1997), though such interdisciplinary explorations remain largely underdeveloped. Instances of conceptual convergence are likely to become clearer to the reader as they burrow more deeply into each one of the chapters in this part of the book. In an effort to shed light on the promise American pragmatism holds for enriching critical management research, we have organised our arguments as follows.

This chapter begins by commenting upon the origins of American pragmatism before going into its main features more deeply. In discussing the most striking facets of pragmatist theory, we concentrate on the publications of one of the key founders of American Pragmatism: namely, John Dewey. We spotlight John Dewey's approach for we believe him to be not only a central founding figure of American pragmatism, but also the most influential and controversial pragmatist philosopher. We then review the legacy of Dewey's work and its relevance for critical management research. In so doing, we detail a number of ways in which American pragmatism has already permeated and continues to permeate organisational theories. With these inroads in mind, we round off the last section of the chapter by broadly sketching out a pragmatist ethnographic orientation towards studying management.

The origins of American pragmatism

Pragmatism is a theory of meaning. In other words, pragmatism asserts that concepts are only relevant in as much as they are relevant for action. Building on this basic insight, pragmatism favours a reality that is in the making, a social model of knowledge, pluralist methodologies of research and an agenda of emancipatory ethics. Underlying these features is the view that rationality is embodied and therefore deeply intertwined with practical action.

Charles Peirce (1839–1914), William James (1842–1910) and John Dewey (1859–1952), the founders of this philosophical school of thought, established American Pragmatism as an alternative to Western rationalism. It is worth stating here that pragmatist thinking is not restricted to the American tradition. As the work of Thayer (1981) illustrates, there is a range of connections and points of divergence between the European and American pragmatist traditions. The progenitors of American pragmatism listed above held various and loosely connected concerns about philosophy, truth, human experience and meaning. For example, Charles Peirce trained as a scientist and, as such, was keen to apply scientific principles to philosophical problems. For Peirce, meaning was established by direct interaction with the sensible effects of one's actions. On a slightly different tack, William James was troubled by the precarious place of humans in the new scientific world. His scholarly interests shifted from logic to moral and psychological matters. The pursuit of truth was less a matter of scientific endeavour and more to do with the 'here and now'; in other words, the context and the individual. John Dewey affirmed Peirce's inquiring critical spirit and logical methods but, like James, his interests were moral, aesthetic, and educational, and his notion of the truth was pluralistic and tolerant of diversity.

Rooted in empiricism, pragmatism challenges the dualistic relationship between knowledge and experience and argues that reality can and should be changed through reason and action. As such, pragmatism goes beyond the shortcomings of positivism and certain versions of postmodernism by insisting that there is a reality out there (however fragile and disputed it might be). Further to this, pragmatism suggests that reality can be changed for the better by applying reason. While subjective interpretations are important in this endeavour, not all of them are equally useful. Usefulness becomes a central concern for the pragmatists, which is defined primarily on two counts:

1 epistemologically, in terms of whether the information or knowledge is credible, well founded, reliable and relevant;
2 normatively, in terms of whether knowledge/theory helps to advance one's cause/project and improve one's immediate circumstances (Wicks and Freeman, 1998).

As mentioned above, the work of the earlier pragmatists (John Dewey, Charles Peirce and William James) has received relatively little attention in organisation and management studies (unlike the work of Richard Rorty that has informed many postmodernist debates on contemporary organisational ethics). While pragmatism has generally been neglected within university business schools, there is evidence to demonstrate the presence of some scholarly interest in pragmatism within the fields of organisational and informational studies (for example, Goles and Hirschheim, 2000; Wicks and Freeman, 1998). However, the concrete contribution made by American pragmatism to the way we conceptualise, research and enact change in organisations has not been unpacked in detail. In order to describe some of these potential contributions we move to sketch out the main features of American pragmatism before providing evidence of its contribution to the management and organisational field.

The features of pragmatism

A reality that is in the making

Pragmatism sees reality, not as a static phenomenon, but constantly in the making, on its way to becoming constituted but never quite 'finalised' (a position shared with versions of postmodernism and queer theory, as outlined in Chapters 4 and 7 respectively). In Dewey's words, pragmatism pictures: 'a universe which is not all closed and settled, which is still in some respects indeterminate and in the making ... an open universe in which uncertainty, choice, hypotheses, novelties and possibilities are naturalised' (1927/1950: 52). This processual ontology is usually coupled with a relational perspective on social concepts. In particular, pragmatism is interested in the interrelationships between social entities rather than in the essence of these social entities. Such interrelations are seen to be fraught with indeterminacy and ambiguity, being difficult to predict, know or control at a distance. Cooper and Law's (1995) approach to organisation shares this concern. It distinguishes between distal and proximal approaches: the distal approach privileges results and outcomes, viewing organisations as a set of self-contained effects, while the proximal approach discloses emergent processes that are continuous and unfinished, viewing organisations as organising. In other words, organisations are viewed as a seamless web of interconnecting, heterogeneous actions.

According to Cooper and Law (1995), there is a tendency in the study of organisations to reduce them to social states (nouns) rather than acknowledging them as processes in the making (verbs), on their way to be constituted but never to be finalised. The proximal line of inquiry is also pursued in Actor Network Theory (ANT) studies of organisations (see for example, Latour, 1996; Suchman, 2000). For the pragmatists, this relational and processual dynamism is ubiquitous and central to social life. The way to resolve its indeterminacy is by actively participating in the situation at hand, applying terms supplied by the community of practice interested in finding solutions to problems. Note that 'community of practice' refers to those stakeholders who have an interest in resolving a particular problem that arises out of a specific context.

A social model of knowledge

For pragmatists, the question of whether truth can be attained or not is not theoretical but practical. The meaning of an idea is the practical consequences of the idea, for knowledge is intrinsically intertwined with human action. What people know about the world is influenced by what they do, can do and want to do in the world, not only as individuals but, more importantly, as collectivities. As such, knowledge cannot be a mere individual achievement, but a social one, for the validity of a theory is assured when that theory makes sense to a certain community of practice. Groups are bound together by similar or shared experiences and are able to reflect on new knowledge via dialogue and deliberation.

Pragmatists recognise that there are many ways of interpreting the world and some are better for this than others. However, one can recognise the superiority of one way over another thanks to practical experience and dialogue. The pragmatist's interest in what works and how and why it works (or doesn't) translates into a notion of knowledge that is antifoundational: one that is directed towards problem solving using the data and understandings available at the time. This form of knowledge can serve a number of knowledge interests among which are description, explanation, critique, innovation, emancipation and dialogue. We will return to these later in the chapter.

A pluralist methodology

Pragmatist philosophy 'gives us a pluralistic restless universe in which no single point of view can ever take in the whole scene' (James, 1897/1956: 177). Pragmatist methodology upholds a reality that does not always lend itself to clear-cut judgements.

A researcher is allowed (indeed encouraged) to use indeterminate truth-values in their attempt to handle situational indeterminacy. The quest for pragmatic certainty sensitises researchers to fuzzy things, multiple realities, paradox and ambiguity. Participant observation and other hands-on methods of data collection and analysis are seen to be the most effective ways to comprehend uncertainty and provide tentative yet workable solutions to problems.

Emancipatory ethics

Pragmatism shows an acute interest in action, not for its own sake but as a way to change existence. Researchers have a moral responsibility in presenting knowledge that has consequences for future applications. The research endeavour should be towards generating knowledge that makes a positive difference and contributes to better practice. Theories cannot be neutral for they have ethical and political implications. A pragmatist ethics counsels tolerance to ambiguity and calls for personal responsibility on the part of researchers. Personal effort in one's immediate community of practice is more important than following universal codes of ethics, for every moral situation is also a unique situation (see Dewey, 1920).

Embodied rationality

For pragmatists, rationality must be embodied if it is to be able to cope effectively with the perennial indeterminacy and contingency with which humans have to struggle in their everyday existence. To think means to experience the world in one way or another; not accounting for this experience means escaping into abstract and useless theory. Experience means not only what has occurred in the past but our visceral and embodied response to the immediate context. In *Experience and Nature* (1929) Dewey writes that experience is about what men do and suffer, what they strive for, believe in and endure, and also how men act and are acted upon, the ways in which they suffer, desire and enjoy, see, believe and imagine. Thus, for Dewey, reason is linked to 'the universe of nonreflectional experience of our doings, sufferings, enjoyments of the world and of one another' (1916: 9). In the pragmatist model, experience is mediated by signs and symbols (see Peirce's Theory of Signs).

Dewey also shows an acute interest in the interrelationships between social entities rather than in the essence of these social entities. These interrelationships are seen as contingent on the specific context. Grasping them allows us to better understand the changing nature of our world, its paradoxes, complexities and general messiness. The world exhibits an 'impressive and irresistible mixture of sufficiencies, tight completedness, order, recurrences which make possible prediction and control, and singularities, ambiguities, uncertain possibilities, processes going on to consequences yet indeterminate' (Dewey, 1958: 47).

The legacy of John Dewey: the community of inquiry

Born in 1859, John Dewey was an American psychologist, philosopher, educator, social critic and political activist. He made seminal contributions to nearly every field and topic in philosophy and psychology on subjects as diverse as pedagogy, the philosophy of the mind, epistemology, logic, the philosophy of science, and social and political theory. He was outspoken on progressive education, educator's rights, domestic and international politics, women's issues and humanism, as well as world peace. His pragmatic approaches to ethics, aesthetics and religion have also remained influential. Arguably, Dewey is one of the greatest thinkers of recent times and a premier philosopher of the twentieth century, along with James, Bradley, Husserl, Wittgenstein, Heidegger and Sartre.

John Dewey opened up a distinctly American approach to philosophy. Here the main use of philosophy was to meet people's needs, to help them deal with problems as they arose without necessarily making recourse to the perennial Cartesian and Platonic dilemmas. The task of the philosopher became a practical one, bearing on social, economic and political problems with a view to ensuring that individuals and communities lived richer and more fulfilling lives (Wicks and Freeman, 1998).

Dewey was not against the economic success of the large corporation but he worried about the effects corporate life would have on its members and the dangers of technocracy. Dewey felt that a participation in corporate American life left people dissatisfied, unfulfilled and insecure. He viewed the corporation as essentially deskilling, controlling and manipulating the individual. The individual could not simply search for meaning and expect to find it in the corporate environment unless some fundamental changes took place in the ways in which corporations and society at large functioned (Evans, 2000). Dewey's sensitive scrutiny of the ills of the corporate world did not however turn him into a pessimist, as he did not accept that such ills were unsolvable. He viewed scientific inquiry/research as an important vehicle in addressing and resolving them.

Thus, one particular strategy to remedy this situation was the idea of a community of inquiry that would take on board the challenges of corporate America. People belonging to such communities of inquiry would be connected by three elements. First, there is the problematic situation, the science needed to resolve that problem and the democratic values to be upheld in coming up with a practical solution. According to Dewey, this focus on a problematic situation is essential for it helps a community to form around the issue requiring resolution. Second, members of a community of inquiry must bring a scientific attitude to the problematic situation and view both theory and method as tools to address the problematic situation. Third, a community of inquiry must be democratic. They must take into account values/ideals such as freedom, equality and efficiency in pursuing their goals and objectives (Evans, 2000).

The contemporary organisation is a site of many struggles. These struggles pose significant challenges to the individual in a search for meaning (be they a senior manager or a local worker). Individual and organisational challenges could become the focus of research ensuring that actors (both academics and practitioners) rally around them, forming a potential community of inquiry. However, the members of a community of inquiry must proceed with a sense of critical optimism and with the belief that there are practical solutions to such problems. Dewey was a strong believer in the capacity of humanity to progress while at the same time accepting that uncertainty and doubt existed in the world. As he stated: 'The scientific attitude may almost be defined as that which is capable of enjoying the doubtful; scientific method is, in one aspect, a technique for making a productive use of doubt by converting it into operations of infinite inquiry' (Dewey, 1929: 228).

Although Dewey applauded science for offering rigorous methods for solving problems and acquiring information about how the world works, science was not regarded as the ultimate or the only way to know the world. According to Dewey, there may be other, equally valid, means of experience (such as art) and the activity of knowing through them could also enrich human understanding (Shield, 2003). For Dewey, the process of inquiry began with and ended in experience. Inquiry as a contingent, open-ended process relied on the positive (or otherwise negative) feedback from the community of inquiry. Dewey again: 'all scientific inquiries, regardless of their field of focus, are natural, situational, grounded in problems, integrations of theory and practice, and evaluative' (in Campbell, 1995: 199). The conclusion of the process of inquiry is not truth, but the best available solution at the time that is always subject to revision. Thus, scientific inquiry is not a means or method to find the truth. It is merely the means/method to reduce doubt and restore balance to a problematic situation. Moreover, knowing the world through experience is instrumental to rearranging it and giving it a form that is more useful to one's purposes.

Dewey's conception of community is closely connected to his understanding of democracy as a kind of co-operative experiment (Seigfried, 1996). Democracy is not necessarily political democracy but a social phenomenon that goes deeper. It is a way of life that emphasises working with others, sharing with others and contributing something positive to humanity. Thus, co-operation among individuals takes place not only in order to achieve certain goals but is itself a priceless addition to life (Dewey, 1938/1998: 342). As such, researchers are urged to respect and account for the interests of all constituent parties, rather than elevate the interests of elites.

From the pragmatist perspectives which have been considered thus far, we can begin to discern points of relevance for management researchers. As the next section shows, although some scholars do not explicitly reference American pragmatism in their work, it can be argued that many organisational scholars already owe an intellectual debt to these early pragmatists.

Pragmatism and organisation studies

A look at organisation theories suggests that American pragmatism has permeated the thinking of management classics and contemporary theorists in a myriad of ways. We provide the following illustrations, presented thematically.

Organisations (and environments) in the making

Pragmatism focuses on the relationship between entities rather than on the entities per se. The view of organisations as open systems (Katz and Kahn, 1978), though subject to intense criticisms, continues to shape the way in which organisations are being conceptualised in the twenty-first century. Weick's (1976) version of open system theory appears to be particularly indebted to pragmatist ideas. Here Weick sees organisations as loosely coupled systems, suggesting the existence of both rationality and indeterminacy, of both distinctiveness and responsiveness in the same system. This loose coupling provides organisations with the flexibility and slack necessary for survival. For Weick, organisations are self-regulating and self-reproducing systems that follow erratic patterns/sequences which are difficult to map out in advance.

In his later work, Weick (1988) goes beyond open system theory by questioning the existence of an *a priori* given environment by advancing the notion of *enacted environment*. With this notion, it becomes clear that the relationship between organisations and their environments is fraught with ambiguity and cannot be explained by causal models of thinking (such as input/output systemic methodologies). To accommodate such ambiguity, Weick proposes that we see organisations as processes based on shared understandings and interactions that enable them to function. Language, culture and history are viewed as central elements in thinking about one's actions in the world and thus the enactment of organisations. Weick accords narratives a central place in processes of organising, interpreting, and enacting, viewing human beings as creators and interpreters of social meaning at the corporation level.

Social and pragmatic organisational knowledge

A significant part of the organisational learning literature shares pragmatist, experimentalist and evolutionary ideas about what counts as knowledge. For the pragmatists, ends and means are often intertwined: mental constructs (knowledge) are endlessly revisable in light of experience and manipulable through imagination.

Consequently, both empirical understandings of the world and values are mental constructs to be tested against experience. For John Dewey in particular, the end as a condition affects the formation of a line of action, but taking an overt action is likely to bring about changes in the end. Argyris and Schön's (1978) single and double loop learning reflects the tension between habit and reflexivity and the interconnection between means and ends. If single loop learning is about reflecting on the outcomes of learning (the ends), being a process steeped in habit, double loop learning is about reflecting on the initial assumptions and premises in order to affect/challenge the outcomes of learning. The interaction of means and ends, combined with an anarchic model of organisational structure, is also embraced by Cohen et al's (1972) garbage can theory of organisations.

The view that knowledge arises through experimentalism (whereby individuals treat prospective action as a hypothesis to be tested against experience) has resonance with a well-established model of learning styles (Kolb et al., 1971). According to Kolb and his followers, a learning style begins with experience: we reflect on and try to make sense of what has happened in order to come up with rules of behaviour in similar situations. We then test these rules out in similar situations to see if they work. When they do we consolidate our learning, and when they don't we begin reflecting again. Kolb's learning styles are usually discussed within the organisational problem-solving context: some styles excel at problem finding, while others do the same in problem solving.

Action learning methodologies have also taken inspiration from this pragmatist stance. While action learning has developed multiple variations since its conception in the 1940s, all its different forms have a number of elements in common: 'all forms of action learning share the elements of real people resolving and taking action on real problems in real time, and learning through questioning and reflection while doing so' (Marquardt and Waddill, 2004: 186). Action learning also seeks to take advantage of individuals' previous experience and 'expertise'. For Revans (1980) learning consists mainly in the re-organisation or re-interpretation of what is already known. Raelin and Schermerhorn (1994) believe that action learning not only encourages practitioners to contribute to knowledge, but also gives them a critical role in determining its usefulness. As they suggest, management and organisational practices are shaped not only by existing theoretical understandings of organisational life but also by reflection on those events in which the individual practitioner has been involved (more on this in Chapter 9).

For pragmatists, knowledge is also social. In the context of organisational learning literature, learning is seen as a collective effort mediated by existing organisational structures, practices and learning tools. The so-called learning organisation is an exemplar of the sociality of organisational knowledge (Senge, 1990). Yet critics warn that the altruistic assumptions of the learning organisation contradict the performative nature of organisational practices and, in fact, the learning organisation is yet another form of managerial control and domination, serving the social agenda of management rather than an all-inclusive social agenda. To counteract such tendencies, learning spaces must be created where difference and diversity, multiple meanings and multiple realities (another feature of a pragmatist ontology) are accepted. Here, learning takes place in an ambiguous and disorganised fashion away from the dominant managerial agenda (Boje and Rosile, 1994).

Pluralist organisational methodology

The emphasis that pragmatism places on pluralism stems from the view that people confront different types of problems and hence have different experiences. As such, multiple research lenses are needed to comprehend rising organisational complexity and diversity. In light of this challenge, the role of researchers becomes that of interpreters – translating, penetrating and investigating different *modes of rationality* (Clegg, 1990). Multi-paradigm research, for example, facilitates this role, linking modern desires for order and stability with postmodern interests in fragmentation and ambiguity (Scherer, 1998). Multi-paradigm inquiry adheres to Kilduff and Mehra's conviction that 'the practice of research should never be a timid adventure' (1997: 476). Multiple research lenses and methods will enable insights into varied facets of organisations, potentially enhancing understandings of how dramatic transformations are intensifying ambiguity, complexity and conflict. Multi-paradigm strategies may guide explorations of pluralism and paradox, fostering the development of a more relevant and comprehensive theory. For the challenges of contemporary academia necessarily reflect those of organisational life:

> **The same paradoxical demands are made of researchers of complex social and cultural processes. They cannot simply adopt existing, standardized approaches. The whimsicality of reality can only be grasped with a multi-perspective approach that combines various methods of data collection, multi-level analysis and the in-built view of paradoxes in the research plan. This calls for creativity, for serendipity-proness, for not being afraid to walk on thin ice, for an attitude of fundamental scepticism about fixed models and solutions and for a critical reflection on one's own actions. (Koot et al., 1996: 211).**

Emancipatory organisational ethics

At the heart of pragmatism is the fundamental ambivalence or tension as to whether institutions and organisations are liberating or repressive (a dilemma shared with postmodernism, feminism and queer theory: see Chapters 4, 6 and 7 respectively). For some theorists, organisations are iron cages (DiMaggio and Powell, 1983), for others organisations are liberating sites (Simmel in Simmel et al., 1997). As early as 1938, Chester Barnard saw organisations as co-operative systems but, in the end, he took a managerial perspective on co-operation, viewing it in performative terms – subsumed to the overarching need to make profits and be efficient in business. Pragmatism emphasises the importance of the individual development of moral and intellectual capacity within a social milieu. For Dewey, the social nature of human beings leads to an emphasis on the importance of social co-operation to solve collective problems and on democracy as the means to achieve this social co-operation.

Fritsche and Becker's (1984) research on how individual managers think about ethical dilemmas at work found that most managers followed a utilitarian orientation, evaluating behaviour in terms of social consequences. In contrast to this growing, utilitarian stream of business ethics, postmodern approaches to business ethics (Parker, 1998) deny the possibility of unmediated knowing in the contextually shifting, power-laden structures and discourses that make up organisations. Managers' attempts to construct rules of ethical behaviour are intertwined with the acknowledgement of ambiguity and difference at work, a position which invites an alternative politics and ethics of managing by sustaining an ongoing dialogue and interaction with 'otherness', rather than denying and concealing it. This is not an all-or-nothing attitude towards ethical codes, but a heightened sensitivity towards the location of moralities in the concrete practices in which they are used or enacted in organisations.

Towards an emancipatory pragmatist ethnography

The preceding analysis of how pragmatism has impinged upon organisational studies bears testimony to pragmatism's strong, though often unacknowledged, influence on organisational theory. As a way of illustrating how theoretical insights derived from American pragmatism may shape future research agendas within critical management studies, we briefly suggest one way of adopting a pragmatist inflected approach to ethnographic research on management (for an outline of the ethnographic research tradition, see Chapter 9).

The focus of analysis

Pragmatist ethnographers will concentrate on actions. By studying actions, they can better grasp how individuals and groups render the world meaningful. Researchers will tend to blur the Habermasian distinction between material/instrumental and social/discursive actions. The sayings and doings of an individual are both regarded as actions and therefore worth studying. Moreover, actions must be placed in their practical context in order to avoid atomistic descriptions of individual actions. Practice is seen here as a holistic notion, 'the embodied, material, mediated array of human activity centrally organised around shared practical understandings' (Schatzki, 2001: 2). Thus, practice transcends individual human actions to include material artefacts, language conventions and other material and discursive props that determine which actions are adequate within the practice. This concept of practice might come in handy when solving the problems of unitarist research in, for example, international management (see Hassard et al., 2007) by providing the conceptual space necessary for examining people as centres of action as well as the structures that may influence individual decisions (Graham, 2005, quoted in Hassard et al., 2007).

Taking the example of international management further, the focus of analysis is on both successful and unsuccessful actions. Learning from failure and mistakes is as fruitful as learning from successes. Indeed, much can be learnt from the experiences of those multinational corporations who have failed to tap into local cultures, or from the experiences of senior managers who feel overwhelmed by the multiple, conflicting demands from below and above, and fall ill with stress and burn out (Kunda, 1992). Thus the task of the pragmatist ethnographer is not only to outline and challenge the relationship between agency and structure, but also to provide an account and explanation of change. Why is it, for example, that some people seek change when others placed in the same context are content to accept existing arrangements (Archer, 2003)? Why is it that the Anglo Saxon model of international management is at times accepted and at times resisted by local cultures?

How to theorise

To reiterate an earlier point, the pragmatist ethnographer cannot simply engage with reflection by sitting in the ivory tower of academia. Reflection cannot on its own resolve the issues of a contingent world. Abstract concepts and theories must thus be translated with respect to practice. Pragmatist theorising means an acknowledgement of the full dialectics between knowledge and action. Hence, proper knowledge is knowledgeable action and proper action is actable knowledge. Moreover, the practicalities of knowledge help establish the difference between meaningful and non-meaningful knowledge. In line with the process-oriented participative research advocated by Hassard et al. (2007), the pragmatist ethnographer's closeness to the empirical world via observation and triangulation of sources and methods is a way to counteract an over-emphasis on what people say.

The consequences of theory

'It is astonishing to see how many philosophical disputes collapse into insignificance the moment you subject them to this simple test of tracing a concrete consequence' (James, 1907). For the pragmatist ethnographer, presenting knowledge that has consequences for future applications is a moral responsibility. S/he may choose to describe and explain the practical world of international management but this will ultimately serve to suggest alternative ways to view the practice of international management in the light of more democratic principles of organisation. As well as developing new theoretical perspectives and conceptualisations of organisational practice, a researcher must make central workers' struggles for human dignity and meaning at work.

A focus on the future

The pragmatist ethnographer must show a genuine interest in the future, in the alternatives that may just happen, and in perspectives that are not yet realised. Pragmatic thinking is thinking towards the future consequences rather than about the past. Acting in the present is about anticipation and projection rather than about evaluating the past. Thus research on management, in an international context or otherwise, must be concerned with imagining a future that is more capable of solving the struggles of the local against the global, of the individual against the corporation, of culture against politics. This requires a great deal of critical optimism and a faith in progress, however local and contingent, as a real possibility.

Summary

The aim of this chapter was to introduce the reader to American pragmatism. Drawing upon Dewey's writings, we have set out what we consider to be some of American pragmatism's most useful conceptual components, building up a picture of what research interventions within critical management studies might look like if they adopt pragmatist principles. What is more, affinities exist between pragmatism and other critical theories discussed in Part I of this book; most particularly with feminism. However, these interdisciplinary relations remain under-developed.

Equally and relatedly American pragmatism has a low profile within CMS, though it would not be entirely true to say that American pragmatism has not influenced organisational studies. As we have been at pains to show, the tenets of early American pragmatist thought have percolated into organisational studies over the decades, though their influence is seldom acknowledged. More than anything, though, we have presented American pragmatism here because within pragmatist thought political and social action stand above (though not in isolation to) abstract theory. For management researchers, this idea might be very appealing because a research project characterised by pragmatism could focus sharply on the richness of human experience within organisations, experiences that are not always fully accounted for within organisational studies. For Dewey, focusing on experience would lead to the identification and formulation of connections between individuals and communities. Viewed in this way, pragmatism's concern for experience as a route to knowledge and theorising strikes us as harbouring enormous promise for management researchers wishing to develop anti-oppressive/emancipatory forms of research. Arguably, in many ways, aspects of American pragmatism foreshadow some of those key tenets of postmodernist thought (originating in the postmodern architecture movement) that gradually emerged following John Dewey's death. It is to postmodern theories that we now turn in Chapter 4.

Further reading

John Dewey's original works are indispensable in any exploration of early pragmatist theory: *How We Think* (1910), *Democracy and Education* (1916), *Experience and Nature* (1925) and *Logic: The Theory of Inquiry* (1938) represent a very small selection. Dewey also published numerous essays. Modern reprints of these texts are readily available and a number of edited collections of his work have been published. For instance, Jo Ann Boydston has edited a number of books that usefully assemble Dewey's works chronologically. As noted above, while Dewey's writings have engaged the minds of philosophers for many years, his work is less well known within those scholarly circles occupied by organisational theorists and feminists (to name just two). For a scholarly account of the possible interconnections between feminism and American pragmatism, try Seigfried (1996) *Pragmatism and Feminism: Reweaving the Social Fabric* (Chicago: Chicago University Press).

4

Postmodernism

Introduction

In Chapter 3 we outlined some of the most striking features of American pragmatism as a source of theoretical inspiration for management researchers. One observation of much of John Dewey's work is that he was passionate about helping individuals to develop the capacity to view the world in a critical fashion. In one way, Dewey's philosophy finds more than a dull resonance with those aspects of postmodern theory that also encourage us to think critically about the lifeworlds we occupy. Of course, there are significant ways in which these two bodies of theory diverge, but it is tantalising to think that there may well be a rendezvous between the two.

In this chapter we wish to explore the contribution of postmodernism to management theory. Unlike American pragmatism, postmodernism has an established history as a critical force within organisation studies. However, its popularity among business school scholars has not been consistent; indeed, to many organisation scholars postmodernism is a dirty word that signifies armchair theorising, monstrous relativism and pretentious posturing. For its supporters, notably David Boje (2006), postmodernism (after an encouraging start within the fine arts and then the social sciences) has splintered into different strands of theorising. As Boje observes, the ideals held by early postmodernist thinkers for reforming capitalistic societies have dissipated into vaporous strands of theorising. It might be argued that postmodernism has lost its momentum. However, like Boje, we believe that postmodernism is still a theoretical force to be reckoned with, one that has much to offer critical management researchers looking to develop emancipatory forms of research.

With the above in mind, this chapter outlines the most important features of postmodernism by making reference to the organisation studies literature. It is not our intention here to put forward the one 'true' version of postmodernism or one that harbours most salience for the critical study of management. To seek clarity within such debates about what postmodernism is (if it is at all possible to do so) might well lead to privileging some brands of postmodernist thought over others – a prospect many postmodernists would shudder at. In order to avoid rigid classifications, we work up Wittgenstein's concept of family resemblance which purports that two objects may belong to the same classification and, yet, may have very few features in common if any at all. Thus exemplars that appear to stand in opposition to one another could in fact belong to a broadly defined version of postmodernism. The chapter then looks at what lies outside postmodernism before moving on to sketch out the challenges confronted by researchers wishing to engage in the postmodern scientific enterprise.

Postmodern times

Postmodernism is all around us. A trendy catchword since the late 1980s, postmodernism simply refuses to go away. Its discourse and mode of engagement have reached academic domains as diverse as music, international relations, media studies, geography, psychology, architecture, sociology, mathematics, development studies, politics and more recently organisation studies. For many commentators, the focus of postmodernism is on images, copies and other simulacra that supplant what they are supposed to represent (Goldman and Papson, 1994). Desire and unwavering consumption, the blurring between high and mass culture, and the time-space compression are all features of a postmodern world. Postmodernism has, according to many, altered the way we live, organise ourselves, interact with each other and so on. But more importantly, postmodernism has changed the way we think about the human condition.

The literature is replete with postmodernist typologies: for example, Hal Foster divides postmodernism into neoconservative and poststructuralist variants; Pauline Rosenau talks about affirmative and skeptical postmodernism; Richard Rorty about deconstructionist and bourgeois postmodernism; while Mark Hoffman splits postmodernism into critical and radical interpretivist postmodernism (all cited by Darryl, 1998). Perhaps the most influential typology in organisation studies comes from Martin Parker (1992) who suggests that post-modernism (with a hyphen) refers to an epoch of change that presupposes new economic, technological, political and spatial configurations. Postmodernism (without a hyphen) refers to a new epistemological sensitivity that challenges the status quo of social science.

Despite its proliferation throughout the social sciences and humanities, postmodernism remains a curious lexeme of essentially contested concepts, disparate ideas, obtuse meanings and political agendas (Darryl, 1998). Indeed, there are as many versions of postmodernism as there are commentators on the subject: Jean-François Lyotard, for example, sees postmodernism as a general condition of knowledge in the contemporary informational regime; for Ihab Hassan, postmodernism is regarded as a stage on the road to the spiritual unification of humankind; Frederic Jameson views postmodernism as the cultural logic of late capitalism; Jean Baudrillard conceptualises postmodernism as a sea of signs and simulacra that has killed its points of reference; while for Jacques Derrida postmodernism is about challenging the Western metaphysics of presence through textuality. Elsewhere, Michel Foucault sees the postmodern agenda as concerned with unearthing the complicities of power/truth regimes and the resulting subjectivities. Interestingly, the likes of Foucault and Derrida, labeled by some commentators as 'postmodernists' or 'poststructuralists', rejected these terms in a typical postmodern/poststructuralist gesture of refusing the imprisonment of paradigmatic classification.

Mapping postmodernism

As we have stated above, there is no single approach to understanding or capturing the 'essence' of postmodernism; instead, there are many different strands of postmodern theorising (Boje, 2006). Limitations of space prevent a full account here of each variant of postmodern thought. Instead, driven to a large degree by a pragmatic agenda, we outline some of the key features postmodern theorising might be said to embrace. As such, and in broad terms, we view postmodernism as an affirmative, emancipatory research enterprise that asserts the possibility of meaning, the importance of theory and the necessity of practical action. Six main features are crucial to this approach: fluidity, ambiguity, pluralism, literary language, non-linear progress, and localisation. These are outlined below.

Fluidity

Postmodernism shows an acute interest in processes rather than outcomes. In other words, in *organising* rather than *organisation*. As such, it views organisational reality as constantly being in the making, on the way to being constituted, rather than something static and observable at a glance. Postmodernism calls attention to the fluid and slippery nature of the processes that go into the making of organisational reality. Organisations are no longer seen as collections of stable and static entities (people, material resources, ideologies and so on) but as shifting networks in a permanent state of flux and transformation. Postmodernism also posits the end of the strong, stable, coherent and unified subject. Individuals have multiple, fluid, contradictory identities: particular identities take precedence over others, as individuals go in and out of various allegiances and groups. For example, Fournier and Kelemen's (2001) study of a women's learning set explores the fluidity of the identity work performed by its members in an attempt to temporarily suspend, re-negotiate and reconcile the incongruity of their dual position as women and senior managers. Here gender is not seen as a static category, something that is just brought to organisations; instead gender is performed, reproduced and, occasionally, transgressed in organisations (Gherardi, 1995). Thinking about gender as something which is performed rather than given (biologically or culturally) alerts us not only to the complex processes that contribute to constructing and maintaining gender positions and gender difference, but also to the fragility and fluidity of gender dualisms, and the possibility of transgressing them.

Ambiguity

Postmodernism sensitises us 'to a universe which is not all closed and settled, which is still in some respects indeterminate and in the making ... an open universe in which uncertainty, choice, hypotheses, novelties and possibilities are naturalized' (Dewey quoted in Shalin, 1992). It demands that we become accustomed to indeterminacy, as any attempt to close it off is highly problematic. Indeterminacy arises from one of the main functions of language: that of naming (Bauman, 1991). To name means to draw boundaries around an object or an idea, by setting things apart, by including some and excluding others from the 'named' province. The very aim of naming is thus to give the world a clear structure in order to prevent ambiguity. However, the act of naming is ambivalent as it splits the world into two imprecise spheres: the named and the non-named. To ensure that the boundaries are set definitively, one needs an ever more precise name and thus the very effort to jettison indeterminacy creates a space where ambiguity flourishes.

Any attempt to fix meaning is highly suspicious and any chase for the ultimate meaning is riddled with ambiguity. In our quest for precision, more and more ambiguity is created. As we have already shown in Chapter 1, Kelemen's (2000) study explores the ambiguity of the TQM language in four UK service organisations. To reiterate one key finding, Kelemen demonstrates that while ambiguity could potentially facilitate managerial control to be exercised more effectively, at the same time it creates spaces for resistance. In other words, the effects of ambiguity cannot be predicted and known beforehand. Moreover, ambiguity is not only inherent in language, but also in material artifacts that organisational members must read in order to make calculations (Munro, 1995).

Pluralism

Postmodernism celebrates ontological, epistemological and methodological pluralism. The social world is seen as complex, multi-faceted and contradictory, and therefore no single point of view can ever take in the whole scene. In order to recapture as much as possible, one has to change position, mental gears and frames of analysis. Postmodernism encourages multi-paradigmatic and contrasting representations, which could offer 'insights into the characteristic contradictions and tensions embodied in contemporary organizations' (Reed, 1985: 201). Calls for devotion to paradigmatic unity are seen as perilous because they reduce the ability to combine diverse approaches and remove social science from the concerns of a wide variety of stakeholders (Kilduff and Mehra, 1997). Postmodernist researchers are free to apply whatever combinations of research methods they deem useful and are urged not to regard the research process as a timid adventure (ibid.). The use of multiple paradigms, for example, encourages greater awareness of theoretical alternatives fostering greater understandings of organisational plurality and paradox (Lewis and Kelemen, 2002). One of the most important multi-paradigm studies in the UK (Hassard, 1991, 1993) displays postmodern characteristics in the ways in which the author mixes four different organisational paradigms, various research methodologies and styles of writing in his study of work behaviour in the UK's Fire Service.

Literary language

Postmodernism questions the neutrality of language. It argues that the language of management research and therefore of social science is literary and can be interpreted like any other text. Postmodernists embrace the idea that 'knowledge can only be produced in "small stories" or "modest narratives," mindful of their locality in space and time and capable of adapting or disappearing as needed' (Calás and Smircich, 1999: 651). Postmodernist stances draw attention to the rhetorical nature of management science and advocate the role of irony, parody and allusion in refining researchers' sensitivity to differences and their ability to tolerate ambiguity and paradox. If, for many, irony and parody are seen to be signs of disengagement on the part of an apolitical, transcendental ego that floats above historical reality, for LaCapra 'a certain use of irony and parody may play a role both in the critique of ideology and in the anticipation of a polity wherein commitment does not exclude but accompanies an ability to achieve critical distance on one's deepest commitment and desires' (1987: 128). Lilley's (2001) study on management research funding in the UK draws on irony, parody and mockery to explore the role played by conspiracies in the process of knowledge generation and legitimation. Lilley examines the relationship of the funding and ownership of the means of production with the ownership and control of 'scientific knowledge', through a number of stories that surround his own involvement/detachment in producing knowledge for the Economic and Social Research Council, the organisation that funds much of the UK's state-sponsored research in the management science arena.

Elsewhere, Karen Legge (1995, 2005) points out that from a critical postmodern perspective, human resource management is viewed as a set of discourses. In a Foucauldian sense, discourses comprise of images, beliefs, concepts, language and actions (Foucault, 1978; see also Chapter 6). As such, the discourses on HRM are mobilised and (re)produced by its proponents to present HRM as a 'coherent new strategy that paves the way to achieving competitive advantage' (Legge, 2005: 351). These discourses not only justify the practices that underpin HRM, but also the harsh effect these practices have on those on the receiving end (Mabey et al., 1998). Legge is not the only HRM scholar to remark upon the managerialist undertone to contemporary discourses on HRM.

Taking the Foucauldian notion of discourse with its links to power and knowledge, and employing it in a paper on the potential of Foucauldian theory for (re)analysing HRM, Barbara Townley (1993a) has created something of a stir within scholarly circles. Townley's textual analysis reframed HRM practices (for example, selection, performance appraisal, job design, and so on) as technologies of power used by employers to discipline workers. For example, in relation to performance management systems, Townley (see also 1992, 1993b) argues that the performance appraisal is a site in which a worker's behaviour is rendered visible, and their contributions quantifiable and thus susceptible to being ranked. One consequence of this 'serial ordering' (1993a: 529) of individuals is that they may be classified around 'two poles – one negative, the other positive' (ibid.). In so doing, labour can be differentiated hierarchically along the lines of work outputs, and valued or discarded accordingly. Somewhat similarly, recruitment and selection procedures can be seen as practices that split, quantify, sift and rank applicants. In both cases, the power of normative judgement is exercised, whereby workers and applicants discipline their own behaviours vis-à-vis the hierarchical observations of appraisers and selectors in order to meet normative templates of the 'ideal employee'. In these instances, individuals are positioned as disciplined subjects within the subjective realms of their managers and (potential) employers, realms in which managerialist concerns about worker performance reign supreme.

Thus, from a postmodern point of view, HRM practices seek to discipline, order and control workers, although these forms of government are imperfect. In the same Foucauldian vein, it is also possible that workers can engage in acts of resistance that can disrupt and even overturn the designs of management. In other words, the exercise of power is not a zero-sum game that solely works to the advantage of managers. Power may be exercised productively by workers as it can be by managers, though the field of discursive constraints that mediate the exercise of power in each case may well be different (also see Newton and Findlay, 1996). In summary, Townley's groundbreaking paper is a brilliant example of how critical postmodern theory has been used to rethink an aspect of organisation in order to denaturalise its coherent and legitimate appearance. In this case, Townley's Foucauldian analysis refocused HRM as the construction and production of knowledge that 'serves to render organizations and their participants calculable arenas, offering, through a variety of technologies, the means by which activities and individuals become knowable and governable' (1993a: 526).

Non-linear progress

Postmodernism attacks the view of progress as linear development. In fact, the more we know the more we realise we do not know, and thus we progress to an even greater knowledge of our ignorance (Kilduff and Mehra, 1997). Management knowledge does not 'grow' according to some linear cumulative model: processes of double hermeneutics (Giddens, 1987) make such a scenario highly dubious. Within double hermeneutics, the first loop is one in which researchers study and interpret the organisational world. This loop is also characteristic of research in the natural sciences. The second loop is specific to the arena of the social sciences: it is that process where the subjects reflect on the research interactions and findings and change their behaviour in unpredictable ways. Thus the object of study in organisation studies is not static, predictable and coherent but in continuous transformation and is, therefore, difficult to predict. Postmodernism does not reject scientific advances but it draws attention to the rhetorical devices by which theories are arrived at, as well as to the social and political relations that help establish what counts as knowledge at a particular point in time and within a particular context. Knorr-Cetina's ethnographic (1983) study of the social conditioning of scientific knowledge led to some surprising findings: laboratory scientists were driven by a concern to make things work rather than by the abstract quest for 'truth' customarily ascribed to science and scientists. Knorr-Cetina concludes that the products of science are the result of mundane routines occurring in the laboratory. These routines obscure and, at the same time, lend credibility to the processes by which scientists are able to transform the subjective into the objective, the unbelievable into the believed, the fabricated into the finding and the painstakingly constructed into the objective scientific fact.

Localisation

Postmodernism emphasises the importance of the local above any globalising tendencies. The local may refer, among other things, to one's neighbourhood, organisation, region, country, ethnicity or religion. As such, it is a contested resource. Indeed allegiance to the local is by no means unproblematic. Individuals bring with them different expectations and meanings, transforming the local into a site of continuous struggle. Globalisation, deregulation and the erosion of the Cold War geographical systems have helped fuel new aspirations and struggles for local autonomy and assertions of collective identity against freely moving capital, jobs, people and images (Antonio, 2000). Antonio calls this process 'new tribalism', viewing it as a consequence of the postmodern drive towards cultural fragmentation, anti-universalism and identity politics. While we might be witnessing the resurgence of neopopulist group identity anchored in ethnic community, we dispute the claim that the nation state has withered away its utility, sovereignty and political jurisdiction (Elkins, 1995). For a while, on the one hand, we have witnessed the formation of new territorial alliances and the removal of trade and work barriers (within the European Union and the NAFTA countries, for example), in an era that seems to know no boundaries; on the other hand, we are being faced with more ferocious systems for protecting national boundaries against those who are not seen to have the right to belong (economic and political immigrants), as well as more and more armed conflicts aimed, precisely, at defending the boundaries of sovereign states.

What lies outside postmodernism

This section explores what lies outside postmodernism by arguing that postmodernism is neither anti-science nor armchair theorising. In that regard we counter the strong criticisms levelled at postmodernism that suggest it leads to an 'anything goes' approach, that it advocates a wholesale rejection of modernism and that it has become the very thing it despises – a meta-narrative.

Postmodernism is not anti-science

Postmodernists do not dismiss science. They simply question its production (and consumption) in a sympathetic manner. If normal/consensual science is at the heart of modernism, postmodernism challenges the neutrality of the process by which scientific consensus is achieved by focusing on the power relations that help constitute what counts as science at a particular point in time. In general, postmodernism sees theory and science as a constellation of perspectivist narratives arising from, justifying and reproducing hegemonic relations and identities of specific socio-cultural relations. This is not to say that postmodernists would abandon all truth claims and reject references to a reality external to the theoretical text, or that they embrace the view that perspectives from divergent locations are incommensurable and thus impervious to intersubjective consensus. In fact, many postmodernists (Calás and Smircich, 1999; Deetz, 1996; Kilduff and Mehra, 1997) view incommensurability as a modernist legacy and would urge researchers to engage in cross-paradigm communication and research.

If the project of modernist science is built on the myth of the heroic individual who, armed with objective procedures and methods of research, proceeds to discover the 'truth', postmodernism views science as *emerging* from the workings of heterogeneous networks of humans, material, ideologies and traditions that come together at a particular point in time within a particular context (Latour, 1987). Hence, the outcome (or what we may call the scientific product) cannot be known beforehand or indeed predicted and managed according to a grand plan. Latour's ethnography sheds light on the transient and unpredictable constitution of such networks and their workings, by making more apparent the 'messiness' of the processes that contribute to the production of scientific results in a laboratory. His work casts doubt on the rational character of science: the view that science is value free and the result of applying objective procedures methodically to the object of study. In a similar vein, postmodernists argue that partisan values play a central part in producing knowledge but usually the results and processes are neutralised and described in a technical language.

Postmodernism is not armchair theorising

For many critics postmodernism is synonymous with abstract levels of theorising which bear little or no relation to the surrounding management reality. The postmodern management theorist is thought to be a meditative, contemplative and occasionally romantic person, who sits in his/her professorial chair from where he/she engages in theoretical acrobatics. Although we accept that some writings that are labeled 'postmodern' are indeed unwieldy and loquacious, postmodernist writing in management and organisation studies does not have to be abstract or garrulous, and is by no means anti-empirical work. In fact one of the most illustrious, contemporary, organisational ethnographies is an empirically-driven postmodern analysis of contemporary management practices (Kunda, 1992). Kunda's work documents the tensions and conflicts between the individual self and the organisational self, and the ways in which the self is the unpredictable result of personal and organisational contingencies coming together. Postmodernist research employs a plethora of research methods in an attempt to turn theory and practice into a site of denaturalising critique.

Contemporary criticism also asserts that postmodernism has no theory of agency that enables a move into political action (cf. Hutcheon, 1989). This is by no means the case: many management theorists are also activists who try to bring about social and political change in the worlds around them (Boje and Dennehy, 1993). In fact, many postmodernist management researchers care deeply about the social, economic, political and aesthetic consequences of their work. They view common opinion or 'the voice of nature' as cultural representations. They often work hard to challenge the neutral façade of management theory in order to make visible the positive and negative effects it has upon the way we understand and approach organisations.

For instance, Judy Wajcman's (1998) study is a fine example of postmodern analysis that challenges taken-for-granted views about gender and management. Her analysis draws on triangulated evidence collected as part of a survey involving male and female senior managers in five organisations, selected because of their 'exemplary' equal opportunities programmes. Wajcman also constructed a more in-depth qualitative case study carried out in 'Chips', an American-owned, multi-national, high-tech corporation. Wajcman's study scrutinises those practices that make possible the creation and maintenance of gender regimes of management, by investigating whether men and women have distinct styles of management and whether the experiences of men and women in senior management positions are different and if so for what reasons. Her findings suggest that despite a relatively positive attitude towards female managers, women are far from being totally accepted in senior management positions. The reason behind that is not that women are better or worse than men: organisations are circumscribed to a 'male standard' and this positions women as out of place – as travellers in a foreign land (see also Gherardi, 1995). As long as the rules of interaction in organisations are male biased, women will find themselves in the precarious position of having to constantly negotiate their position as managers and women. The study concludes that only by challenging and debunking such rules can organisations achieve success in equal opportunities programmes.

Not 'anything goes' for postmodernists

It has been suggested by many critics that postmodernism adopts a naïve, relativist, 'anything goes' approach. This position suggests that since there are no standards by which to assess which account is more truthful than others, one collapses into a position of endless pluralism and/or nihilism. Jean-François Lyotard's work is typically associated with this position. While Lyotard wages war on totality by celebrating difference and embracing local knowledge, he does not (viewpoints to the contrary) suggest that anything goes. In *The Postmodern Condition: A Report on Knowledge* (1984), Lyotard argues that no scientific discourse can dominate all others by making recourse to a meta-narrative authority to ensure its legitimacy. The postmodern condition presupposes the existence of many *petit recit*-s ('small narratives'), each of them possessing its own specific, local way of representing the world. But Lyotard views the small narrative as the 'quintessential form of imaginative invention, particularly in science' (1984: 60) and the communication between small narratives as a necessary, albeit contingent, function of scientific action. As there are no meta-narratives to regulate such communication, this is an area where, according to Lyotard, a researcher has to be 'active', by taking on the job of the 'philosopher' and not just that of the 'scientist'. In so doing, researchers should attempt to seek out new idioms which can 'speak for the silent', guarantee the conditions for 'participating in conversation', and write about the world 'in the service of the unknown'. Thus, Lyotard's position is not one which invites nihilism but one which encourages active participation in deciding the rules of the game.

Postmodernism does not deny the existence of universal rules; rather, it suggests that different communities of practice interpret such rules differently. Knowledge, or what is considered to be true and valid, is a matter of agreement among the members of the scientific community and depends to a large extent on the sanctioned vocabulary, procedures and mechanisms of inquiry and justification. Scientific communities usually display a high degree of sophistication and complexity with respect to the rules and methodologies that have to be mustered by their members. Initiation into the language game of the community requires special and extensive training. Willful departures from established rules and procedures might be perceived as irrational, especially if they fail to produce findings that align themselves with the expectation of the scientific community. Yet such departures are welcomed by postmodernism as they could lead to novel insights into the fluid, ambiguous and plural social reality. At the same time, they may also trigger the exclusion of certain members from the scientific community.

Postmodernism does not reject modernism

Postmodernism does not represent a total rupture from modernism. *Post*modernism, as the label implies, is neither 'anti-modernism' nor 'non-modernism' but a more sceptical continuation and refinement of modernism. Postmodernism is a particular perspective on modernity and is itself dependent on it (Tester, 1993: 28). It is a condition that only makes sense regarding the extent that it is considered in relationship with the modern. Here a parallel can be drawn with poststructuralism. As we assert in Chapter 5, poststructuralism cannot be understood in isolation from structuralism. Like poststructuralism, postmodernism can never step completely outside of the modern heritage from which it must borrow its tools, its history and language in an attempt to destroy that heritage (Manzo, 1991). As such, postmodernism is the unfolding of the modernist tapestry; talk about the postmodern age is merely talk about the consequences of modernity (Giddens, 1991). Moreover, the postmodern is always implied in the modern, and its potentiality can only be realised in the modern (Lyotard, 1984). Modernism and postmodernism mutually define each other, with their mutuality being in a constant state of tension and difference. Any attempt to periodise the modern/postmodern in a linear fashion is fraught with difficulties. For example, Nietzsche's and Dewey's works display many of the postmodern features discussed above, yet they were created at a time when the whole philosophical establishment was staunchly upholding modernist standards of thought.

Postmodernism is not a meta-narrative

It has been suggested that the postmodern denial of meta-naratives is itself a narrative. According to the critics, to postulate the 'death of the author' and to uphold the 'crisis of representation' is synonymous with hypothesising in the modernist tradition. Postmodernism does not suggest the death of all meta-narratives. Rather, it suggests ways in which such meta-narratives could be resisted and opposed locally. We can turn to Foucault's thoughts on power and resistance for inspiration. In Foucault's work, disciplinary power is the overarching meta-narrative that brings and keeps individuals together. For Foucault (1977), disciplinary power refers to those techniques/technologies that make possible the control of the individual by others or by oneself:

> **Discipline ... is a type of power, a modality of its exercise comprising a whole set of instruments, techniques, procedures, levels of application, targets; it is a physics or an anatomy of power. (p. 215)**

Furthermore, disciplinary power resides in every perception, judgment and act, and therefore any prospects of escaping it are limited to both the advantaged and the disadvantaged (Hardy and Leiba-O'Sullivan, 1998). One becomes a subject – namely, gains knowledge about the self and the Other by taking part in such disciplinary power structures. Disciplinary power transforms individuals into subjects who 'secure their sense of meaning and reality through participation in (certain) practices' (Knights and Morgan, 1995: 194). What Foucault suggests is that rather than simply complying with the demands of disciplinary power, one could manipulate, comply selectively or put up resistances against its practices in order to make discipline work more in favour of the individual.

The challenges of postmodernism

It is argued here that postmodernism has a great deal to offer to management and organisation studies. But management researchers seeking to realise its potential in that respect will be confronted by a number of challenges, as outlined below.

How to avoid orthodoxy

Postmodernism has moved from a rather marginal position only a few decades ago to a more central position in the social sciences. In order to retain its liveliness and usefulness, postmodernism must constantly challenge its own assumptions and search for novel forms of inquiry. Such novel forms of inquiry have to be empirically grounded. Many postmodernists would argue that postmodernism cannot be considered in a purely conceptual manner and needs to be subject to both theoretical and empirical criticism (Strinati, 1993). Esping-Andersen (2000) advocates intentional and purposeful empiricism, for if there is a microcosm in the making, one cannot identify it by trying abstractly to imagine a hidden Gestalt. A far better strategy is to examine empirically what is happening in the organisational world and to report it in a reflexive and useful way to wider audiences. The important thing is that postmodernism does not become complacent. If it is going to revive management and organisation studies it has to continue to disrupt, re-inscribe and re-think the world of organisation.

Emancipation

Postmodernist researchers should view practical action as crucial. Many management theorists would do well to descend from their ivory towers and attend to the unheard and the unseen. This is not to say that those subjects in a more visible position (namely, managers) are to be ignored entirely by management research. Rather they need to be inscribed with new faculties and placed in a more equal relation to marginal subjects. In other words, it is not enough to study workers, women, non-heterosexuals, and so on. One has to study and eventually affect their relation with managers, non-heterosexuals and women (and so on) respectively. Some postmodernist researchers take an anti-managerialist stance by suggesting that providing managers with tools for understanding the concerns of the marginalised Others would in fact reinforce managers' centrality and dominance. Therefore, researchers should not attempt to engage practitioners but should instead confine their theories to academic conferences and publications (Nord and Jermier, 1992). However, this stance is highly modernist in that it preserves the ivory tower of those researchers who are not interested in stepping down in order to engage with the immediate, the contingent and the local. Our version of postmodernism emphasises the importance of pragmatic action and the central role of the reflexive practitioner/manager in transforming organisations in better, more democratic, workplaces. Consequently, the role of postmodernist social science is to successfully adapt to the contingencies and exigencies of experience.

Playfulness

There is nothing worse than boring social science. Postmodernism reverses this trend in that it encourages playfulness in the service of inquiry. This is not to suggest that postmodernism necessarily encourages us to engage in play for its own sake. Play can never be 'free-play' that operates outside a zone of power relations. Our efforts at play are mediated by the constraints that exist within relations of power. This is to say that while play can be liberating it can also be limited in the form it takes. This is an important point because the postmodern notion of play within research has been severely chided by some postmodern critics. Playfulness within scholarly inquiry is a sort of playfulness of the mind that allows one to think of a subject in all sorts of strange ways. Put differently, playfulness can help us to make the familiar 'strange'. Postmodernist writing in management and organisation studies can be playful, eclectic and, to some extent, exhilarating (Kuspit, 1990). But its critics view playfulness as a passive, reactionary position, one of letting the world go by like a play/carnival that has previously been scripted and in which the ending never changes. Others view playfulness as a thinly disguised façade that spares postmodernist theory the embarrassment of revealing its a-theoretical impression and meaningless nature (Huyssen, 1984). We, however, strongly disagree. Playfulness is an active project, one that seeks not only to gather insights into the world, but also to change it for the better by interrogating and disrupting modernist logic.

The place of the individual

Another challenge facing postmodernism is to redefine the place of the individual and his/her relation with structures of authority. Modernism emphasises versions of the individual as being in control of the world or individuals being trapped by broader social structures. Postmodernism celebrates the individual uniqueness resulting from individuals' ability to choose the structures that enable or constrain them. The acknowledgement of individual choice has seen renewed interest in cognition and perception. Individuality is the result of difference, requiring the presence of the Other. Being with the Other and for the Other are postmodern prerogatives of becoming an individual (Bauman, 1995). In addition to being a product of time, chance, and historical and political circumstances, the individual is also an aesthetic product, made of heterogeneous materials, relations and traditions which are put together by the self in an attempt to cope with day-to-day practical contingencies.

Summary

This chapter has argued for the relevance of postmodernism in doing critical management research. Despite the widespread suspicion within some academic quarters about what postmodernism might lead to (for example, relativism and armchair theorising), we view postmodernism as a vibrant body of theoretical perspectives that holds much potential for cultivating open-ended forms of empirical inquiry (see also Hassard, 1995). Rather than shy away from the animating impulses within postmodernism to shake up what we regard as taken-for-granted in the world around us, we embrace the insistence within postmodernism to re-think familiar ideas, images, ways of becoming and relating to others.

As we have stated above, postmodernism is generative in that respect – it enables us to question, re-invent and re-imagine. It is not, as some might have us believe, an unconstrained playground for destruction. In outlining the case for postmodernism within critical management research we hope to have demonstrated postmodernism's potential in that regard, as well as the aspects that are prone to attack. Although the limitations of space prevent us from entering into postmodernist debates more deeply, like some other supporters of organisational postmodern inquiry (Cooper and Burrell, 1988), we duly sound a final optimistic note for the postmodern project as one that helps us to usefully examine paradox, ambiguity and contradiction within management. In the next chapter we outline one analytical approach that bears the postmodern concern for highlighting paradox, ambiguity and contradiction – this is deconstruction.

Further reading

Though challenging and intricate, Jean-François Lyotard's *The Postmodern Condition: A Report on Knowledge* (1984) (Minneapolis: University of Minnesota Press) is regarded by many as a classic on postmodernism. For a useful review of Lyotard's work on postmodernism and its application within organisational studies, read Jones (2003) 'Theory after the postmodern condition', in *Organization*, 10 (3): 503–525.

One of the most influential and readable articles on postmodernism in organisational studies is Parker (1992) 'Post-modern organizations or postmodern organization theory?', in *Organization Studies*, 13 (1): 1–17. Another seminal article which explores the potential of postmodernism for reshaping organisational research is Kilduff and Mehra (1997) 'Postmodernism and organizational research', in *The Academy of Management Review*, 22 (2): 453–481. David Boje, a well-known supporter of postmodernism, has also written a number of articles on postmodernism and organisation studies. One of the most useful (for its overview of the developments within postmodern theory) is Boje (2006) 'What happened on the way to postmodern?', in *Qualitative Research in Organizations and Management: An International Journal*, 1 (1): 22–40.

Finally, we heartily recommend reading Townley (1993a) 'Foucault, power/knowledge, and its relevance for human resource management', in *Academy of Management Review*, 18 (3): 518–545.

5

Deconstructionism

Introduction

Having (re)established postmodernism as a relevant and critical conceptual resource for management researchers in Chapter 4, we now turn to examine deconstructionism: a critical approach that has much in common with one of postmodernism's ambitions to make what is familiar in the world around us extraordinary. The discursive turn in management studies signals the centrality of language in understanding and constructing theories about the organisational world. Some authors are interested in the study of social/organisational text (both talk and written text) in its social action context; elsewhere, others focus on the study of social reality as discursively constructed and maintained. In other words, they focus on the mechanisms by which language constructs and is in turn constructed by social reality (cf. Alvesson and Karreman, 2000).

These approaches, loosely termed 'discourse analysis', refer to the critical reading and interpretation of a text (problem, situation) by making its assumptions explicit and asking certain epistemological questions. Although this type of questioning can be traced back to the ancient philosophers, discourse analysis is typically associated with the postmodern turn in the social sciences. There are numerous types of discourse analysis, for example Jacques Derrida's deconstruction is for many the most influential one. However, of equal importance are also Michel Foucault's conceptualisation of discourse (see Chapter 4), Julia Kristeva's feminist interpretation of social practice and Fredric Jameson's Marxist analysis of postmodernism. It is French philosopher Jacques Derrida's approach to discourse to which we turn our attention in this chapter.

This chapter is organised as follows. To begin with we provide a very short overview of Derrida and introduce some of his key concepts that are relevant to this chapter: discourse and deconstruction. This background information is useful for contextualising one of the key aims of this chapter, that is to demonstrate the possibilities for deconstructing management texts. To do this, we refer to a deconstructive analysis carried out by Kilduff and Kelemen (2004) on a seminal early text, *The Functions of the Executive*

(1938) by Chester Barnard. We then sketch out a short history of Barnard's life before returning again to the notion of deconstruction. Here we provide more detail about some of deconstruction's underpinning conceptual resources; notably, resources deployed in Kilduff and Kelemen's (2004) deconstructive analysis of Barnard's *The Function of the Executive*. In so doing, we offer one possible approach to deconstruction that may be applied to similar texts on management, as well as the documentation, images and symbols that permeate contemporary work organisations. The chapter's main points are then summarised.

Jacques Derrida

Opinions about the work of Jacques Derrida (1930–2004) are divided. Arguably, there are few other comparable figures within the tradition of twentieth century philosophy that have radically influenced not just the field of philosophy, but also related disciplines such as literary criticism. He remains – as a quick review of the copious writings produced by his supporters and opponents amply shows – a controversial figure. Arguments for and against his eclectic styles of writing, his innovative ideas and his desire to expose the messiness and arbitrariness of systems of language run strong in both directions. Even after his death in 2004, column inches within the populist press, journals, newspapers and scholarly publications, are still devoted to debating Derrida's legacy. Given the capacious volume of his work and the extraordinary sophistication of his ideas and arguments, Derrida and his work resist straightforward summation. Indeed, for some of Derrida's fiercest critics the apparent complexity of his work is purported to be nothing more than a smokescreen for intellectual trickery and gimmicks, as vehemently expressed by the Cambridge University professors who once petitioned against the university's decision in 1992 to award Derrida an honorary doctorate. To be sure, even supporters of Derrida's work acknowledge that some of his texts are dense, challenging, even bewildering (Jones, 2004). But this should not discourage us from engaging with his work. Despite assertions that Derrida used complicated wordsmithery to wilfully befuddle and shock his readers, like others before us, we suggest that Derrida's work aims to destabilise commonplace cultural ideas about ways of seeing, reading and writing. Clearly, it is the way in which the challenging nature and purpose of Derrida's work are understood that distinguishes those who find his work abstruse and nihilistic from those who describe his work as invigorating and profound.

Like other organisation scholars who are sympathetic to Derrida's work (Jones, 2003, 2004; Learmonth, 1999), we find much merit in Derrida's ideas, particularly his concept of deconstruction upon which this chapter pivots. Indeed, Derrida is probably best remembered for formulating the ideas that surround deconstruction across three of his most illuminating, albeit challenging, texts: *Of Grammatology*, *Writing and Difference* and *Speech and Phenomena*. All three texts were published in 1967, of which *Of Grammatology* is generally regarded as being Derrida's most influential publication. Although Derrida drew inspiration from major philosophical movements such as phenomenology, existentialism and structuralism that were well established during the early part of his life, he gradually moved away from these schools of thought as he developed the notion of deconstruction. Simply put, deconstruction served as a major (destabilising) challenge to the tradition of Western philosophy because it showed up the binary oppositions that structure conventional ways of thinking, reading and writing. (We come back to this idea later on in the chapter.) Turning to Norris, the challenge posed by Derrida's strategy of deconstruction may be expressed thus:

> **One way of describing this challenge is to say that Derrida refuses to grant philosophy the kind of privileged status it has always claimed as the sovereign dispenser of reason. Derrida confronts this preemptive claim on its own chosen ground. He argues that philosophers have been able to impose their various systems of thought only by ignoring, or suppressing, the disruptive effects of language. (2002: 18)**

We agree with Norris's appraisal. Deconstruction shows up the deficiencies of those philosophical perspectives that claim they can dispense with examining the role of language. Like postmodernism (Chapter 4) and, as we will demonstrate in regard to poststructuralism (Chapter 6), deconstruction shares a concern for centralising and interrogating the role of language in (re)constituting the social world.

As such, discourse is a concept central to much of Derrida's work. It is not altogether remarkable that Derrida (1976) argued that all forms of discourse are textual. Spoken language is a species of writing (text). Speech does not precede writing and is not necessarily spontaneous but rehearsed and inscribed in a written text. Derrida throws light on the ambiguous relationship between speech and writing (or between reality and text) by arguing that writing gives rise to inscriptions that not only describe but also, more importantly, constitute the activities or discourses they are supposed to merely represent.

With this notion of discourse in mind, Derrida's deconstructionist approach aims to uproot, decompose, undo, dismantle and overturn Western rationality through the sustained and multiple textual analysis of (seminal) writings (Derrida, 1976). The objective is not a complete dismissal of Western rationalism, since Derrida recognises this to be impossible, but an attempt to transform taken-for-granted concepts with a view to opening up new possibilities of thought. It is no coincidence that we can already see a connection with postmodernist perspectives that seek to do the same. As we have already mentioned in Chapter 4, some scholars have branded Derrida a 'postmodernist' while others seek to claim him as a 'poststructuralist' (Derrida himself vehemently rejected such labels). Finding clarity in such debates can be extremely difficult and it is not our intention to distil such vexed discussions here. Rather, we would underscore the importance of viewing this naming exercise as a discursive project, one that reveals the arbitrariness and incompleteness of systems of language and meaning.

Putting to one side the disputations over whether Derrida may be a postmodernist or poststructuralist, it is crucial to note that deconstruction attempts to displace the taken-for-granted meanings of the text by exploiting the possibilities of other meanings while accounting for the impossibility of a final interpretation (Calás and Smircich, 1991). Deconstruction focuses on suppressed conflicts and multiple interpretations of a text in order to destabilise all claims to objective truth (Martin, 1990). Deconstruction cannot, and does not, claim to reveal the 'truth' about what the author of a text intended to communicate. Rather, it permits the reader to question the limits that authorship may have imposed upon knowledge and opens up the possibility of enacting different alternatives.

According to Derrida, deconstruction is a stance of sceptical criticism and, at the same time, of genuine sympathy for the text. The text is like a little universe and must be first understood, felt for and then deconstructed. The text may wrestle with serious difficulties and researchers need to surface and interpret these within the textual context at hand, rather than according to some grand method of deconstruction (Kilduff, 1993). For example, Kilduff (1993) deconstructs a classic text, *Organizations* (1958) by March and Simon, and shows how the text simultaneously rejects and accepts the traditions the authors thought to surpass.

With these thoughts on Derrida and deconstruction in mind, we should begin to explore the potential of deconstruction for cultivating critical perspectives on management. In what remains of this chapter we aim to convey something of the richness and complexity of deconstructive analysis, offering up ideas that might inspire management researchers to become deconstructors of texts that relate to or circulate within organisations. To stir up such ambition among some of our readers we offer up a demonstration of deconstructive analysis. In the next section we draw upon a deconstructive work by Kilduff and Kelemen (2004) that takes Chester Barnard's *The Functions of the Executive* (1938) as the object of deconstructive analysis. We begin by providing some background information to Barnard before returning to Derrida's concept of deconstruction in more detail. We then present a deconstructive reading of Barnard's classic text, one that aims to craft fresh interpretations of the text.

Chester Barnard and *The Functions of the Executive*

The Functions of the Executive (1938) is self-described as being based on the author's own experience as an executive: 'So far as I am definitely aware, the notions here expressed [in the *Functions of the Executive*] arise chiefly from reflection upon experience' (quoted in Wolf, 1994: 1042). Beginning his business career in 1910, Barnard became president of New Jersey Bell in 1927, a position he held until 1948. Barnard's executive experience was paralleled and followed by a career in public service. During World War II he was president of the United Service Organisation (USO) whose purpose was to support the morale of American troops. He also held numerous other positions, including chairman of the National Science Foundation and president of the Rockefeller Foundation.

What sets Barnard apart from other organisational theorists is his executive experience combined with an absence of advanced academic training. Although he attended Harvard University, Barnard left after three years without a degree. His intellectual debts to Harvard were many, however. At the time, he was close to a large number of outstanding intellectuals at the Harvard Business School, including Elton Mayo, Alfred North Whitehead, Talcott Parsons, Robert Merton, Lloyd Warner, George Homans, William F. Whyte, B.F. Skinner and Fritz Roethlisberger. These intellectuals were members of the so-called 'Pareto Circle Dining Club' at Harvard in the 1930s and, clearly, Barnard's interactions with them formed the intellectual background out of which the ideas in *The Functions of the Executive* emerged. In fact, Barnard was heavily influenced by the Pareto's rather elitist views as expressed in 'The Manifesto for the Social Engineering of Sentiments'. According to this manifesto, elites could manage better if they understood the irrationalities of ordinary human beings (Parker, 2000). In the same vein, executives represent for Barnard an elite who are capable of understanding and managing the informal features of the organisation in order to mobilise workers' emotions and sentiments toward the achievement of organisational goals (co-operation, for example).

Barnard is, therefore, an example of that rarity in our field: a relatively self-educated practitioner-theorist who derived from his business experiences a systematic approach to organisations that was encouraged and validated by the leading intellectuals of the day. So what kinds of experiences formed the basis for Barnard's theorising? As president of New Jersey Bell during the 1930s, Barnard confronted a series of economic and technological changes. During the Depression years, with returns on investment declining, Barnard announced a planned reduction in working hours for employees, a plan that avoided lay-offs at the cost of reduced worker income. Barnard oversaw the expansion of the company and the development of numerous technical innovations in the post-war years. But his go-slow approach to some new developments, such as the rotary dial phone, may also have contributed to a large drop in net income in 1947. Overall, therefore, Barnard's corporate career has been judged as neither a disaster nor a brilliant success (Scott, 1992: 74).

Barnard's public service work during the Depression was characterised by a disapproval of the New Deal policies of Roosevelt and a preference for 'voluntary national coordination and industrial cooperation inspired by the moral authority of leaders in private enterprise' (Scott, 1992, p. 75). He impressed people with his wide knowledge and humane policies. But he has also been described as 'aloof and daunting' (1992: 84), and as someone whose 'intolerant, often vague, genius was unappealing to his peers' (1992: 87).

Described by many as 'confusing and ambiguous' (Feldman, 1996), Barnard's writing requires numerous readings to 'decipher'. This is not necessarily a shortcoming (not least of all in Barnard's view) but rather is a necessary feature of any sort of pioneering work that concerns itself with complex matters of inquiry. Apparently, it was Barnard's belief that rigorous scholarship presupposes the reading and re-reading of a book a number of times in order to grasp its subtle distinctions. Referring to the Pareto's work, Barnard said that, given its complexity and conceptual nature, 'depending on the man, 5 and 10 critical readings would be required' (Barnard, quoted in Wolf, 1994). In line with the academic writing conventions of the day, Barnard employed a style of writing that could be described as dry, cumbersome and, rather surprisingly, lacking in examples from the modern corporate world in which he operated. It is evident the book was mainly targeted at academics and not at practitioners. In the author's preface, Barnard acknowledges that the book is 'deficient in clarity and illustrations' (1938: xxxiii) and, as such, practitioners may find it difficult to understand and implement, however that social scientists may be more inclined to test and follow up his ideas.

Indeed, more than sixty years after its publication, Barnard's book stands by itself as a foundational document in organisational theory, a monograph commonly credited with initiating the formal analysis of organisations. The number of insights discovered by commentators on Barnard's book include some of the greatest hits of the last half-century's social science: bounded rationality; cognitive dissonance theory; self-perception theory; balance theory; goal setting; equity theory; and a host of other innovative approaches to informal organisation, communication and motivation (see Scott, 1992, for a summary). This notwithstanding, the book that opened the floodgates to work on formal organisation and management studies is itself curiously preoccupied neither with formal organisation nor managerial action, but with relatively solitary and pre-industrial activities (Kilduff and Kelemen, 2004).

More on deconstruction

Building on the general outline of deconstruction provided above, we now flesh out a little more detail on a possible deconstructive strategy of analysis. According to Derrida, deconstruction cannot be boiled down to a universal formula. Its characteristic moves are manifold and highly varied. Only an outline of these moves can be offered here, but the reader is referred to the works of Derrida (1976, 1978, 1988) for examples of how logic, close reading and scholarship can illuminate texts.

As we have already hinted at, deconstruction pays special attention to all claims to scientific truth, to obvious principles, to matters too evident to be debated, to arguments so patently clear to everyone that they are relegated to mere footnotes, to gaps in logic, to missing assumptions and to avoided conclusions. In short, deconstruction is interested in what is absent from the text as much as what is present in the text. Deconstruction, in one of its most original enquiries, asks – Why is this left out? The absence or slighting of inconvenient or apparently negligible issues offers deconstruction an opportunity to uncover all that the text has carefully hidden from our view. A characteristic deconstructive gesture is to reintroduce into the discourse the absent Other, the missing reference, the excluded category, or the avoided conclusion, and to thereby expose the apparently seamless prose as being steeped in rhetorical moves. One of the standard opening rhetorical flourishes in the social sciences, for example, is the claim, nearly always present in the first few paragraphs of a text, about an absence in the extant literature that is waiting to be filled by the providentially provided text in question. Without such a lacuna the implication is that the text in question could not be written, would not be accepted and would not be scientific. To pose as science, the text must insist that its presence fills an absence.

Another of the hidden aspects of texts that Derrida has alerted us to is the dependence of the text on sets of hierarchically-ordered binary oppositions. Examples of such binary oppositions include: woman/man, leader/follower, inside/outside, reason/emotion, speech/writing, and so on. From a deconstruction perspective, these binary oppositions are organised in *opposition* to one another as well as being well arranged *hierarchically*: one element of the dualism is privileged over another that is marginalised or suppressed. For example, reason is privileged over passion in traditional Western philosophical thinking, as numerous feminist commentators have shown (Cixous and Clément, 1986; Lloyd, 1984). Also, in an example familiar to many of us, a text may persist in calling all the participants by the male gender, excluding all women from consideration. Or the text may implicitly or explicitly privilege the mind over the body, the organic over the mechanistic and those who write programmes over those whose working lives are programmed (see Kilduff, 1993, for an example of such a deconstruction). What is more, as Derrida points out, the hierarchically-ordered elements in these binary formations are sites of conflict and contestation as one element seeks to gain ascendancy over another. Thus the relationship between the two components is highly volatile, unstable and arbitrary.

A deconstructive strategy aims to loosen us from thinking in such oppositional and hierarchically-ordered ways, though such a project is not straightforward. The dismantling of binary oppositions can generate further disorientation as we are required to let go of preconceived ideas and develop alternative, multiple and open-ended ways of thinking about the how the world around us is discursively constituted. Yet to assume that deconstruction is merely a textual strategy that contains no emancipatory impulse is to miss a point on which Derrida was consistently adamant:

> **I refuse to denounce the great classical discourse of emancipation. I believe that there is an enormous amount today for emancipation, in all domains and all the areas of the world and society. Even if I would not wish to inscribe the discourse of emancipation into a teleology, a metaphysics, an eschatology, or even a classical messianism, I none the less believe that there is no ethico-political decision or gesture without what I would call a 'yes' to emancipation. (Derrida, 1996: 82)**

Thus the deconstruction of the structure of language can help to prevent or rupture the privileging of binary oppositions that have oppressive effects on how individuals understand the world around them. One implication of this is that organisational and managerial discourses that appear to be normative within certain work contexts can be denaturalised – that is, regarded as sites of contestation, paradox, uncertainty and even violence, rather than politically neutral and common (business) sense representations of the world around them (see Learmonth, 1999).

A standard deconstructive procedure is to examine carefully the examples used to illustrate the major concepts or processes present in the text. For example, if the text is concerned with the ways in which speech preceded and gave birth to writing, it is important to notice that the examples given to illustrate the characteristics of speech are in fact all examples taken from written rather than spoken statements (Derrida, 1978). It may also become apparent that the text habitually illustrates the privileged member of a hierarchically-ordered pair by falling back on the disparaged member of the pair, indicating, at the very least, a discrepancy in the analytical scheme being presented.

Perhaps the most powerful deconstructive gesture of all is to reveal to the startled reader a hidden text, glossed over countless times by inattentive eyes, but suddenly present for all to see only too clearly once its boundaries, its syntax, its phrasings and its hiding places are abstracted from the protective embeddedness of the surrounding rhetoric. The hidden text, so mysteriously absent and yet so powerfully present, may contradict the explicit text, may even undermine the message that the authors have been at such pains to articulate. By bringing the different parts of the hidden text together, the critic is like an archaeologist who reconstructs the skeletons of vanished creatures and brings them to life, creatures that the authors had assured us were banished forever, but who now claim attention from the very pages that the authors have laboured to write. In this sense, deconstruction can be a profoundly creative process that enriches our understanding of texts rather than impoverishing them.

However, deconstruction must follow the contours of the text itself. It cannot impose the critic's political beliefs or prejudices, it cannot follow a rigid code of rules, it cannot be the same from one text to another, it cannot depend on a set of preformed clichés borrowed from other critics, other sources. The deconstructive process is as much a textual appreciation as it is a riveting set of analytical procedures (see also Kilduff and Kelemen, 2004, for a more detailed explanation). Taking some of these Derridean deconstructive impulses, we now turn to providing an example of the critical power of deconstructive analysis using Barnard's *The Functions of the Executive.*

Deconstructing *The Functions of the Executive*

Barnard's concept of a formal organisation was eclectic enough to include 'families and businesses of more than one person' (1938: 4). Because Barnard believed that 'fundamentally the same principles that govern simple organizations may be conceived as governing the structure of complex organizations' (p. 95), much of his book is premised on the analysis of not just any simple organisation but of apparently pre-industrial organisations, some of which appear to consist of just one solitary individual (p. 14). The irony of Barnard's book, therefore, is that conclusions about industrial corporations are derived from the analysis of simple pre-industrial activities. When reaching for examples, Barnard repeatedly falls back on illustrations that are not just simple in their narrative structure, but are almost child-like in their appeals to our credulity. To demonstrate his axioms concerning the management of large bureaucracies, Barnard offers illustrations from a world untouched by bureaucracy of any kind.

We are told about the boy 'who wants an apple' from the 'farmer's tree – not one at home or in the store' (p. 18). A page later, one is introduced to an evidently prehistoric hunter with no shoes who, 'running to catch an animal for food gives off heat energy to the atmosphere, pulverizes a small amount of gravel, tears off a bit of skin, and somewhat increases his need for food while attempting to secure it' (p. 19). This man's sad fate pales in comparison to his companion of the same paragraph who, we are informed, 'starts an avalanche which destroys his family, or his dwelling, or his stock of stored food'. What, one may ask, do any of these examples have to tell us about administration, executives, or, indeed, the conditions of work in the industrialised West?

Barnard persists throughout the book with his lonely figures engaged in sometimes futile and sometimes comical tasks. In the dry and abstract prose that characterises his delivery of weighty conclusions, the lonely figures that illustrate his points take on a remarkable life of their own. One of his obsessive themes, for example, is the man who again and again faces the task of moving a stone – for instance, the 'Stone too large for man,' then the 'Man too small for stone' (pp. 23–24). The deliberately simplified

English of these equivalent discourses presages the impoverished narratives themselves. In either discourse a man is frustrated and seeks out a companion to help him move a stone. According to Barnard, this signals the birth of co-operation. The possibility that co-operation naturally preceded the effort to move the stone, but that co-operation might be an end in itself is specifically ruled out, together with all other purposes that are 'social in character' (p. 25). Barnard wants to focus our attention solely on the biological man, alone on the stage, pushing in vain either because he is too small or because the stone is too large.

The possibility that this individual might use technology of some kind to get the stone moving is not, at this stage in the man's developing narrative, allowed by Barnard. We are introduced to a universe where the gods ordain trials of strength that must be undertaken with no outside help. This same pitiless universe created and controlled by Barnard allows him to systematically examine the limitations of humans considered as mere biological animals. These proto-humans survive in a world with only the rudiments of comfort. When houses or food or family are referred to, they are likely to be used as stage props to increase the grief and loneliness of the individual who, as we have seen, succeeds in moving his stone only to have it precipitate an avalanche that destroys the house, the food or the family. But the lonely man may be a mere anthropomorphic projection from our universe onto the oddly functioning world of Barnard's where, apparently, companionship may be naught but an 'unsought-for consequence' of the objective 'such as moving a stone' (p. 45).

In Barnard's universe of isolated automatons, successful organisational co-operation is *abnormal*: 'successful cooperation in or by formal organizations is the abnormal, not the normal, condition' (p. 5). Bearing in mind that formal organisations consist, according to Barnard, not only of families but also of 'associations, clubs, societies, fraternities' and 'many millions of formal organisations of short duration, a few hours at most' (p. 4), his vision of co-operation in organisations as an abnormal condition seems difficult to defend. How can it be that people consistently and continually co-operate in family groups, in clubs, in basketball games and in work organisations if the prevalence of co-operation is an 'illusion' (p. 5)?

In order to problematise co-operation, to demonstrate that executives are necessary for the motivation and control of purposive organisations, Barnard reduces human beings to bundles of biological and physical characteristics, to 'automatons which we manipulate' (p. 23). Under these conditions of 'artificial simplicity' (p. 36), humans engage in co-operation only in order to overcome physical limitations, to move stones too large for one person, for example. Humans considered as biological caricatures untroubled by any need for association are dominated by the need to consume: 'Everything that an individual does is for consumption' (p. 33). These proto-humans come together to move stones, to plant seeds, to store food and to make weapons such as clubs (p. 32). As each limitation of the environment is overcome and the automatons, having moved the stones, look at each other wondering what to do next, 'special organs known as executives' emerge to provide new purposes, to prevent the disintegration of co-operation (p. 37). Thus, the proto-humans invent formal organisations complete with co-operative and executive systems purely from egotistical motives of personal consumption.

This intellectual horror story allows Barnard to derive the necessity of executive action from the most primitive behaviour. The implication seems to be that purposive, formal organisations run by executives are impersonal solutions to consumption problems faced by machine-like drones. Only at this point does Barnard acknowledge what is surely obvious to all: co-operation among humans is *normal*, not the abnormal state of affairs. Barnard begins his fourth chapter by acknowledging the omnipresence of the social factors he repeatedly excluded in the first three chapters: 'In all actual cooperative systems, however, factors thus excluded are always present' (p. 38). He ends the fourth chapter with almost the same words: 'social factors are always present in cooperation', and he goes on to an apparent contradiction of his earlier insistence that co-operation was the essential work of executives. Co-operation, he tells us, is, for individuals a personal desire and for 'systems of cooperation ... a social fact' (p. 45). Even more astounding, in the last few words of the crucial fourth chapter, he recognises that the social factors so rigorously excluded from his depiction of the proto-humans 'determine cooperation itself' (p. 45). Co-operation is no longer driven by consumption needs and organised by executives. It is now a self-perpetuating system that rewards its members with personal and sociological 'satisfactions'.

The exclusion and inclusion of 'social factors' from the concept of cooperation, the argument that co-operation was both an abnormal condition and yet an ever-present motivation that perpetuated itself in co-operative systems, these apparent contradictions indicate the difficulties Barnard ran into as he attempted to build a theory of organisation that justified executive control.

Perhaps the most famous contribution by Barnard was his definition of organisation. But we should recognise that, mirroring the conflicted nature of his arguments, he gave us three alternative versions of his definition. First, he argued that 'persons' be excluded from his definition because 'the personal point of view has no pertinence here' (p. 43), given that organisations consist of human activities and forces and not individual humans: 'An organization is defined as *a system of consciously coordinated personal activities or force*' (p. 72, emphasis in original). But he no sooner banishes persons from organisations than he reintroduces them in a slightly different definition on the next page, that he calls the 'central hypothesis of this book ... embodied in the definition of a formal organization as a *system of consciously coordinated activities or forces of two or more persons*' (p. 73). So persons are both absent (in the first definition) except as shadows encapsulated in the adjective 'personal', and present (in the second definition that restores the persons) albeit only to the extent that these persons exhibit themselves as 'activities or forces'. Later on we have another definition that removes both the 'personal' and the 'persons' to emphasise that, after all, 'organization, simple or complex, is always *an impersonal system of coordinated human efforts*' (p. 94).

Note that this definition applies to all organisations, including families: 'Fundamentally the same principles that govern simple organizations may be conceived as governing the structure of complex organizations' (p. 95). The iron hand of bureaucracy reaches deep into the simple family structure and governs it as an 'impersonal system'. Co-operation itself becomes reified. Once it comes into existence, like Frankenstein's monster, 'cooperation requires something to do' (p. 52). Co-operation takes centre stage as a devilish agent in its own right: it 'organizes' (p. 58), and its efficiency 'depends upon what it secures and produces ... and how it distributes its resources and how it changes motives' (p. 59). It applies forces to factors in order to be able to furnish 'inducements or satisfactions' (p. 59). Co-operation itself, it seems, is the invisible executive to which the persons must submit, either as '*objects* to be *manipulated* ... or as *subjects* to be *satisfied*' (p. 40, emphasis in original).

The reification of co-operation as the self-perpetuating system to which persons as either objects or subjects must submit puts Barnard in the difficult position of both removing persons from his conception of organisation and yet promoting certain persons – executives – as the practitioners of the arts and sciences of administration. Barnard starts his book with a quotation that exalts the importance of the leader who brings order where otherwise there is chaos: 'For the efficiency of an army consists partly in the order and partly in the general: but chiefly in the latter, because he does not depend upon the order but the order depends on him' (Aristotle, *Metaphysics*). For Barnard, order is synonymous with formal organisation. Order is privileged, disorder is denigrated; order is what counts, disorder is the unimportant Other, an Other that needs to be appropriated, managed, organised and transformed into order.

The privileging of order and the nervous remarks throughout the text concerning the 'unrest of the present day' (p. 3), the instability of human desire and human environments (p. 149), and the totalitarian solutions (such as fascism) to such instabilities (p. 9) help explain, perhaps, Barnard's insistence that, after all, it is to the art and craft of specific human actors that co-operative systems owe their survival. Whereas the mass of humanity are helpless victims of random forces, dependent on chance outcomes that they can neither foresee nor control, the executive, like Plato's philosopher kings or Nietzche's 'superman', achieves a mastery of affairs that, even at the end of the book, remains mysterious. Consider this concluding quotation: ' ... in human affairs, chance is everything ... [but] art should be there also: for I should say that in a storm there must be surely a great advantage in having the aid of the pilot's art. You would agree?' (Plato, *Laws*).

Thus the book begins and ends with a recognition of the disorder that characterises ordinary 'human affairs' and praise for the exemplary figures who find order even in chaos. The romanticism of Barnard's exaltation of the executive is at odds with the persistent depersonalisation of his portrayal of organisations. Whereas the executive is the pilot in the storm, the organisation is an impersonal electromagnetic field of forces (p. 75). Executive 'organization personality' is quite distinct from 'individual personality' (p. 174), enabling executives to overcome in an heroic fashion the 'opposed facts ... opposed thought and emotions of human beings' (p. 21). Rather than being tossed around on the storm of emotions and contradictory forces, the executive, like the switchboard operator who showed 'great moral courage' in continuing to provide uninterrupted service while watching from her office window her mother's house burn down with the mother inside (p. 269), rises godlike above such emotions as pity and fear. The executive is in thrall to co-operation to such an extent that coercion (including homicide) may be regarded as justifiable to persuade others to submit to authority (p. 151).

As the embodiment of the organisation's personality, as the human agent through which impersonal co-operation takes action, the executive represents 'the good of the organization' (p. 171) and must therefore take extreme action when evil threatens. Barnard recognises that his romantic portrayal of the executive as the embodiment of superior authority is a 'fiction' (p. 170), albeit one that is necessary to protect the illusion that co-operation is natural and inevitable. What is this evil that threatens the acceptance of co-operative authority? It is the situation when 'objective authority is flouted for arbitrary or merely temperamental reasons' (p. 171). Human temperaments have no place in the co-operative system, as they threaten the survival of impersonal functions and represent hostile elements that must be destroyed.

In one of the most remarkable passages in the book, Barnard suggests what should be done to people who bring their individual fallibilities into organisational settings, who threaten the fiction of superior authority, whose behaviour falls outside that coldly impersonal zone of indifference to which employees have surrendered their moral rights of rebellion: 'To fail in an obligation intentionally is an act of hostility. This no organization can permit; and it must respond with punitive action if it can, even to the point of incarcerating or *executing the culprit*' (ibid., emphasis added). Barnard further continues, so that we are in no doubt what he is referring to: 'Leaving an organization in the lurch is not often tolerable' (ibid.). Better to let the mother burn than to leave the organisation's telephone system, so necessary for co-operation, unattended – even for a moment.

Barnard's vision of organisation?

So, bearing the above deconstructive analysis in mind, what might we say about Barnard's perspective on work organisations? Based on the deconstructive analysis above, one reading is that Barnard sounds the first notes of a theme later developed by the Carnegie school of theorists (Herbert Simon, James March and Richard Cyert in particular): a siren-like discourse that has seduced the ears of many managerialists. For Barnard, employees are objects to be manipulated or subjects to be satisfied, theory is a powerful tool in the service of the executive and authority must be insinuated through systems of co-operation. The modern corporation functions much like an army in which the personality of the individual is subjugated to the rationalised systems of offices and objectives. In an army, troops march at the command of officers, and in the corporation workers obey within wide latitudes the commands of the executive, irrespective of whether they understand the specific objectives of their orders, their actions, or their routines. Above all else the organisation strives to survive and to do this it must overcome the natural inclination of the solitary individual to pursue selfish and unstable desires. The executive must inculcate a belief in the real existence of common goals in the service of organisational personality. Through the inculcation of motives, employees become capable of ignoring their own interests in order to enact the routines of the organisation, exhibiting at times 'extraordinary moral courage' (Barnard, 1938: 269).

In organisations, according to Barnard, the average human being is able to overcome an inherent avoidance of decision making (p. 189) through training in the routine delivery of 'technologically correct conduct' (p. 192). Thus the average human is privileged to be part of a formal organisation's 'superlative degree' of logical processing (p. 186) planned and executed by top executives, a processing that contrasts favourably with the illogicality of the informal activities that average humans, when left to themselves, engage in.

This vision of a superlative organisation run by guardian-like executives who inculcate motives through benign propaganda aimed at narrow-minded employees (cf. p. 190) has powerful echoes throughout organisation theory. In our radical re-reading of Barnard's text, we focused not on these more familiar themes but on the privileging of organisational behaviour itself, in contrast with private individual behaviour. Whether floating in boats, moving stones, pursuing apples or precipitating catastrophes, the lonely mythical figures that flit through Barnard's book illustrate the absence of formal organisation, even as they ostensibly serve as paradigmatic examples of co-operation. Can it be that Barnard's discourse, his celebration of organisational rationality and co-operation, rests not on the mysterious systemic power of formal systems but on the inherent co-operative camaraderie of individual persons?

Summary

In this chapter we have considered the potential of deconstruction for generating critical perspectives on management. We have suggested that there is much value in crafting deconstructive analyses because they open up possibilities for viewing afresh what is already familiar. We have illustrated the generative impulse within deconstruction by taking Barnard's influential text *The Functions of the Executive* (1938) and cultivating alternative, deconstructed, readings. This does not, as our earlier comments indicated, mean that we simply demolish the text. The art of deconstruction hinges on a sense of sympathy for the text in question. As we have shown, deconstruction allows multiple meanings to emerge, some of which may resist dominant cultural ideas or, in this case, hegemonic readings of Barnard's classic work. Also of note here is that we do not offer up a universal formula for deconstructive analysis. Deconstruction is a complex strategy for (re)reading and (re)analysing texts that does not rely upon a singular approach (see Chapter 9 for more detail on deconstructive methodologies). What we offer up in this chapter is a brief demonstration of (not a recipe for) how deconstructive analysis might help generate critical perspectives on management.

For management researchers, deconstruction is a potentially powerful means for critiquing facets of organisational worlds. For example, in addition to the relevance deconstruction has for deconstructing much lauded management texts, a deconstructivist approach may be applied to organisational documentation produced by managers (Learmonth, 1999), company artefacts, narratives and memorabilia (Boje, 1995), as well as other discursive arrangements such as identities. In regard to the latter, a deconstructive analysis of identity would point up the lack of any stable foundation to identity by highlighting its provisionality, fragility, fluidity and its reliance on the Other for its construction. Given its critique of conventional modes of thinking about such matters as identity, deconstruction has fostered some of the most fascinating analyses of organisations, despite not being afforded the intellectual headroom it deserves within management studies (Weitzner, 2007).

As we have hinted at above, the emphasis deconstruction places on language, and therefore textual analysis, is also apparent in some feminist theories. As we show in the next chapter, feminism is a multifaceted body of theory, where some strands, in drawing their inspiration from the works of Derrida and Foucault, display a proclivity for discursive forms of analysis. How these might be of relevance to critical management researchers is the focal point of Chapter 6.

Further reading

While we would encourage readers to head straight to Derrida's original works, we are mindful that these texts are challenging. The principles of deconstruction are elaborated (by demonstration rather than prescription) over three works published in 1967: *Of Grammatology*, *Writing and Difference* and *Speech and Phenomena*. As with most of the 'hard-hitting' French philosophers, over the last few decades we have witnessed a boom in secondary texts that offer a 'helping hand' into the content of these texts. For those not yet adventurous enough, these secondary sources can serve a useful purpose; otherwise, plunge into Derrida directly – *Of Grammatology* is a good place to start. One scholar who has shown great sensitivity to Derrida's corpus of work is Campbell Jones. He provides a careful and concise overview of Derrida and his work in Linstead (2004) (ed.) *Organization Theory and Postmodern Thought* (London: Sage). Also worth reading is Jones's analysis of Derrida's relevance for business ethics: see Jones (2003) 'As if business ethics were possible, "within Such Limits"...', in *Organization*, 10 (2): 223–248.

Martin Kilduff has also written lucidly on Derridean deconstruction and its application in organisational studies. Kilduff's work is both informative and accessible and represents a good position from which to take off and explore deconstruction. Try Kilduff (1993) 'Deconstructing organizations', in *The Academy of Management Review*, 18 (1): 13–31. For a recent overview of Derrida's philosophy and ideas, including deconstructive analysis and its potential application in economic and organisational theory, read Weitzner (2007) 'Deconstruction revisited: implications of theory over methodology', in *Journal of Management Inquiry*, 16 (1): 43–54.

6

Poststructuralist Feminism

Introduction

Feminist theory is incredibly diverse. The number of feminist-inspired theories that may be used as a lens through which to explore the complexities of women's (and men's) lives has increased appreciably. There is a plethora of feminist ideas and just as many labels to catalogue its conceptual heterogeneity. In any comprehensive publication on feminist theory the uninitiated reader is faced with the challenge of getting to know 'liberal feminism', 'socialist feminism', 'radical feminism', 'postmodern feminism', 'poststructuralist feminism', 'eco-feminism', and so on. Feminist commentators are also working at forging links between feminism and bodies of theory such as critical realism. There are, of course, a good many other texts that will help the reader navigate their way through this constellation of paradigms and their feminist progenitors (for example, Beasley, 2005).

From this stock of feminist theory, we now select poststructuralist feminism as an example of an approach that has made significant contributions to the critical study of management. In selecting this strand of theory it is not our intention to privilege it over all others (notably, we do talk more expansively about feminism in Chapters 9 and 10). Such a manoeuvre would not be in keeping with our philosophy of encouraging paradigmatic plurality. Rather, poststructuralist feminism has close affinities with the critical theories we have already presented thus far. For example, poststructuralist feminism also places emphasis on a discursive approach to analysing management in a somewhat similar way to some postmodern (Chapter 4) and deconstructive (Chapter 5) perspectives. This might be of some value to readers looking for points of connection with postmodernism, deconstruction and, possibly, American pragmatism. Placing poststructuralist feminism centre-stage for this reason, as well as for its focus on gender in organisation, we are not oblivious to the relevance of other feminist theories that prefer to view the world of organisation in non-discursive 'realist' terms (see Lawson, 1999). What we offer in this chapter is a very small window into feminist theorising;

nonetheless, we see it as a good starting place to consider the relevance of feminist theory for critical management researchers.

This chapter begins by briefly outlining the relationship between feminism and poststructuralism. We then single out the influence and relevance of Michel Foucault (a key 'poststructuralist' thinker) for feminist theorising. The compatibility of Foucault's work with feminism's emancipatory goals is contestable. As we go on to show, poststructuralist feminists have handled Foucault's ideas with considerable care, showing how they may be deployed in ways that support poststructuralist feminism's epistemological concerns. Having established a number of insights into poststructuralist feminism's conceptual resources, we then demonstrate how this collection of feminist perspectives may allow researchers to accentuate certain aspects of managers' lives that are otherwise obscured within mainstream/'malestream' management theory. While the focus on gender is a key concern in these studies, they also explore the Foucauldian relationship between power/knowledge/resistance in their illustrations of how individual identities and subjectivities are (re)constructed. Finally, we sum up the chapter's main themes.

Poststructuralism and feminism

Of all the various types of feminist theorising that have proliferated over the years, poststructuralist feminisms have gained ascendancy within many academic spheres. One reason for the rise of this type of feminist critique is because poststructuralist feminism offers a set of conceptual resources that seem to overcome essentialist understandings of women's lives and forms of inequality. Poststructuralist feminisms have taken exception to feminist modes of thinking about gender that adopt the liberal principle of sameness, which posits women as the *same as* or *equal to* men, without interrogating the male norm to which women are being compared or equalised. While poststructuralist feminist approaches largely start from the shared notion of thinking about gender in terms of *difference* rather than *sameness*, by scrutinising gender in relational terms and calling into question the connections between and the universal categories of 'woman' and 'man', they are by no means an harmonious chorus of voices. Poststructuralist feminism is varied not least of all because the poststructuralist theoretical groundwork on which it rests is multifaceted.

A detailed overview of poststructuralism is beyond the scope of this chapter and will only be briefly set out here. What is important to note is some of the main streams of philosophical thought that collectively, if not rather loosely, compose what is largely understood as poststructuralism. In so doing, we proceed here with a measure of caution. Like 'postmodernism', 'poststructuralism' is a notoriously difficult term to define because as a corpus of intellectual work it refuses to deal in absolutes. As we have already stated in Chapter 4, poststructuralism and postmodernism share many of the same preoccupations with, for example, the role of language and interrogating claims to truth (which we consider later). Some people use the terms interchangeably, while academics such as Linstead (2004) include poststructuralism under the term 'postmodernism'.

However, we are minded to follow the poststructuralist feminist Lois McNay, who argues that while these two paradigms are closely tethered, they are in significant ways conceptually distinct. McNay makes this distinction abundantly clear in her analysis of the interrelationship between poststructuralist Michel Foucault's work, feminism and postmodernism, arguing that Foucault does not altogether abandon 'Enlightenment notions of autonomy, domination and self-determination' (1992: 117). In other words, Foucault may be read as *reworking* some of the key ideas of the Enlightenment that some hardcore postmodernisms reject outright. When viewed in this way, we come to appreciate that poststructuralism diverges from postmodernism in some respects, but this is not at the expense of imposing restrictive labels on ideas that might 'count' as poststructuralist or postmodern in their tendencies. As such, we do not wish to 'fix' the definition of poststructuralism by simple paradigmatic classification, since one of the oft-cited, anti-foundational tenets of poststructuralist theorising is that there are no stable and unproblematic representations of reality. As such, poststructuralism itself becomes a site of contestation not least in terms of its meaning. For one thing, there is no clear consensus, written or otherwise documented, about what constitutes poststructuralism, partly because it is such a voluminous body of complex conceptual resources.

What we can say, however, is that as a philosophical movement that emerged in the 1960s, poststructuralist theorists responded critically to a range of intellectual, political, cultural and economic stimuli in French society in particular, and within the West more broadly. As such, poststructuralism has been a highly fertile territory in which to mine ideas and develop anti-essentialist, anti-foundationist and anti-totalising forms of theory and politics. In general terms then, poststructuralism maintains a deep suspicion of Enlightenment conceptions of the individual as unified, rational, all knowing, and possessing an essence of humanity.

One helpful way in which to approach poststructuralism is to think about its relationship with structuralism. Since poststructuralism is often regarded as a series of critiques directed at its philosophical forbears, namely structuralists Ferdinand de Saussure and Claude Levi-Strauss, poststructuralism then constitutes a multiplicity of connected (but an uneven and sometimes competing) range of critical responses to aspects of structuralist philosophy. As such, poststructuralism cannot be *fully* understood in isolation to structuralism since many of the figures heavily identified as 'poststructuralist' – namely the heavyweight French intellectuals Jacques Derrida, Michel Foucault, Gilles Deleuze and Julia Kristeva – have drawn upon and expanded structuralist ideas concerning, for example, how the role of language is understood. Indeed, holding structuralism and poststructuralism in the same frame can help to identify some of the ideas that knit together different threads of poststructuralist theory. As poststructuralist feminist Chris

Weedon asserts, there are distinct assumptions commonly made by poststructuralists regarding language, meaning and subjectivity.

In *Feminist Practice and Poststructuralist Theory* (1987/1997), Weedon argues that the work of linguist Ferdinand de Saussure has proved highly influential for poststructuralists, since Saussure's structural theory of language claims that reality is a system of signs. In other words, reality is not an objective property that independently exists: a state where the individual or researcher is positioned externally in relation to reality. The work of Saussure was a radical departure from this point of view because Saussure suggested that language is arbitrary, a constructed system of signs that hold no intrinsic meaning. Put differently, this is to say that language does not simply reflect reality. Signs (words, images, sounds, objects, and so on) only become signs when they are invested with meaning. If we accept this idea, then we open up the possibility for thinking about the (un)conscious role people play in investing certain signs with meaning, which leads us to the notion that reality is a series of constructions. As Weedon points out, poststructuralists adopted and developed Saussure's conceptual insights into language to argue that, and this is one perspicuous marker of difference between poststructuralism and structuralism, signs may be inhered with *multiple* meanings. For instance, how we interpret the sign of 'feminine' or 'masculine' will waver from one individual to the next, and these interpretations will change over time in any given location. In contrast, Saussurean linguistic theory regards signs as having a fixed meaning, and the role of the individual in relation to language is said to be mostly unconscious.

Poststructuralists contest both these ideas, arguing that individuals may *consciously* imbue language with *multiple* meanings. In this way, individuals may draw upon language in dissimilar ways, using linguistic resources such as discourses (a concept we discuss below) to assemble a plurality of identities. How we go about this over time, often in ways competing with each another, varies enormously. This line of thought allows poststructuralists to consider carefully the myriad ways in which people *continuously* make sense and thus provide meaning to aspects of their lives. This process is called subjectivity, as Weedon explains:

> **Subjectivity is most obviously the site of the consensual regulation of individuals. This occurs through the identification by the individual with particular subject positions within discourses. But the discursive constitution of subjectivity is much more than this. It is a constantly repeated process, which begins at birth and is repeated continually throughout life. (1997: 108)**

It is, perhaps, already easy to see why poststructuralism has sparked some heated reactions from its objectors, who frequently cite its theoretical opacity and its dissenting politics as its chief failings. This is not to say that poststructuralism represents one example of intellectual navel-gazing. In our view, poststructuralism is concerned with putting theory into practice through crafting and implementing critical modes of analysis, as we have already demonstrated in Chapter 4. Poststructuralism encompasses a range of stimulating analytical practices, and so it is of no surprise to anyone that some feminists have borrowed from poststructuralism's bank of conceptual resources in developing discursive theories of gender and sexuality. For some feminists, Foucault's conceptual resources are of particular appeal, just as some feminists have reached into the works of Jacques Derrida to theorise gender difference (see for example Irigaray, Cixous, Kristeva). For our purposes here, though, we now discuss the feminist approaches to poststructuralism that have mobilised certain ideas from the writings of Michel Foucault, since these feminist perspectives have gained a certain prominence in recent times within some segments of critical management and organisational theory. Before we discuss the contributions these feminist researchers have made in advancing knowledge within these academic domains, we shall first examine some of the main conceptual concerns that poststructuralist feminist analyses exhibit.

Foucault and feminist theorising

If we can draw one conclusion from the rash of publications on the life and works of French philosopher Michel Foucault, it is that his influence on the intellectual landscape of twentieth-century theory has been both titanic and contentious. His work is expansive and demanding, and many of his publications have achieved iconic status. Early examples include *Birth of the Clinic* (1973) and *The Order of Things* (1970), while from the middle of his scholarly career *Discipline and Punish* (1977) and the first of the projected six volumes of *The History of Sexuality* (1978) are especially noteworthy. The second volume, *The Uses of Pleasure* (1985), and the third, *The Care of the Self* (1986), in *The History of Sexuality* series were published towards the very end of his life, and received as much critical acclaim as they did criticism.

Indeed, even after death, Foucault continues to cut a controversial figure when it comes to evaluating the intellectual impact of his work. His ideas on the relational aspects of knowledge, power, subjectivity and resistance have been applied widely and across numerous academic disciplines, including the field of critical management studies. Doubtless there is much of interest in Foucault's work, and not least of all for many feminist theorists. During his lifetime and in the years since his death in 1984, feminists have critically responded to his ideas in various ways. Not all, as we shall see in the discussion that follows, appraise his work positively. However, in the remainder of this section we largely draw upon the influential work of some of those feminists (Lois McNay, Jana Sawicki, Chris Weedon) who have tried to bridge the chasm that divides Foucault from his most eremitic feminist critics.

It is crucial to note that while feminists have a well-established track record of searching Foucault's scholarly oeuvre for theoretical insights that may be pressed into the service of explaining and analysing women's oppression, such conceptual borrowing is not without cost, or at least some sizeable degree of risk. As feminist Lois McNay rightly points out in *Foucault and Feminism* (1992), feminists are 'acutely aware' (p. 3) of the shortcomings in Foucault's theorising. After all, Foucauldian theory has come under heavy fire from many feminists. However, the invectives of Linda Alcoff (1992) and others (Benhabib, 1992; Hartsock, 1990) while unsympathetic are nonetheless compelling, and it is wise to have some understanding about why some feminist theorists are minded to argue that Foucault's ideas are moribund for feminist theorising. By doing so, we may regard these criticisms as challenges facing those management and organisation researchers wishing to activate the ideas of poststructuralist feminist theorists.

Gender troubles?

As diverse as feminism is, it may be said that one principal concern connecting the numerous currents within feminist scholarship is to denaturalise the deeply entrenched idea that gender is derived from biological sex. Feminists have targeted this dichotomous line of thinking in different ways, and one result of corrective feminist analyses of the sex/gender dichotomy has been the proliferation of theories of gender, sex and sexuality. In a succinct review of the main tenets of liberal and radical feminist theorising, Weedon (1987/1997) sketches out the contribution poststructuralist feminist theorising has made to the debates on gender and sex:

> **Poststructuralist feminism requires attention to historical specificity in the production, for women, of subject positions and modes of femininity and their place in the overall network of social power relations. In the process of constituting subjectivity, the meaning of biological sex is never finally fixed. It is a site of contest over meaning and the exercise of patriarchal power. (p. 131)**

Weedon's quote refers to the Foucauldian idea that by focusing on the linkages between discourse, power and knowledge, identity and subjectivity are seen to be the *effects* of how subjects engage with discourse. Foucault was preoccupied with the concept of discourse throughout his intellectual career, and while his conceptualisation of discourse is capacious, it generally refers to the means by which knowledge can be specified: that is, sets of loosely coherent statements and utterances that have been and continue to be invested with meaning. Discourses circulate within societies, but specific discourses may circulate more intensely and widely than others, and so some discourses may become marginal.

For poststructuralist feminists, the Foucauldian concept of discourse is arresting because it permits an analysis of how men and women attribute meaning to certain discourses, and relatedly, how some discourses carry in them a knowledge of what 'counts' as 'masculine' or 'feminine' in any given context. From a feminist point of view, some knowledge carried in discourse may be considered patriarchal, and therefore damaging to women. With all this in mind, gender may be seen as a *discursive effect*, as opposed to an *essential property* of individuals and their interactions. As Weedon suggests, how gender is understood may change over time and, as Foucault urges us in much of his work, historical specificity is critical in any analysis of how power and knowledge are related and exercised. What this then shows is that Foucault was more concerned with analysing the connections between power, knowledge and discourse, rather than providing a grand theory on sexuality, or even gender. For poststructuralist feminists, Foucault's import is precisely because he avoids producing a meta-narrative of gender, one that would risk essentialising and universalising meanings of gender. However, other feminists disagree. They regard Foucault's apparent lack of concern with theorising gender as a sign of gender-blindness.

Lois McNay captures the wider concern of those feminist theorists who complain that Foucault neglects to theorise gender. Some go as far as to accuse Foucault of being androcentric. These complaints tend to find weight in how Foucault is said to conceptualise the disciplinary effects of power on the body. As McNay suggests, Foucault's notion of gender as an 'effect of dominant power relations which is imposed on the inert bodies of individuals' (1992: 71) appears to reverse his anti-totalising theorising, insomuch as when gender is imported into this frame, gender is assumed to be 'unproblematic and total' (ibid.). Yet, for McNay at least, Foucault's ideas regarding the linkages between power and the body, explicated in the text *Discipline and Punish*, harbour a more worrying fault. McNay says: 'I argue that a more serious flaw is the definition of individuals as "docile" bodies which cannot explain many of the experiences of women in modern society and results in an impoverished and over-stable account of the formation of gender identity' (1992: 47). For McNay, Foucault's work on the body contains a paradox that is damaging to the feminist plight of overturning the cultural image of women as passive victims. By moving to show how bodies are culturally constructed, disciplined and historically situated, Foucault ends up overstating the case in McNay's opinion: his line of reasoning regarding the docile body circumvents women themselves, rendering them passive.

How poststructuralist feminists such as McNay surmount these criticisms partly hinges on how McNay and others develop Foucault's ideas. For McNay, how agency is understood is pivotal to assessing how much of Foucauldian theory is valuable for feminist theorists, as demonstrated in *Gender and Agency* (2000). Why the matter of agency is a critical and urgent one for feminism more broadly is discussed next.

'All that's solid melts into air'? Foucault, identity and agency

Feminist Ladelle McWhorter (1999) points to another problem feminists have with Foucault. Feminists have discredited Foucault's work on the basis that it fails to provide a solid platform on which feminist political action can be taken. McWhorter uses the gay and lesbian community as an example, showing how Foucault's anti-essentialist notion of identity (which undermines the idea that there is an ahistorical, essential gay and lesbian identity) has been read by his critics as tantamount to the dissolution of all possibilities of political practice. Such protestations are premised on an idea of political action being viable only when it is grounded in fixed identities that function as rallying points. Within this line of reasoning is a concept of community that is reliant on a sense of identity that is widely shared among individuals for growth. Likewise, from a feminist perspective, accepting the admonition of those who allege Foucault indulges in an acute form of anti-essentialist theorising might, understandably, lead to anxieties regarding how women mobilise feminist values and experiences as the basis for political action. McNay exposes this worry among some feminists, citing (as many commentators do) Nancy Hartsock who raises the question: 'Why is it that just at the moment when so many of us who have been silenced begin to demand the right to name ourselves, to act as subjects rather than objects of history, that just then the concept of subjecthood becomes problematic?' (1987: 196). At the heart of Hartsock's protest is the conviction that in order to generate solidarity among women a coherent identity is needed, which at first glance seems to find little accommodation in Foucault's thinking on the constructedness of identity. Martha Nussbaum (1992) echoes Hartsock's alarm call, seeing in poststructuralism nothing more than a rejection of the material dimension of life that fails to make any substantial connection with the everyday lives of women.

For Hartsock and Nussbaum, who both handsomely invest their hopes for combating gendered inequalities between men and women in being able to identify an essence of womanhood that can be used to engender a politically charged sense of 'sisterhood', Foucault's theories on identity and, relatedly, the notion of the 'de-centred subject', run counter to their efforts. As Weedon (1987/1997) remarks, feminists have accused Foucault of anti-humanism insofar as they assume that one of the effects of thinking about the self in discursive terms is that women are displaced under the sign 'woman', which itself is dissolved, or so we are led to believe. Some of the most persuasive feminist criticism to be brought to bear on Foucault forcefully asserts that his anti-humanist critique sweeps away the agentic capacity of individuals. Foucault does indeed encourage us, especially in his later works on the practices of the self, to see identities as constructs, always open to (re)construction and, thus, contestation in terms of the meanings attached to them. The case, however, for suggesting that Foucault vaporises all possibilities of agency, as they might find expression in forms of political action arising from such artistry of the self, is somewhat overstated.

Both McWhorter (1999) and McNay (1992) offer a more measured appraisal. Taking McWhorter first, Foucauldian theorising is not equal to the destruction of identity: 'Foucault does not suggest that all dangerous things or even hurtful things are things to be destroyed' (1999: 80). McWhorter reminds us that we must carefully consider the networks of power which certain identities are dependent upon for their construction and codification at any given time. This is a crucial point because, in Foucauldian terms, subjects cannot externally exist to relations of power. Thus subjects generate identities and subjectivities as they exercise power by, for example, drawing upon discourse to construct identities that relate to work, gender, race, and so on. For McWhorter, spaces for political action exist within relations of power, because Foucault tells us that power is intimately bound up with resistance – the discursive means by which subjects can mobilise politically. We talk more about Foucauldian debates on resistance below, but for now it is sufficient to trace the rest of McWhorter's argument. Disrupting identity, especially identities that have the appearance of coherence, stability and solidity (such as a 'heterosexual' sexual identity), can have the effect of rupturing the relations of power within which such identities are formed. Such discursive practices hold political promise, as McNay articulates in more detail: 'I suggest that it is more fruitful ... to ... ask how his work presents a challenge to feminists to think of an ethics which does not rest on a fixed or naturalized notion of "woman"' (1992: 112).

Here McNay steers our attention towards the work of feminists such as Judith Butler (more on Butler in Chapter 7), who in *Gender Trouble* (1990) argues against treating the identity category of 'feminist' and 'woman' as monolithic, suggesting that feminists should instead look to develop a type of politics that comes about when subjects engage in disruptive, reiterative performances of identity. Such identity practices destabilise normative discourses that relate to, for example, masculinity or femininity. Jana Sawicki (1991: 103) also notes the 'troublemaking' potential of Foucault's theorising on identity and agency, and calls it a 'politics of uncertainty'. As Sawicki elaborates, Foucault's notion of agency is useful because it does not set out a limitless horizon of possibilities, as many women are no doubt already aware from their personal experiences of negotiating forms of patriarchal knowledge and power. In this vein, agency has its limits, which is not to say that we are overly constrained by discursive arrangements in society, as Sawicki neatly sums up:

> **Foucault's account of subjectivity does not introduce any obstacles to feminist praxis that were not already there. Feminist praxis is continually caught between appeals to a free subject and an awareness of victimization. Foucault suggests that this tension may be permanent, that both views are partially correct, and that living in this uncomfortable tension is an important catalyst for resistance and wariness. (1991: 104)**

As the above quotation reveals, within discursive arrangements that produce an 'uncomfortable tension' for some subjects are possibilities for agency not least of all manifest in forms of resistance, which we now turn to consider.

Power and resistance

Foucault's notion of power is radical. Responding to theories of power that had previously accounted for it in the possession of a group of people or at an identifiable point of origin, signalled clearly in Marxist theories of power, Foucault wrote about relations of power existing within a network. Writing on power in the first volume of *The History of Sexuality*, Foucault says: 'Power is everywhere; not because it embraces everything, but because it is produced from one moment to the next, at every point, or rather in every relation from one point to another' (1978: 93). Poststructuralist feminist analyses have robustly contested criticisms levelled at Foucault for providing a totalising view of power in which subjects are rendered helpless against its enveloping embrace. Accepting this line of argument might spell disaster for feminist theorising and politics because any notion of agency is wiped out in such a deterministic rendering of Foucault's analysis. However, feminist poststructuralist theorists have, by careful appraisal and modification of Foucault's ideas, amply shown that his notion of power does not automatically result in the death of agency.

From a poststructuralist feminist perspective, although Foucault asserts that 'power is everywhere', it would be misleading to think that we are all trapped in its vice-like grip. As McWhorter sees it, in Foucault's mind 'power exists only in its exercise' (1999: 77). When read in this way, Foucault's capillary-like concept of power is particularly useful. Because power is relational, which is in one sense to say that power is bound up with knowledge and discourse, it has a productive – especially *generative* – effect. This becomes apparent in how Foucault conceives of the link between power and discourse:

> **Discourses are not once and for all subservient to power or raised up against it, any more than silences are. We must make allowances for the complex and unstable process whereby discourse can be both an instrument and an effect of power, but also a hindrance, a stumbling block, a point of resistance and a starting point for an opposing strategy. (1978: 101)**

With the above quotation in mind, two observations are worth mentioning. First, the way in which Foucault conceptualises power exhibits an openness that characterises much of his analytical insight. Here, as Weedon (1987/1997) avers, Foucault's notion of power does not pre-empt what forms power might take, a point that has rankled with many of his critics. The second point is related to the first. Foucault's theorisation of power does not obliterate agency for the reason that, as Foucault insists, 'points of resistance are present everywhere in the power network' (1978: 96). By prising open the possibility for resistance at the very same time power is exercised, Foucault offers up a way of thinking about a politics of possibility: that is, a way of thinking about how competing discourses can be taken up by subjects to continuously (re)construct alternative identities and subjectivities. This is the generative effect of exercising power. Foucault again says:

> **There is not, on the one side, a discourse of power, and opposite it, another discourse that runs counter to it. Discourses are tactical elements or blocks operating in the field of force relations; there can exist different and even contradictory discourses within the same strategy. (pp. 101–102)**

In the discursive spaces that are exposed when power is exercised, there exist, however momentarily, opportunities for agency. In the same first volume of *The History of Sexuality*, Foucault explicitly states that within any given discursive arrangement are contained the same discursive resources that may nourish competing discourses. One oft-cited illustration of this line of argument is Foucault's genealogical analysis of the figure of the 'homosexual'. As supporters of Foucault's work have publicised, by reconceptualisng the 'homosexual' as a category of knowledge, and thus a subject position rather than an essential identity, this allows Foucault to give emphasis to the formation of a reverse discourse: 'homosexuality began to speak on its own behalf, to demand that its legitimacy or "naturality" be acknowledged, often in the same vocabulary, using the same categories by which it was medically disqualified' (1978: 101).

For poststructuralist feminists, what Foucault's insights into power and resistance offer is a sizeable measure of hope for realising a feminist politics energised on notions of difference and resistance. Instead of treating women as homogeneous, or as passive victims, poststructuralist feminists can point both to how women engage differently with discourses of gender, as well as how they exercise resistance: creating their own discursive spaces to construct new identities, ways of relating and subjectivities that are not 'man-made'. At the same time, however, such analyses can also signal the limits of resistance (and of power) by underscoring how the discursive actions of women can be complicitous within normative discourses that disadvantage women. While a sympathetic evaluation of Foucault's ideas of power and resistance is clearly possible, it is important to state that his theorising on resistance is partial. Many poststructuralist feminists have noted this deficiency and have proceeded with a more cautious view about the limits of Foucauldian theory when it comes, for example, to analysing the conditions that are required in order to make possible certain expressions of resistance (Bartky, 1988). Yet Foucault's claims about power and resistance have inspired many feminists to apply and develop his ideas within empirical domains. In the following section, we outline some of this work within the field of management and organisation studies.

Poststructuralist feminist theorising and management

Gender and management

As with other feminist theories that have been used by researchers to analyse organisations and management, poststructuralist feminism starts from the notion that organisations are not gender neutral. That gender and sexuality have been ignored within mainstream management and organisation studies is a well-rehearsed argument within the circles occupied by feminist scholars. More than most, feminist theorists have drawn to our attention the hitherto unacknowledged influence of gender and sexuality within classic mainstream organisation and management theory. Linstead and Thomas (2002), for example, in an article on poststructuralist feminism and management, highlight that seminal studies of managers and management within management theory (they cite Fayol, 1949; Hales, 1993; Mintzberg, 1973; Stewart, 1989) have little or nothing to say about the influence of gender. Indeed, that the subject of gender has now received the mixed critical attention it so richly deserves is clearly evident in some of the published, scholarly reviews of the gender and management literature which we recommend reading (for example, see Brewis and Linstead, 2004).

While feminist analyses of management and organisation differ in their analytical foci, they are broadly united by their commitment to expose the masculine assumptions and power relations that undergird the seemingly gender-neutral appearance of traditional management studies. However, a shift in feminist analyses of organisation and management has occurred in recent times. A number of feminist theorists have taken issue with rigid accounts of gender hierarchies (see Walby, 1990) and structural explanations of gender in work organisations (for a well-cited example, see Kanter, 1977), arguing that such analyses tend to neglect agency and the fluidity of gendered power relations or deposit gender outside of the organisation. A number of feminists cognisant of these theoretical limits, and the shortcomings in other types of feminism more generally, have adopted poststructuralist perspectives to approach the realm of work in discursive terms, exploring what constitutes 'managers', 'management', 'work', 'job roles', 'work identities' and so on, in any given work context.

As mentioned earlier, adopting poststructuralist theories allows feminist researchers to problematise essentialist notions of gender and power that have pervaded some previous feminist theorising. Turning their attention to the workplace, poststructuralist feminists have produced fruitful ways of viewing gender as an unstable and historically specific category of knowledge within which the gendered subject is formed. Following Foucauldian theory, since gendered discourses (like all discourses) exist within a matrix of power relations, poststructuralist feminists conceive the workplace as one site in which subjects are constituted within asymmetrical, ever shifting, power relations. Accordingly, as Collinson and Hearn (1996) remark, poststructuralist feminism draws us close to 'men's and women's diverse, fragmented and contradictory lives in and around organizations' (p. 10). The following selection of examples illustrates the contribution such analyses have made in that respect.

Managerial identities and subjectivities

Pauline Leonard's (2003) study of doctors and nurses in the British National Health Service (NHS) employs a poststructuralist feminist approach to explore the contradictions and ambiguities that arise when these workers engage with gendered organisational discourses. One feature of Leonard's research, and a characteristic of much poststructuralist feminist analysis, is the close attention paid to examining the ways in which subjects engage with competing discourses, particularly the inconsistencies, contradictions and paradoxes that occur when discourses are used to construct multiple subject positions. For example, some of the interview accounts reveal the tensions in how doctors and nurses understand and take up discourses of professionalism. Simply illustrated by one nurse in Leonard's study, who identifies the nursing staff as being 'far more pragmatic in the way they handle things' than doctors, at the same time she is aware of how doctors may position them as 'powerless' workers, whose 'job it is to clear up after them' (pp. 226–227).

For Leonard, poststructuralist feminist methodological perspectives have several distinct advantages. They allow researchers to gain insight into the 'different ways in which [subjects] position themselves' within a 'fluctuating range of competing discourses' (p. 219). Here, the self is understood in Foucauldian terms as a discursive construction, and as such calls attention to the ways in which organisations influence the fashioning of the self at work. As Leonard goes on to say, such insights are valuable for organisations since they serve as a reminder of the fragile relationship between workers and organisational culture, a point seldom acknowledged in the wholesale efforts of many organisations to transform employees 'through larger processes of cultural change' (ibid.). Another benefit is that poststructuralist feminist approaches aim to underline the plurality of voices, especially those belonging to marginalised groups and individuals, not least of all but by no means limited to women.

Elsewhere, in an empirical study of middle managers' identities, Linstead and Thomas (2002) employ poststructuralist feminist perspectives to remedy what they identify as univocal and homogeneous accounts of identities and subjectivities in previous studies of middle management. As they go on to argue, distinctions between middle managers in terms of gender are obscured and, as such, individual differences are suppressed. In the spirit of poststructuralism, especially in its emphasis on polyvocality and difference, Linstead and Thomas utilise feminist poststructuralism as a mode of analysis that 'focuses more specifically on the issue of difference', whereby managers are seen to 'construct and deconstruct difference, sameness and identity' (p. 2). In so doing, Linstead and Thomas stress the fluid and fractured identity work undertaken by the middle managers they interviewed in a private sector organisation in the UK. Understanding that, in poststructuralist terms, identity is not an immutable and essential property of individuals, Linstead and Thomas's analysis goes beyond prior studies of middle managers' identities as being relatively stable. In this vein, Linstead and Thomas depict how middle managers take up gendered managerial discourses to legitimise their roles and purpose, and how identity masks are a necessary instrument in the identity work of becoming a middle manager.

What is more, the study reveals how identity constructions are not always effortless or seamless. As such, a poststructuralist feminist methodology facilitates comment upon the contradictions, paradoxes and tensions that surface when gendered managerial masks are continuously (re)constructed, especially when middle managers steal time from their home lives to satisfy the burgeoning demands of work. Or, in the case of one female middle manager called 'Jackie', the researchers reveal how she creates a 'self-identity which is durable and transferable from one work situation to the next – that of the de-gendered professional manager' (p. 12), which disassociates Jackie from traditional discourses of femininity. Yet Jackie's de-gendered identity performance 'may actually preserve the dominance of control systems which are masculinist and patriarchal in their nature and effects' (ibid.). Arguably, the identity effects of such de-gendered performances might (not) be seen as worth sustaining. In summary, Linstead and Thomas's (2002) analysis is a fine example of a poststructuralist feminist approach to the analysis of management in terms of the fragility, fluidity and indeterminacy of managerial identity constructions.

Power and resistance

Taking the same approach to conceptualising managerial identities as provisional, Thomas and Davies (2005) outline the relevance and advantages of using feminist poststructuralist perspectives in analysing micro-level practices of resistance among managers within organisational settings. Research carried out into how public sector professionals draw upon discourses of new public sector management to construct identities and subjectivities, Thomas and Davies utilise feminist poststructuralist perspectives to cultivate a 'far more textured, detailed and nuanced understanding of individual agency' (p. 723). Their approach stands in contrast to frameworks of resistance derived from, for example, Marxist and labour process theories. Like Linstead and Thomas, they also offer a spirited defence of poststructuralist feminism as a frame for analysing the unstable and multi-dimensional discursive arrangements within organisational contexts. The focus on localised practices of resistance illuminates the dialectical relationship between constraint and freedom, and what types of resistance are produced as a result of shifts in power relations that impact the dynamic of the dialectic.

A number of examples are paraded in front of the reader, including one manager ('Dave') who, rather than acquiescing to his superior's preferences, questions 'pointless bureaucratic' organisational processes when he sees them hindering departmental effectiveness (p. 729). Another manager ('Frances') 'operates with a different set of performance criteria for her team', namely the criterion of being 'good enough' (ibid.) and no more than that, which acts as a countervailing criterion to those endorsed by the dominant discourses of new public sector management.

By the writers' own admission these examples of resistance in their study may be 'small and somewhat constrained' (p. 728) but they are, nonetheless, empowering at an individual level. As they go on to argue:

> **Individual dissent through identity work can contribute to destabilising truths, and the resistance of managers, who play a significant role in constructing the organization, may influence and make more generally acceptable other ways of 'being'. (ibid.)**

Theorising resistance within a Foucauldian frame, which holds resistance as an event of power, permits Thomas and Davies to document a finer-grained analysis of localised practices of resistance. As they conclude, poststructuralist feminist perspectives help to account for the 'resisting subject' (p. 732), one who may engage in multiple resistances depending on how they position themselves, and/or are positioned by others in relation to discourses of gender, or in this case particularly, new public sector management.

Elsewhere, Silvia Gherardi's work (1994, 1995, 1996) also exhibits poststructuralist sensibilities in the way she explores how organisational cultures vary according to their gendered dynamics. Gherardi treats gender as a relational concept, as well as viewing it as a performance. In that respect, gender relations are said to exist in discursive terms and may be observable in 'forms of thought and language' (1995: 3). Gherardi takes some of her conceptual cues from the work of Derrida and French feminists such as Julia Kristeva and Luce Irigaray to conceptualise gender as a politics of discursive difference: men and women are culturally constructed and positioned in a relationship of separation and hierarchy where one (men) is privileged over the 'Other' (women). This is what Gherardi calls the 'symbolic order of gender': an order founded on the appearance of separateness and difference. For Gherardi, language and discourse help maintain a symbolic order of gender in which men and especially women (re)produce traditional gender differences in their everyday actions. Gherardi describes these activities, performed by men and women on a continuous basis, as 'ceremonial work'.

Turning to examine the position of women in the workplace, Gherardi argues that the presence of women in organisations disturbs the symbolic order of gender. Women may be viewed, as narrative accounts of the experiences of women at work attest, as travellers in male organisational worlds (see Gherardi, 1996), which in extreme situations may lead to women feeling like they are 'intruders' or 'fraudsters'. In order to clear up the ambiguities that may be generated by the gendered actions and identities of female 'interlopers' who are out of place within the symbolic order of gender, women and men undertake 'remedial work'. For instance, a woman may dress in certain ways that are considered 'feminine' in order to show that she has not 'lost out' on femininity. While such gendered practices may help to repair the rupture to the symbolic order of gender, remedial work may also be used as a strategy of resistance and/or transgression.

Fournier and Kelemen (2001) point out that the concept of remedial work draws very close to Foucault's conception of a power and resistance dynamic. As Fournier and Kelemen go on to argue, remedial work can allow women to use femininity as a resource within the workplace. Women may perform femininity in specific ways to achieve competence and, at the same time, may gain pleasure from flirtatious performances of femininity, for example. Yet, as is typical of forms of resistance (at least in the Foucauldian sense), the outcomes of remedial work cannot be predetermined. Fournier and Kelemen's empirical (2001) analysis of a learning set established by a group of senior women managers in the UK is a case in point. The learning set afforded the women a number of opportunities to undertake remedial work to reconcile their conflicting identities as 'manager' and 'woman'. Although the endeavour allowed the women to mobilise images of community to provide forms of collegial support, the learning set did not help some women to address the pressures associated with being a 'woman' *and* a 'manager'. In that regard, the women's remedial work carried with it a number of unresolved tensions and ambiguities.

Poststructuralist feminism and men

Notable here, perhaps, is that the above-cited poststructuralist feminist research has been carried out by women. Arguably, this is hardly surprising given that popular perception suggests that feminism is the sole preserve of women. At worst, in the extreme tabloidisation of men's relationship with feminism, men are led to believe that feminism can offer them nothing or little more than man-hating feminists. Yet men can have a critical role to play in advancing feminism's broad aim of dismantling normative gender regimes.

Stephen Whitehead is one example of a large number of pro-feminist scholars who seek 'to contribute to the critical interrogation of men's practices while both illuminating and deconstructing the gendered relationship that exists between men, masculinities and organisational life' (1998: 201). Whitehead and other pro-feminist scholars (for example, Jeff Hearn, David Knights) have mobilised poststructuralist feminist perspectives to inform their analyses of how male and female managers construct and give meaning to their gendered identities, especially in relation to wider organisational discourses of management. It is doubtless that the role of men within feminism has been and continues to be fervently debated. We do not map these discussions here, but we do wish to support Whitehead's thoughts on the theoretical and political possibilities for conducting feminist research derived from poststructuralist feminism's misgivings on a feminist standpoint epistemology: an epistemology that contains a claim, that by virtue of their experiences within patriarchy, women occupy a unique position (as the disadvantaged) to critique the practices of men (see Hartsock, 1983). Such an assertion unhelpfully excludes men from such critiques, as Whitehead (2001) argues. By contrast, poststructuralist feminism's questioning of a female standpoint epistemology opens up opportunities for the role of men to work in parallel with feminists to 'transform the existing "gender order"' (p. 73).

Referring to Whitehead's (2001) research, study findings show the discontinuities and contradictions in how male and female further education managers construct their identities and subjectivities. The study similarly provides insights into the diverse and fragmented managerial lives of male and female managers reported in Linstead and Thomas (2002) Whitehead uses some of the conceptual resources from feminist poststructuralists, including Sawicki (1991), Weedon (1987/1997) and McNay (1992), to accentuate the ways in which male and female further education managers resist dominant discourses that carry localised knowledge about conventional ways of being a man/manager. Such findings also find a connection with Thomas and Davies's (2005) study cited above. Taken together, Whitehead's research on the complex discursive practices of managerial selves in the further education sector enables him to articulate a series of concerns for transforming managerial domains, that privilege that which Whitehead and co-author Deborah Kerfoot (1998, 2000) name elsewhere, as a rational and instrumental set of managerial practices that has gained currency in many managerial contexts. One major stumbling block to changing gender power relations, as Whitehead's (2001) research reveals, is that gendered self-reflexivity, a key component of change as far as Whitehead is concerned, seems hard for men to engage in, as they typically fail to see 'their own gender as a factor in inequality' (p. 79).

Summary

This chapter has outlined some of the helpful contributions poststructuralist feminists have made in forwarding the critical study of management. In particular, we have centred our attention on those feminists who have engaged with the writings of Michel Foucault to formulate a discursive approach to exploring the realm of management. Gender is of prime importance in these analyses, but the matter of gender is not confined solely to the concerns of women. Because Foucauldian theorising encourages us to consider the interrelationships between power, knowledge and discourse, in which the subject is endlessly (re)constituted, how men engage with organisational discourses of gender and management is of equal critical concern. This is a valuable, if not trouble-free, shift in analytical emphasis. If we are to interrogate men's roles in organisations generally and within management in particular, with a critical eye to understanding the differences between and among men and women so that we may dismantle organisational inequalities, then men are required to fully participate in this critical endeavour as much as women. Poststructuralist feminisms offer some flexible critical tools for male and female researchers to do exactly that.

A point worth reiterating at this closing stage is that poststructuralist feminist writing reflects a high level of consideration for the conceptual antagonisms that Foucault's work might inflame when aligned with feminist theories. For critically-minded researchers of gender and management, it is not simply a matter of raiding Foucault's work for ideas without any regard for how feminist theories might converge or conflict with some of Foucault's notions about, for example, agency. Much poststructuralist theorising continually questions the extent to which feminists can use Foucault's work. In that regard, this scholarship displays a level of reflexivity that is not only typical of feminist research more widely, but as we see it, is a necessary practice of any critical research into management and organisation. In extending the possibilities of developing reflexive and self-critical forms of research, we now turn to examine queer theory. With a close affinity to poststructuralist feminism perspectives as well as postmodernism and deconstruction, queer theory may be seen as something of a theoretical amalgam of some of the key concepts that thread together much of the theoretical work presented in Part II of this book.

Further reading

Since we have focused exclusively on poststructuralist feminism in this chapter we would urge those readers interested in feminist theorising to read some further material. One recent text that covers the diversity of feminist theorising in an accessible and introductory fashion (as well as including commentaries on sexuality studies) is Beasley (2005) *Gender & Sexuality: Critical Theories, Critical Thinkers* (London: Sage). For an accessible and stimulating account of how Foucault's ideas can be applied within feminist theory, try Sawicki (1991) *Disciplining Foucault: Feminism, Power and the Body* (New York: Routledge). Texts by Lois McNay also explore the tensions and possible points of connection between feminism and Foucauldian theory in a scholarly fashion. McNay's (2000) *Foucault and Feminism: Power, Gender and the Self* (Cambridge: Polity Press) is a good place to start. For an entry point into Foucault's work, many readers start with the first volume of *The History of Sexuality* (1978). For a more detailed overview of poststructuralist feminism then the classic is Weedon's (1987) *Feminist Practice and Poststructuralist Theory* (Oxford: Blackwell – there is also a second edition published in 1997). From the materials we have cited above that apply poststructuralist feminist theory within organisational studies, a particularly thorough exploration is: Linstead and Thomas's (2002) 'What do you want from me? A poststructuralist feminist reading of middle managers' identities', in *Culture and Organization,* 8 (1): 1–20.

7

Queer Theory

Introduction

This is the final chapter in Part II. As we stated in the previous chapter, queer theory might be usefully viewed as a body of theoretical perspectives that draws inspiration from many of the theories we have explored so far. As a child of postmodernism, queer theory has a number of prominent bloodlines that originate in feminism, poststructuralism and deconstruction, as well as specific areas such as gay and lesbian studies. It may also have potential points of connection with American pragmatist theory (Parker, 2001; Seidman, 1997).

While such affinities have yet to be sketched out in some detail, it is true to say that, like American pragmatism, queer theory has made a limited impact on organisational studies. Often confined to studies of sexuality and organisation, most particularly those that explore the work experiences of non-heterosexuals, queer theory occupies the outer margins of the more radical arm of CMS. We see this as a shortcoming, a missed opportunity and a disappointment. In our minds, queer theory finds a wider resonance beyond the empirical analyses that use queer theory to inform their explorations of the linkages between sexuality, gender and work organisations. Its destabilising impulse, its concern for the relationship between power and knowledge and its deconstructive approach to matters such as identity (to mention but a few of its qualities) all make queer theory capable of questioning the normative facets of organisational life.

With these comments in mind, the broad aim of this chapter is to sketch out some of queer theory's most prominent and productive conceptual resources that strike us as holding relevance for the critical examination of management. To begin this exploration, we consider the various ways in which queer theory has been understood and deployed, and to what effect. We then turn our attention to identifying some of queer theory's key progenitors and their works, and summarising some of the chief criticisms levelled at queer theory by its opponents. Since there is no well-established tradition of using queer theory perspectives in the study of management and organisation, we then move to point up the *potential* queer theory carries for aiding researchers who work within such academic domains.

It is worth commenting upon this point in more detail. Our aim here is not simply to rehearse debates about queer theory. More than this, we borrow from such discussions insights and concepts in order to stimulate thinking about how management researchers might employ ideas and perspectives within queer theory to understand and analyse work organisations afresh. We do this, not because we regard or seek to introduce queer as a fashion or fad within critical management studies (though some commentators do hint that queer is something of a novelty). Rather we consider queer theory as having the potential to offer researchers an imaginative, politically charged and sustainable set of conceptual tools with which to craft critical and penetrating modes of analysis.

At this point in the chapter, we detail some of the research that forms part of a small trickle of studies that have begun to apply queer theory within organisational studies. We finish by briefly outlining some of the main challenges facing management researchers who wish to adopt queer theory.

Mapping queer theory

'Queer' is a multifaceted term. Ever since its début within Teresa de Lauretis's commentary in a special edition of the feminist journal *differences* in 1991, the term 'queer theory' has stoked up the imaginations of countless scholars within the humanities. Additionally, its influence on theorising gay and lesbian lives and politics has been far reaching. Over the years, then, it has been, and continues to be, attributed different meanings by different people for different reasons. For example, it has been deployed as a derogatory slur typically in relation to gay men and lesbians. In the most extreme cases it has a direct link to homophobic violence: 'queer bashing' resulted in the ignominious death of Matthew Shepard in the USA and such incidents are still reported in parts of the UK.

In this spirit, to be designated 'queer' is to be constituted within language distinctively, and such modes of articulation have clear, material, effects for those individuals labelled as such. As Patrick Dilley (1999) remarks, the term 'queer' can be used as both a noun and adjective to identify individuals who belong to a minority group (based on sexuality) and, at the same time, to connote the abnormality of that membership insomuch as queer means 'not normal or, more specifically, not heterosexual' (p. 457). The personal costs for some individuals positioned as queer are well documented: depression, isolation, self-harm and loathing, even death (Russell, 2003; Vincke and Bolton, 1994); in relation to 'queers' in the workplace: truncated career trajectories, job losses and the use of identity disclosure strategies to evade homophobia (Hall, 1989; Ward and Winstanley, 2003; Woods and Lucas, 1993). Even though queer has the capacity to be mobilised and understood within discourses of homophobia, so it may be attributed different meanings by other non-heterosexuals who draw upon competing cultural discourses.

For many, queer is shorthand for 'gay' and 'lesbian', representing a welcome departure from the negative connotations the identity categories of 'gay' and 'lesbian' sometimes evoke. Indeed, the hijacking of queer by non-heterosexuals intent on transforming it into an inclusive, non-specific identity category bears more than an echo of how the term 'gay' was appropriated by gay men and some lesbians in a subversive political move to affirm a positive sexual identity and way of life that the term 'homosexual' did not signify. Gay and lesbian identity categories have become rallying points for minority, rights-based political groups ever since, as some historians of sexuality and sexual politics have well documented (Altman, 1982; Gamson, 1996; Weeks, 1985). Yet one perspective is that queer can never be wholly reclaimed as a sign of pure affirmation; arguably, it can never shake off its association with shame and hatred. In that respect, queer partly derives its potency as an anti-normalising politics and set of ideas.

Queer, then, can operate as a compendious, but voluminous, gender-neutral and inclusive sign for a diversity of sexual dissidents. As such, it reflects the limitations of identity categories and the struggles of some individuals to resist being compartmentalised into identity categories they find meaningless and moribund. For instance, there may be more room within queer for assembling members of other minority groups such as transgender persons and transsexuals who have frequently been excluded from mainstream gay and lesbian politics and theories (Namaste, 1996, 2000). While we maintain that senses of belonging do grow in and around identity categories such as queer, it is important to be mindful that there is also a line of reasoning that questions why certain people may be linked to others just because they share a marginalised sexual and gender identity. This raises a number of questions concerning the restrictions of identity categories, one example of which may be expressed thus: why should transgender and transsexual persons be affiliated to gay men and lesbians under the term 'queer' (for detail, see Namaste, 2000)? The non-specificity of queer, often regarded as its greatest strength, is also its Achilles' heel, according to some scholars. For instance, Max Kirsch (2001) avers that queer should not be unquestionably taken as a coherent way of linking different minority groups of peoples. For Kirsch, queer theory and politics may lead to a potentially catastrophic reversal in the growth of important communities that have built up around identity categories such as gay and lesbian. Insomuch as the very term and politics of queer may split asunder communities of people who seek to congregate and mobilise around its indistinct insignia. Such complaints are significant but crucially remain unsettled.

Our approach here takes into consideration such scholarly misgivings but also holds open the countervailing views of queer theorists (Jagose, 1996) who argue that queer is not best seen as a unifying term that brings together various sexual outlaws. Even if some individuals doubtless attribute meaning to queer as a totem around which they and others can muster. For one reason, as queer theorist Michael Warner (1993: 22, cited in Jagose, 1996: 126) notes, queer, gay and lesbian can co-exist as identity categories: 'Queer activists are also lesbian and gays in other contexts – as for example where leverage can be gained through bourgeois propriety, or through minority-rights discourse, or through more gender-marked language'. Importantly, queer theory, as Warner and we understand it, does not seek to supplant 'lesbian' and 'gay' as identity categories and install itself in their stead.

Rather, its main concern (if it can be said to have just one main concern) is to cast into suspicion how and why certain identity categories are constructed, given meaning and used for securing political gains. Queer theory invites us to (re)think our claims to certain identity categories. However, because queer is concerned with matters of identity categories and it seems to be inevitably imbricated in endless debates about identity politics as they relate to gay, lesbian, bisexual, transgender and transsexual people. There may be a sense in which queer is unhelpfully caught up in a vortex of semantic arguments about the virtues and vices of deploying various linguistic markers. David Halperin also acknowledges this:

> **... endless and fruitless debates among lesbians and gay men over the respective merits of 'gay' or 'lesbian' versus 'queer' have not only wasted a lot of energy and generated a lot of ill feeling but, more important, have inhibited careful evaluation of the strategic functioning of those terms. (1995: 63)**

With the above in mind, we suggest that one useful way in which to approach queer, rather than as a noun or adjective, is in terms of a positionality: not one that is stable and so becomes an essential and easily identifiable position, but one that is reliant on and exists in tension with normativity. As such, it is usefully regarded as an indeterminate approach, chronically unstable, ambitious in its purpose and relentless in its interrogation of a social category of 'normal' in specific cultural contexts at any given time. Halperin again:

> **... 'queer' does not name some natural kind or refer to some determinate object; it acquires its meaning from its oppositional relation to the norm. Queer is by definition whatever is at odds with the normal, the legitimate, the dominant. (1995: 62)**

Halperin's commentary emphasises queer theory's fluidity and indeterminacy, and in sum, its resistance to definition. If, for instance, queer signifies an identity, then it is one 'without an essence' (ibid.) and always in motion, as a term and theory that is in a permanent state of (re)construction. Viewed in this way, queer theory is an animating impulse for a generation of critical modes of analysis because in one respect it militates against the formation of arguments that are held in an 'either/or' frame.

Queer theory is also extremely proficient at highlighting dilemmas, tensions and problems, but not in resolving them and, thus, being fixed to one position or another. Rather, queer theory can help researchers to unearth problems, question taken-for-granted assumptions and, in so doing, develop critical practice that is mindful of a range of competing perspectives. It is, if you like, using a prism to view a problem: what comes into view is an intricate pattern of issues that may require the researcher to adopt multiple perspectives to make sense of them. Understood as such, we need to comprehend something about the attributes that make queer theory a slippery constellation of concepts and how its indeterminacy might be of great use to management researchers.

Denaturalising

Alan Petersen (1998), writing on the postmodern and poststructuralist challenge to viewing masculine identity as a fixed and essential property of individuals, argues that the ascendancy of queer theory reflects the latest turn in a 'crisis in the epistemology of sexuality' (p. 97). Viewed in this way, queer theory is explicitly seen to concern itself with the problems of identity categories that arise as a result of the operation of the heterosexual/homosexual binary opposition. Indeed, while queer theory is partly parented by postmodern thought, sharing its suspicion of truth claims and upholding the value in viewing knowledge as historically situated, it diverges from postmodernism in its crisp focus on sexuality as a key epistemic category of analysis. One primary objective for queer theorists has been to denaturalise the heterosexual/homosexual binary by highlighting its constructed nature. The influence of French poststructuralist theorising, particularly the work of Michel Foucault, is clearly evident in that respect.

Foucault's (1978) *The History of Sexuality, Volume 1* has accrued legions of supporters among queer theorists because it skilfully demonstrated that heterosexuality and homosexuality are not the natural, fixed properties of individuals, but are historically contingent categories of knowledge. In this regard, 'homosexuality' and 'heterosexuality' have specific cultural currency, as, for example, when in the latter part of the nineteenth century homosexuality first appeared in the published political discourses of Karl Maria Kertbeny in 1869 (see also Tobin, 2005). One of the major implications of Foucault's theorising was the constructedness of sexuality and its relationship with power and knowledge. As Halperin explores in *Saint Foucault: Towards a Gay Hagiography* (1995), Foucault's radical (re)theorising of homosexuality and heterosexuality as discursive effects generated a vital aperture for political and theoretical advancements within the field of sexuality. From within this framework, queer theory could emerge and find sustenance in

Foucauldian ideas of how sexuality, as a category of knowledge, may also operate as a technology of power, insomuch as certain discourses of sexuality circulate to give the impression that heterosexuality is both 'natural' and stable. In this respect, many queer theorists regard sexuality as disciplinary knowledge.

The legacy of Foucault's work for queer theorising is not to be underestimated. In the way that Foucault's ideas are seen to denaturalise traditional understandings of sexuality (see Jagose, 1996), so, too, does the writing of celebrated and oft-cited queer theorist/feminist Eve Kosofsky Sedgwick. Drawing upon Foucault's insights, Sedgwick (1990) provides a deconstructive literary exploration of the operation and interdependence of the heterosexual/homosexual binary opposition. This is explicitly articulated in her book's opening page: 'The book will argue that an understanding of virtually any aspect of modern Western culture must be, not merely incomplete, but damaged in its central substance to the degree that it does not incorporate a critical analysis of modern homo/heterosexual definition' (1990: 1). This aim advances an epistemological understanding of the heterosexual/homosexual binary, a binary that has extensively shaped the cultural contours of Western societies. Or, as Epstein (1996: 155) expresses it, *Epistemology of the Closet* 'seeks to analyze how various ways of constructing sexual marginality shape the self-understanding of the culture as a whole'. For Epstein and others (see Warner, 1993), the muscle in Sedgwick's writing is located in the genealogical analysis of the homo/heterosexual binary to not only show up the incoherencies in definitions of sexuality, but also to demonstrate how the concept of the 'closet' is a site of origin for the operation of a multiplicity of binaries, including 'secrecy/disclosure', 'public/private', 'masculine/feminine', 'majority/minority', 'innocence/initiation', 'natural/artificial', 'new/old', and so on (Sedgwick, 1990: 11).

In Sedgwick's work a denaturalising impulse is evident. In a similar way to that of Foucault, Sedgwick shows that knowledge is never complete: it is always shifting, historically situated and operating in ways that regulate the identification practices of individuals. Accepting this contention, we become cognisant of how the terms 'homosexuality' and 'heterosexuality' are differently attributed meaning by individuals in different societies and at different times. In this way, definitions of sexuality (and its practices) that become over determined, to the point of demonstrating seamless coherence, are cast into doubt. Such an impulse is useful for management researchers because it encourages a deeper questioning of what is constructed as normal in specific work or managerial contexts. The concern does not have to be with sexuality per se. For example (as Sedgwick's work gestures), a queer lens can be applied to the epistemological workings of other binary oppositions in organisations such as 'public/private' or 'leader/follower'. The denaturalising drive of queer theory is a valuable critical tool because it never releases us from exposing what appears to be self-evident as a matter of construction while, at the same time, generating resistance to normative (organisational) discourses.

Deconstruction

Queer theory has a strong connection with deconstruction (see Chapter 5). The deconstructive impulse in queer theory sensitises us to the importance and limitations of identity categories. Most significantly, queer theory reminds us that identities are not best understood using essentialist perspectives that, according to feminist Diana Fuss (1989: 2), are predicated on a 'belief in true essence – that which is most irreducible, unchanging, and therefore constitutive of a thing or person'. As we have mentioned earlier, the postmodern turn in the social sciences stands against essentialist theories that naturalise identity as a stable property of the individual. As Steven Seidman (1997: 148) writes, one inimical effect of using essentialism to conceptualise gay and lesbian identities is that 'the heterosexual/homosexual binary' is left intact as a 'master framework for constructing the self, sexual knowledge, and social institutions'. On this point some queer theorists (Warner, 1993) and feminists (Sedgwick, 1990) converge. Sharing postmodernism's and poststructuralism's misgivings about essentialism, queer theory may be seen to push debates about identity into the realm of the discursive. As Sedgwick's (1990) work illustrates, treating sexuality as an unstable category of knowledge reveals the heterosexual/ homosexual binary as mutable and fragile. It is within this line of theorising that a deconstructive approach to thinking about identity emerges.

Sedgwick's (1990) *Epistemology of the Closet* is one example of a text that offers a deconstructive analysis of binaries and identity. It advertises the limits of binary oppositions by employing a deconstructive analysis, which in Sedgwick's text operates within the field of literature. Recognising the problems associated with essentialism, Diana Fuss in the widely cited (1991) text *Inside/Out* provides a similar deconstructive, textual analysis of identity. Seizing on the ideas of Jacques Derrida, Fuss argues that the heterosexual/homosexual binary is closely tethered to another: namely, inside/outside:

> **The homo in relation to the hetero, much like the feminine in relation to the masculine, operates as an indispensable interior exclusion – an outside which is inside interiority making the articulation of the latter possible, a transgression of the border which is necessary to constitute the border as such. (1991: 3)**

In a deconstructive gesture, Fuss argues that both terms within each binary are mutually dependent on each other for definition, though this state of mutual dependence is always concealed, and that the borders between heterosexual/homosexual and its attendant binary of inside/outside are porous. Here, identity is conceptualised as difference because, as Fuss (1989: 103) explains: 'identity always contains the spectre of non-identity within it, the subject is always divided and identity is always purchased at the price of the exclusion of the Other'. Deconstructive analysis not only exposes the dependency and confusion around such binaries as they relate to practices of Othering, but it also seeks to force them, as Fuss puts it, to 'the point of collapse' (1991: 1). Such deconstructivist approaches to identity have been dubbed by opposers as a form of anti-identity politics, a claim that Fuss (1989) contests. These debates are intense, complex and continue to rage on.

As we have stated in Chapter 5, deconstructive analysis can be challenging, so gaining traction on such procedures is sometimes difficult, especially in terms of how they might be translated into empirical contexts. However, as Petersen (1998) usefully suggests, queer informed deconstructive analyses can be productive, particularly when interwoven with other perspectives such as those from sociology (see Seidman, 1996). The deconstructive conception of identity based on difference (or *différance* using Derrida's take on identity) is potentially enlivening. As Seidman (1996) asserts, deconstruction can support a line of thought for picturing how identity is 'permanently open' (p. 12) in how it is built and assigned meaning. Furthermore, queer informed deconstructivist approaches (like poststructuralist feminist perspectives) might be of enormous value for researching organisations insofar as they could, for instance, question the assumption of shared identities among and between employers and workers, and how the heterosexual/homosexual and inside/outside binaries (to name but a few) within dominant organisational discourses operate to shape corporate cultures and organise people within the workplace. In summary, the Derridean interest in exposing the instability and conflict in how one element of a binary opposition is at once parasitic and needs to stand above the other element is also a matter of interest for queer theorists.

Performativity

If there is one feminist more than any other who has inspired queer theorists the world over, then it is Judith Butler. In not a dissimilar way to how Michel Foucault's *The History of Sexuality* has been pored over by innumerable scholars to the extent that both the text and its author have gained iconic status, so too has Judith Butler and her work, especially the 1990 publication *Gender Trouble*. Butler's writings are thought provoking and demanding, and while we briefly consider just two examples here, readers of this book are encouraged to explore her work more widely (see Butler, 1990, 1993, 2004). *Gender Trouble*, regarded by many as one of several core texts on queer theory (despite the curious fact that *it* makes no direct reference to queer theory) is primarily a *feminist* tract on how gender may be understood in performative terms (see also Osborne and Segal, 1994). The promotion of Butler into the pantheon of queer theorists and the transplantation of her work into a queer canon of literature has partly come about by what queer theorists see in Butler's performative theory of gender. For Butler gender is not a one-dimensional or single performance, say in the manner of acting out a part in a play where the act or performance pre-empts the individual. Rather, gender is considered a 'stylized repetition of acts' over time, and it is within the iteration of performances that gender is signified (Butler, 1990: 179). Thus, historically specific acts and gestures that signify gender are 'performative in the sense that the essence or identity that they otherwise purport to express are fabrications manufactured and sustained through corporeal signs and other discursive means' (p. 173).

Related to the argument of gender as being performative is the attendant notion of 'drag', which Butler uses to illustrate the performativity of gender. Drag is one of Butler's most cherished concepts among her followers because it appears to be the exemplar for the theatricality of gender and, as such, a seemingly powerful way of transgressing gender norms. Yet, as Butler famously argued in her follow-up (1993) book *Bodies that Matter*, 'drag' and 'peformativity' were two terms grossly misunderstood by many of *Gender Trouble*'s readers. Radical feminist Shelia Jeffreys (2003), for example, takes Butler's performative gender theory to be simply the ability to cast gender on and off at will, in the manner with which one might choose garments to wear from a wardrobe. Butler has been at pains to clarify herself in that respect, (re)asserting that 'performativity is neither free play nor theatrical performance; nor can it simply be equated with performance' (1993: 95). Not least of all because such reiterations are generated within a field of power, and therefore, are subject to constraint.

Butler's radical theorising of gender has attracted, and continues to attract, criticism from other feminist detractors (for example, see Nussbaum, 2000) and celebration from her supporters. For queer studies scholars, Butler's intellectual explorations shatter the notion that gender is derived from sex and, in particular, in one of her latest offerings *Undoing Gender* (2004), the possibilities and conditions for undoing gender norms. For organisational researchers, Butler's corpus of work is not without relevance and merit even though, as Borgerson (2005) remarks, Butler has little to say about corporations. In one respect, as Borgerson implies, Butler's theorising on gender has direct relevance for queer theory researchers wishing to study workplace gender and sexual relations. But the notion of performativity is equally useful for alerting us to the efforts made by some individuals at work to generate seamless and coherent displays of identity as they relate to specific aspects of work. For instance, Hodgson's (2005) analysis of the performativity of professionalism among project managers in the UK is a noteworthy example of the translation of Butler's theoretical insights into an empirical analysis. In the context of Hodgson's study the use of performativity illuminates issues regarding (and the linkages between) agency and power. Hodgson's analysis foregrounds instances of resistance among project managers generated in the discontinuities in the reiteration of the acts and gestures that signify professionalism.

Queering management and organisation

Despite the proliferation of queer theory texts, especially those that aim to queer films, periods of history, people's lives, aspects of popular culture and so on, there is a paucity of literature about queering management and organisation. Heap on top of this observation the barrage of criticism regarding queer theory's indeterminacy, opaque language and concepts, its failure to deliver social change and its apparent narrow focus on sexual minority groups, and it is little wonder that queer theory might not be the first tool of choice in the kitbag of management researchers. We appreciate the complaints put forward by many of queer theory's opponents but we also caution that care is needed not to overstate the critique of queer theory. Much of this evaluation is too harsh and often one-dimensional.

Positively, some scholars have made efforts to evaluate the potential of queer theory in advancing the project of critiquing management and organisation. For example, Martin Parker's (2002b) article, 'Queering management and organization' (from which we borrow for the title of this section), offers up a series of ideas regarding the promise queer theory harbours for challenging management as an occupation, discipline and array of practices. Taking his lead from Butler (1990), Sedgwick (1990) and Seidman (1996), Parker's essay explores the intervention queer theory could make into (re)thinking current ideas about management and organisation (also see Parker, 2001). As to why we might wish to critically rethink management, Parker makes a forceful argument in his monograph *Against Management* (2002a). One of the book's chief lines of argumentation is that alternative ways of conceptualising organisations and modes of organising are being stifled 'through the generalized application of managerialism as the one best way' (p. 184). Parker identifies three forms of management that have been applied that, collectively, produce and sustain a 'hegemonic model of organization', a template that has a 'certain air of inevitability to it' (ibid.). One type relates to the contributions of academics employed within university business schools, outputs that bolster the hegemony of management in the ways Parker describes. One consequence of all this scholarly activity is that it sizeably contributes to a narrow and 'dangerous' mode of thought that (un)wittingly underlines the necessity of 'control' within management practices: a form of discourse which is being used in some organisations to conceal 'inequalities' and legitimise 'cruel' managerial regimes (p. 8).

With the above in mind, it is possible to clearly envisage how queer theory might be of considerable value. As Parker (2002b) asserts, queer theory is brilliant at exposing the production of knowledge within the academy as political practice. As such, queer theory can illuminate the political contours of knowledge production within university business schools and, thus, of theory formation itself. In this way, as Warner (1993) notes, queer has the ability to 'mess up ... [the] normal business in the academy' (p. xxvi). We agree with Warner and Parker regarding the productivity of such a venture. Activating Butler's concept of drag, Parker elaborates:

> **A university (or even management department) which dressed in drag, and recognized its own economy of secrecy and disclosure, its economy of repression and freedom, might be an institution that worked against itself in some rather playful and productive ways. (2002b: 162)**

In this capacity, queer theory can generate a reflexivity that channels attention to how academic discourses are value-laden and 'regard the management of everyday life with scepticism' (2002b: 161). Enormous potential exists here for unsettling the conventions of management practices. Importantly, Parker does not install queer in opposition to management in the shape of a binary opposition. Rather, as queer can only operate within the rules of convention or normativity because they both constitute each other, so, too, does queer and management. The relationship is relational, fluid and dynamic, as well as creative and conformist. In summary, Parker's essay carefully hints at the horizon of possibilities for doing queer in management and organisational locales.

Elsewhere, Cindy Rottmann's (2006) essay on queering educational leadership shadows Parker's commentary in both the suggestion that queer theory can generate critical dialogues and in the proposal that such critical modes of analysis can destabilise and disrupt normative models of organising and leadership. Like Parker, Rottmann establishes queer theory as a contender for dealing with some major problems associated with forms of work and organisation: first, the vulnerability of sexual minority students within the US education system as targets of homophobia and heterosexism; second, the paucity of non-hegemonic dialogues within educational curricula regarding sexuality; and lastly, the poor challenge mounted by queer theorists and activists regarding heterosexist models of educational leadership. For Rottmann, queer theory can move to support the type of critical dialogue that operates to rupture and displace a ubiquitous template of the 'effective leader' as 'strong, charismatic, dedicated, dynamic', as well as one who is adept at 'problem solving' and who can act as an agent of organisational change and justice (p. 13). In the attempt to demystify such forms of leadership, queer theory's theoretical anchors within the realms of feminist, poststructuralist and deconstructivist theorising give it strength and force. These conceptual bases support in differing measures and in different ways a disruption of dichotomous thinking, whether it concerns notions of leaders/followers or a heterosexual/homosexual binary.

Plainly, debates of the kind we have sketched out above largely explore queering aspects of organisational life in conceptual terms. In this regard, many questions about how this might be experienced by those individuals whose everyday work routines are influenced by heteronormative forms of organising remain empirically open. And yet, there is a small stream of studies that have begun to fill that lacuna, employing queer theory in empirical domains as they attempt to critique heteronormative discourses within work organisations. For example, Hugh Lee's (2004) research into the work lives of gay, male, senior managers within voluntary sector organisations in the men's sexual health promotion field shows how the men avail themselves of heteronormative discourses of management in order to construct identities as competent managers. Lee highlights how identity formation is provisional, riddled with the tensions and ambiguities that arise in gay men's managerial work lives. Most particularly as they relate to the adoption of 'straight male' identities by the men in order to project their managerial competence within organisational sites populated by gay men who provide information services to men who have sex with men. Here, queer theory gives some purchase for understanding how the impetus of becoming 'normal' operates within gay men's work lives.

Likewise, Rumens's qualitative (2005) study into the work lives of a group of gay men in the National Health Service in the UK provides insights into the identity dilemmas experienced by gay men seeking normalcy in their work lives. Elsewhere, Rumens (2007, 2008a, 2008b) explores how gay men's workplace friendships may generate discursive spaces for individuals to queer intimate relationships of their work lives. In other words, the ways gay men and their workplace friends negotiate issues of individual difference, as they pertain to work roles, gender and sexuality, open up and foreclose opportunities for individuals to critique normative organisational discourses of sexuality and gender.

The challenges of using queer theory

As the previous section shows, queer theory has much to offer for the advancement of the critical examination of management and organisation. However, mobilising queer theory is no small matter. Accordingly, what we offer below is a brief consideration of some of the main issues that researchers must address in that endeavour.

Who can use queer theory?

It has been apparent that research undertaken by queer theorists has been about and for other 'queers,' if we use that term to identify members of sexual minority groups, including gay men, lesbians, bisexuals, transsexuals, transgender people, and so on. One very good reason for this is that for many decades the identities and subjectivities of non-heterosexuals have remained invisible, and their experiences in different social settings are largely undocumented. Queer theorists along with feminists, gay and lesbians studies scholars and some sociologists have not only examined heterosexist and homophobic structures in society (Weeks, 1995), but have also analysed how members of sexual minority groups are creative in forging identities, subjectivities, forms of desire and belonging in all aspects of their life worlds (Weeks et al., 2001).

More than most, queer theory has done a far better job of exposing the dilemmas of gay and lesbian normalisation (see Seidman, 2002; Warner, 1999) and such analyses are starting to develop in relation to the particular position of gay men in the workplace (see Rumens, 2005). Wrestling with the difficulties of normalisation, queer theorists have found that they have becoming increasingly remote from some gay men and lesbians, especially those who enjoy the comforts of normalcy. Political commentator and writer Andrew Sullivan (1995) is one such person, frequently regarded as promoting the very liberal, rights-based politics that bolsters gay and lesbian normalisation. While queer theorists like Warner question this brand of gay and lesbian politics, one key point we wish to make here is that queer theory does not have an automatic relationship with non-heterosexuals. To elide queer theory purely with the desires and interests of non-heterosexuals is very restrictive. It reverses several decades or so of theorising the differences within and between sexual minority groups.

Building on this point, it is not that queer theory is only about the study of the lives of non-heterosexuals. Rather, queer theory is about questioning what is considered to be 'normal'. Taking this on board, 'doing' queer theory is an expansive activity, one that shifts from operating within select empirical locales and discrete groups of people, so as to avoid establishing a false dichotomy between 'queer' and 'heterosexual' research. Given queer theory's non-specificity, it follows that a wide range of people can access queer's conceptual resources. In saying that, there are, of course, issues regarding why certain people might adopt such tools, especially in regard to heterosexuals.

'Straight' US academic Calvin Thomas (2000: 12), writing on his participation in queer theory, asks: 'Other than voyeurism, appropriation, theoretical trendiness, or the desire to be the "good," responsible heterosexual critic, what might the draw of queer theory for straights be?' This is a poignant question, one that seems to produce a good deal of disquiet, not least of all in the minds of many heterosexual, male researchers. Indeed, what we also find striking about Parker's (2002b) observations on queering management and organisation is the undertone of defensiveness that is evident (and signposted) in his essay. Arguably, it reveals less about the writer's own apprehension with participating within queer studies, and more about the anxieties of those sceptics for whom queer in the hands of a white, straight, middle-class man is little more than intellectual posturing.

Whether such scepticism might be warranted is a moot point. That heterosexuals should gesture their interest in expanding queer dialogues when many occupy a position of cultural privilege – an advantage that is sustained in opposition to a homosexual Other – does seem puzzling. As Thomas questions, for what gain would heterosexuals partake in doing queer theory if the primary aim of queer is to unsettle the very normative regimes upon which heterosexual privilege rests? One rationale for undertaking such a journey is because not all heterosexuals find a clear resonance with heteronormativity in their life worlds. An obvious corollary of this is that not all heterosexual men are the same. For one thing, the strong current of homophobia and sexism that runs through many overlapping heteronormative discourses is as repellent to many members of sexual minority groups as it is to large numbers of heterosexuals. Queer theory might well serve as a 'critical process' through which heterosexuals can learn about the (re) production of heteronormativity, as Thomas (2000) writes:

> **… if there is any political value in straight queer aspiration … it may only be this: to assist in working the weakness in the heterosexual norm, to inhabit the practice of heterosexuality's rearticulation and inhibit its hegemonic dominance. (p. 31)**

Plainly, gender and sexual outlaws do not have to be, for example, 'gay' or 'lesbian'. Yet it is revealing (and disappointing) that there is still a scarcity of heterosexual researchers, men especially, who are taking part in queer theory research.

Making connections

Queer theorists must be able to make connections across theoretical domains. After all, queer theory is multidimensional and not always easily distinguished from other theoretical paradigms within which it has numerous points of origin, including social constructionism, postmodernism, poststructuralism, gay and lesbian studies, psychoanalysis, deconstructionism and feminist theory. In much the same way we argue that queer theory should not be claimed as a theory for 'queers', then we also opine that queer theory should not be understood within one particular theoretical vein.

Queer studies scholars do not speak as a chorus and so researchers may find they have to search for continuities between each theorist and various sets of theoretical debates. This can be productive as new intersections are being mapped out by academics concerned with developing linkages between queer theory and critical disability studies (McRuer, 2003; Sherry, 2004) and postcolonial theory (Binnie, 2004; Spurlin, 2006). Since queer theory exists in an unending state of (re)construction, researchers must feel comfortable with being mobile and creative in how they interpret and draw upon various conceptual resources, and in what contexts they deploy queer theory. Making connections is also crucial in the face of certain reprimands delivered against queer theory. For example, one of the most prominent objections to queer relates to its tendency to dissolve the 'social' into the 'literary'. Steven Seidman (1993), writing in Michael Warner's *Fear of a Queer Planet,* sounds a cautionary note regarding this variant of queer 'textual idealism'. Such concern, fuelled by a number of reprobations made by queer theory's critics about its theoretical opacity and inattentiveness to social structures, was later to move Seidman to articulate a series of possible connections between queer theory and sociology in an edited collection titled *Queer Theory/Sociology* (1996). Expanding the possible nodes of attachment queer theory may find with other theoretical domains has at least two distinct advantages.

First, it does much to counter the misplaced criticism levelled at queer theorists for being wilfully obscure in their analyses. While some queer scholars are theory specialists and some queer theory is dense and seemingly impenetrable, the writings of queer theorists should not be simply reduced to the fine art of wordsmithery. Second, as Seidman argues in relation to the conjoining of sociology with queer theory, queer theorists would encourage sociologists to (re)examine the assumptions upon which sociology rests: foundations that are heterosexist, as mainstream sociological research in topic areas such as the family attests (Weeks et al., 2001). Likewise, a queer social theory would obtain an empirical richness that is not always present in queer theory analyses. A similar and more recent plea is made by feminist/sociologist/queer theorist Sasha Roseneil (2000). To our minds, both Seidman (1996) and Roseneil (2000) show that these sorts of critical interdisciplinary dialogues are vital in three broad ways: (1) for eroding academic self-enclosure; (2) for nourishing a critical internal dialogue within queer theory to help it challenge its own elitist and normative assumptions; (3) for chasing new ideas that can be put into the service of questioning and challenging normativity.

Another important connection queer theorists must (re)cultivate and maintain is with feminist scholarship. In an obvious sense the connection is crucial given that queer theory is a progeny of certain strands of feminist theorising (for example, the work of Judith Butler, Eve Kosofsky Sedgwick and Teresa de Lauretis). More broadly, both feminism and queer theory share the same aim of debunking the idea that gender and sexuality are derived from biological categories of sex. Yet the relationship between queer theory and feminism remains tense. Despite its shared anti-normalising impulse with some branches of early lesbian feminism, queer theory has often been chided by lesbian feminists for its aggressive, in-your-face approach, reflecting a certain type of gay male politics lurking at its heart. Radical feminist Shelia Jeffreys (2003) is especially scathing of the terms 'queer' and 'queer theory' and has, over many pages of her publications, vehemently attacked queer theory for creating another space for the activation of a gay male agenda that suppresses lesbian experiences. Starting from the same notion, feminist Lillian Faderman (1997: 226) expresses despair over why female queers 'seem to have given up entirely a conceptual space for themselves as lesbians in adopting the term and the concept "queer"'. We cannot, however, entirely follow Jeffrey's invective against queer theory's cover for the advancement of gay male politics. These worries are often conveyed bluntly.

Feminist Kathy Rudy (2000) adopts a more nuanced stance from which she asserts that a 'feminist version of queer theory' is needed to prevent discrimination against women within queer studies and politics. Such a move, or rather a series of moves, is conceptualised by Rudy as a critical process that does not collapse one agenda into another. Instead, Rudy avers that queer theorists and feminists need to develop stronger alliances (conceptually and politically), although some reservations may be retained about Rudy's effort at promoting yet another version of queer. Regardless of this, however, what Rudy does here is to make a valuable point concerning the ties between contrasting anti-homophobic discourses and people – not in a way whereby everyone speaks in unison, but in ways that permit polyvocality and, thus, help us to engage with differences. This would appear to be vital, if queer is to infiltrate research domains where it is currently absent.

Queer theory is not ivory tower intellectualising

Lastly, we reason that queer theory researchers should view empirical inquiry as crucial. Unlike some commentators, we do not altogether regard queer theory as an intellectual enterprise confined to universities and their classrooms, one that eschews the need to explore empirical domains. While it is doubtless that queer theory's emergence first took place within scholarly discourses in the literary and cultural studies departments of universities in the USA, over the intervening years it has seeped into other academic spheres and has established a strong relationship with political action. While there is not the space here to review the permutations of queer politics in the USA and the UK, it is obvious, in one sense at least, that queer theory has become intermeshed within the political dynamics and actions of some organisations (see Seidman, 1997). This is not the same as saying that queer theory has a facile relationship with politics and that it can always deliver social change, as some of its critics have pointed out (Kirsch, 2001). It is, however, to suggest that in the light of our exhortations above, especially in relation to building connections and senses of confederacy with others through doing queer, we can instigate transformations within the everyday realities of people. As Judith Butler (2004) avers, theory alone is not sufficient for

> **... social and political transformation. Something besides theory must take place, such as interventions at social and political levels that involve actions, sustained labor, and institutionalised practice, which are not quite the same as the exercise of theory. (p. 204)**

In this way, the exercise of doing queer to instigate cultural change or emancipation is not solely about challenging organisational norms at a conceptual level. In actuality (and in the workplace), queer theory must also stimulate human action around such issues as the configuration of work, management and organisations, generating a rupturing effect on what is taken-for-granted. Obviously, this is no small matter. But it is likely to be a pragmatic matter; arguably, a matter where pragmatist scholars might lend a helping hand? But we have no desire here to splinter queer theory into mutually exclusive parts that relate to theory and practice. Theory does not pre-exist practice: the two are mutually interconstitutive and if seen in this way we can begin to gain a fuller understanding of the effects of one on the other. Given queer theory's ancestry within postmodern thought, it can be minded to give emphasis to contingency and indeterminacy in theorising people's lives as well as foregrounding the significance of pragmatic action. From this vantage point, queer theory may be used to generate modes of resistance to the organisational norms that impel people to act in certain ways and shape how they make sense of work, management and organisation.

Summary

In this chapter we have proposed something about the usefulness of queer theory perspectives for doing critical management research. Several points should stand out. First, if, as Parker points out, the 'enemy' of (re)thinking about management and organising in all but the narrowest senses is a 'lack of radical imagination' (2002a: 211), then the use of queer theory might make management and organisational studies all the better for it in that respect. Saying this, however, does not equate to positing queer theory, and to borrow the words of Halperin (1995: 66) as 'merely a radicalism for its own sake, a fashionable attachment to whatever may look new in the way of personal or political styles'. We do not treat queer as a mercurial creature of modishness that happens to offer up the latest brand of radicalism. What we do suggest, however, is that because queer theory maintains a 'conceptually unique potential as a necessarily unfixed site of engagement and contestation' (Jagose, 1996: 129), it avails researchers of an exciting and elastic positionality from which to critique what appears familiar and 'normal' within organisational environments. Second, while queer theory's indeterminacy is of great worth to researchers, it necessarily demands a level of self-reflexivity and intellectual dexterity not only to handle its animating impulses, but also to generate research that is critical and stimulating. Doing queer theory then can potentially offer a level of adventure that few other critical approaches can rival.

This chapter is the last one in Part II of this book. Having established our select sample of critical theories, we now move to demonstrate how these theories have influenced quantitative and qualitative research traditions. In doing so, Part III, 'Methodologies of Management Research', shows how critical theory has shaped the methodological approaches taken by researchers to actually doing critical research.

Further reading

As we have noted above, the seminal works associated with queer theory are: Butler (1990) *Gender Trouble: Feminism and the Subversion of Identity* (London: Routledge); Sedgwick (1990) *Epistemology of the Closet* (Berkeley: University of California Press); and de Lauretis (1991) 'Queer theory: lesbian and gay sexualities', in *differences: a Journal of Feminist Cultural Studies*, 3 (2): iii–xviii. Readers might wish to start with the article by de Lauretis before heading off to either Butler or Sedgwick.

Numerous books have been published on queer theory since the early 1990s, and some of the more insightful and provocative texts include: Warner (ed.) (1993) *Fear of a Queer Planet: Queer Politics and Social Theory* (Minneapolis: University of Minnesota Press) (especially the introduction by Warner); Jagose (1996) *Queer Theory: An Introduction* (Melbourne: Melbourne University Press); and Seidman (ed.) (1996) *Queer Theory/Sociology* (Oxford: Blackwell). The edited collection of essays by Seidman is a particularly good resource for scholars wishing to (re)consider how queer theory and sociology might rub shoulders. Material that explores the application of queer theory in organisational studies is sparse, but Parker's (2002b) 'Queering management and organization', in *Gender, Work and Organization*, 9 (2): 146–166, is both a breakthrough in that respect and a stimulating read.

Part III

Methodologies of Management Research

8

Critical Perspectives on Quantitative Research

Introduction

Our overarching purpose in this chapter and the one that follows is to draw upon the theoretical perspectives previously reviewed in Part II, in order to describe the impacts of these theories, already demonstrable or yet to make an impression, on quantitative and qualitative management research. Part III of this book, then, is mainly concerned with exploring how organisational researchers may use their knowledge of these theoretical contributions in the generation of reflexive and anti-oppressive forms of management research.

While we have split our discussion into two halves (namely, one chapter on quantitative research, another on qualitative research), we do not wish this to be read as an indication of an attempt on our part to maintain rigid boundaries between the two. Organising the discussion in this way is done largely for the sake of clear presentation, and thus for the convenience of the reader. However, wherever possible we shore up our argument for moving away from a 'quantitative *versus* qualitative' stance to a more open-ended vantage point from which the researcher can survey a horizon of possible points of contact between the two research traditions.

In this chapter on quantitative research our aim is quite simple: we wish to show why critical researchers (despite the proclivities they might hold towards postmodern forms of research) do not need to dispense with numbers. Or, put differently, why critical management researchers can rely upon and generate quantitative data. To be sure, some of the critical theories that we have touched upon in the second part of this book appear not to have established much contact with quantitative forms of research. For example, deconstruction and queer theory perspectives seem (at first glance) more at home within the qualitative research tradition. But this is not necessarily the case. One message we hope to convey clearly throughout this chapter is that critical theories and critical theorists are neither directly opposed to nor naturally adverse to quantitative forms of research. Such a dichotomy is more reflective of the entrenched quantitative/

qualitative divide within the social sciences rather than the actual behaviours and mindsets of a large number of critical theorists.

In developing this argument we have organised the chapter as follows. First of all, we discuss the quantitative/qualitative divide within the social sciences before moving on to highlight the dominance of positivistic quantitative research agendas within mainstream organisational studies. We put forward and illustrate our concerns about some of the outcomes and drivers of the prevailing tide of traditional positivist management research. We review why quantification processes are of some considerable importance to organisations, paying particular attention to statistics. Offering up a concise discussion of some of the key terms within statistical measurements and types of statistical tests reveals something about the role statistics play in organisations, as well as how statistics are often uncritically presented in mainstream research methods textbooks. For the type of open-ended, multi-paradigm and integrated approach to critical management research we support, the next section of the chapter provides a critique of statistics using three examples: (1) an ethnostatistics approach, as outlined by Gephart (2004, 2006); (2) the issues queering statistical data might bring to the fore; (3) feminist approaches to quantitative research. Feminism is constructed here as a particularly good example of how a critical theory, typically hostile (with good reasons for being so) to quantification processes, can be used to critique existing quantitative data, as well as to develop quantification processes that do not antagonise organisational feminist goals. Given the paucity of scholarly material for demonstrating a deconstructive approach towards or queering of quantitative research, we then underline ethnostatistics and feminism as two examples of how critical researchers can develop and employ quantitative data.

The quantitative/qualitative divide

Traditionally, quantitative research has been characterised by its concern for objective data collection, its emphasis on researcher control, the development of systematic and standardised procedures and counting. For example, Alvesson and Deetz (2000) suggest that 'quantitative research may be defined as research aiming at reducing ambiguity through transforming perceptions into pre-structured, quantifiable categories' (p. 55). As a mind-boggling number of research methods publications bear testimony to, certain research methods have become closely tethered, perhaps inextricably so, with quantitative research. Questionnaires, experiments, surveys and statistical techniques are some of the most commonly cited research tools of those working within the quantitative tradition. How these research tools are used in conjunction with the variety of epistemological positions quantitative researchers adopt makes for a well-furrowed field of inquiry. It is possible to argue that certain themes unite different quantitative

...2000) again write: 'much [quantitative] research ...ty' (p. 56). The idea that we can research and ...versial. Acres of text have been devoted to ...bjective components (for example, presump... from researchers' minds so they may observe ...search purporting to adhere to principles of ...for decades. Yet we already know that certain ...incoherence of objectivity and rejected the ...ng the rug out from underneath academic

...rted to relax the stranglehold of quantita... ...out the 1960s onwards, the zone between ...e research has resembled something of a ...pted over the years as various scholars ...he relay of criticism and counter-criticism ...tive and qualitative forms of research. ...ese aptly named 'paradigm wars' (see ...terms of challenging the mainstays of ...rder to develop new methodological ...s launched by some quantitative and ... on matters such as 'objective truth' ... ha... ...th in the effort to demarcate distinct m... ...d even the experienced) researcher, wa... ... is in many respects, is still easy to get ...hese debates has cooled, scholarly opin... ... the quantitative and qualitative resea... ...vein, there are obvious borderlines betwe... ...and defended from 'invaders'. For examp... ...e introduction of postmodernist perspe... ...ter 4) postmodernism provides a warrant ...ctive truth'. As such, quantitative researche... ...ve often savaged postmodernist perspecti... ...pistemological, ontological and methodol...

What g... ...e. Some researchers might still be inclined ... particular research paradigms at a conceptual ... But we do not put store on such academic guard duty. For one thing, it merely reifies unworkable distinctions between quantitative and qualitative forms of research. To illustrate, questionnaires and surveys are sometimes unthinkingly taken to *be* quantitative research just as interviews and field observation

3M SelfCheck™ System
Circulation system messages:
Patron in file

Title: Critical thinking skills :
ID: 581982
Due: 21/05/2015 24:00
Circulation system messages:
Loan performed

Title: Critical thinking for students :
ID: 597139
Due: 21/05/2015 24:00
Circulation system messages:
Loan performed

Title: An introduction to critical management research /
ID: 543143
Due: 21/05/2015 24:00
Circulation system messages:
Loan performed

Title: Research methods for business students /
ID: 549951
Due: 21/05/2015 24:00
Circulation system messages:
Loan performed

Total items: 4
...4/05/2015 14:51

Circulation system messages:
Missing ID and verification.

Thank you for using the
SelfCheck™ System.

techniques are sometimes taken to *be* qualitative research. This is misleading because research methods do not determine whether a research endeavour is either 'quantitative' or 'qualitative'. For one thing, there is an established history of researchers using multi-method approaches, integrating components of qualitative and quantitative research processes. Quite often, as Bryman (1984) argues, the division between the two research traditions goes incredibly awry, partly explained by the fact that it is the underpinning thinking about what constitutes reality and valid claims to knowledge that shapes whether a route of inquiry may be described as 'quantitative' or 'qualitative'. With this in mind, increasing numbers of academics, among which we include ourselves, do acknowledge the futility of dichotomous modes of thinking about quantitative/qualitative research. Arguing from this position allows us to explore at a paradigmatic level (rather than at the level of research methods) the possible ways in which different forms of research (traditionally labelled as qualitative or quantitative) will converge, diverge and overlap.

Quantitative research on organisations

As noted above, before the 'linguistic turn' in the social sciences took hold, bringing with it a fresh emphasis on exploring language and discourse, positivistic and post-positivistic paradigms held sway. This is easily detectable within current and past organisational research. Up until the linguistic turn, the production of quantitative research went, by and large, unchallenged. Positivist-orientated researchers especially generated quantitative research built upon what Alvesson and Deetz (2000) describe as 'modernist science' (p. 13). The argument here is that the ushering in of the Enlightenment period in Western society brought with it an optimism for and commitment to 'an autonomous subject progressively emancipated by knowledge acquired through scientific methods' (ibid.). Thus, Enlightenment thinkers attached a high premium to uncontaminated human reason over irrationality and emotionality. Under the guiding principles of the Enlightenment, society, it was argued, would progress. As Alvesson and Deetz go on to say, early organisational studies such as those carried out by Federich W. Taylor, which later formed the bedrock of 'Scientific Management', embraced these Enlightenment ideals.

While postmodernism, poststructuralism and other types of critical theory discussed in the earlier chapters were to furnish scholars with the conceptual resources they needed to shed light on the 'dark side' of Western Enlightenment philosophy, the legacy of 'modernist science' within management research can still be felt today. Ever since organisations were conceived in positivistic terms as entities that could be explained by scientific laws, numerous studies have been carried out that have sought to measure and test relationships between the various material factors that shape an organisation's size, capacity for strategy making, culture and so on (Donaldson, 1996). Within this tradition, a concern for quantification is clearly evident. Lex Donaldson, an outspoken proponent of positivism in organisational theory, argues for the role of quantification in management research, suggesting how it can dispel flimsy, commonsensical thinking about, for example, how as organisations grow in size so they become managerially top heavy (see Donaldson, 2003). Donaldson's fervent campaign for positivist organisational theory has not always been well received, attracting derision and scorn from those who diametrically oppose his line of argumentation (Hassard and Parker, 1993). Such counter criticisms though should not be taken as an outright rejection of quantitative research. Positivistic quantitative research, as this chapter will show, is merely one permutation.

What is of particular concern, as articulated by a large number of commentators who have critiqued the positivistic tradition in management research, is the dominance of positivistic quantitative research in the study of management. Alvesson and Deetz (2000) evaluate this in relation to the thousands of positivistic/post positivistic studies on leadership. In their view, such studies have not greatly advanced a deeper understanding of leadership. Since much of this research attempts to reduce the ambiguity of how leadership is understood and attributed meaning by aiming to fix leadership as a singular concept, the multiplicity and the contingent nature of its meaning are lost. Somewhat similarly, we briefly consider the state of human resource management research (HRM).

Karen Legge's critical (2001) appraisal of the present day concerns of HRM researchers vividly highlights the overwhelming popularity of positivistic quantification in the growing number of studies searching for the 'Holy Grail of establishing a causal relationship between HRM and [organisational] performance' (p. 23). Much of this research emanates from the USA (for example, Huselid, 1995, Huselid et al., 1997, Ichniowski et al., 1996), where large-scale postal surveys have been typically used to gather data. As Legge asserts, drawing upon Purcell's critique of such methods, the validity of quantitative data of this sort is questionable. Often tick-box postal surveys of single respondents rely on the individual making judgements about the entire organisation. This can be problematic, especially if the organisation is complex both structurally and culturally, since the data gathered are merely indicative of one person's views – views that are hardly representative of all staff. Furthermore, the approach to causality in many studies adopts an uncomplicated viewpoint, where scant attention is seemingly paid to unlocking the 'black box of the processes that link HRM ... with organizational performance' (2001: 29). Without identifying the key variables within this 'black box', establishing and testing with credibility the resulting cause and effect relationships is highly problematic. These critical remarks (and others) that Legge expresses all lead to one gloomy conclusion: 'much of the research on HR "high commitment/performance" practices and organizational performance is at best confused and, at worst, conceptually and methodologically deeply flawed' (p. 31).

We can take at least two valuable points from Legge's essay. The first, as Legge herself notes, is that quantification is appealing to many UK university business schools. There are 'pay-offs' for researchers who can demonstrate a causal relationship between HRM and organisational performance. Scholars who claim to have found such causality, who then publish their findings in top ranked, refereed American business journals (that still favour positivistic quantifiable research), are thus more likely to garner academic kudos and help boost their employing institution's position in published university league tables. The second point, related to the first, is the sense in which organisations value quantification. Organisational worlds, in all their diversity, share a concern for quantifiable data in one way or another. Bottom lines are conveyed in numerical terms, as are employees' salaries and performance indicators, to mention but a few. Numbers and number crunching also form part of everyday business discourses within meetings, corridor conversations and organisational documentation. Undoubtedly, quantification has a vital part to play in helping organisations to internally manage and improve their everyday activities. However, our contention is that statistics and quantification processes are not viewed often enough (as Legge demonstrates) as being embedded within political and power relations or taken to be cultural/organisational artefacts. It is to this that we turn in the next section.

Quantification in organisations: statistics

The last two decades alone have witnessed a growing emphasis on the precise measurement of organisational performance, in particular financial performance, alongside a discernible shift away from social and interpersonal control mechanisms to numerical ones. Quantification is seen to lie at the heart of competent management and effective and profitable organisational life. Statistics have permeated organisational discourse like never before: averages, ratios, means, modes, medians and tests of significance and best fit are now part of everyday discourses in organisations (Gephart, 1986).

Labovitz and Hagedorn (1971: 65) define statistics as a professional field of inquiry concerned with 'the theories and techniques that have been developed to manipulate data'. In simple terms, statistics refer to any numerical summary that is the outcome of the application of rule-governed calculations. Statistics is a scientific discipline guarded carefully by an army of professionals (the producers of statistical data). Its contribution to economic and social progress is seen as paramount and there is little critical engagement with the assumptions, rationales and interests that are encapsulated in its apparent rationality. The one notable exception is ethnostatistics (Gephart, 1986), a form of quantitative sense making which examines how statistics are constructed and used to represent organisational realities. Before we discuss ethnostatistics in detail, it is useful to outline some of the most commonly used terms within the field of statistics and how they might be used within organisational settings.

Deductive research and statistical evidence

In the deductive tradition, the research process is one that relies on translating concepts into empirical indicators – namely, indicators are based on that which is observable, recordable and measurable in some objective way (Labovitz, 1972). Correspondingly, 'quantification' is possible by using the idea of variables. Even at a relatively crude and modest level, when we count the frequency of the presence or absence of some property, this allows us to describe observations (descriptive statistics) and to infer general conclusions about probabilities on the basis of samples (inferential statistics).

Having established that we may need to use quantitative methods in order to answer specific research questions, there are several issues that we must consider if we want to select the right statistical methods and make the appropriate interpretations. These include scales of measurement, the nature of descriptive statistics and the types of inferential statistics. We deal with each term separately:

Scales of measurement

There are three important properties that make scales of measurement different from one another: magnitude, equal intervals and absolute 0. Magnitude is the property of 'moreness'. A scale has the property of magnitude if we can say that one attribute is more than, less than, or equal to another attribute. The concept of equal intervals is a little more complex. A scale has the property of equal intervals if the difference between two points is uniform along the entire scale. For example, the difference between 5cm and 9cm on a ruler means it is the same difference between 15cm and 19cm. The difference is exactly 4cm in each case. An absolute 0 is obtained when nothing at all exists of the property being measured. The best example of absolute 0 comes from chemistry where it is a point on the Kelvin scale where all molecular activity stops.

Table 8.1 shows that a nominal scale does not have the property of magnitude, equal intervals or absolute 0. The sole purpose of a nominal scale is to name objects. For example, they can be: male, female or workers, middle managers, senior managers.

A scale with the property of magnitude but not the properties of equal intervals or absolute 0 is known as an ordinal scale. An ordinal scale allows us to rank individuals but not to say anything about the meaning of the differences between the ranks. However, for most problems in behavioural science we do not have the precision to measure the exact differences between intervals and so most of the time we use ordinal scales of measurement. For example, Intelligence Quotient (IQ) tests do not have the properties of equal intervals or absolute 0, but do have the property of magnitude.

Table 8.1 Scales of measurement and their properties

	magnitude	equal interval	absolute zero	example
nominal	×	×	×	team strips
ordinal	✓	×	×	ranking
interval	✓	✓	×	temperature (°f)
ratio	✓	✓	✓	temperature (kelvin)

When the scale has the property of magnitude and equal intervals but not the property of an absolute 0, we then refer to it as an interval scale. The most common example of an interval scale is the measurement of temperature in degrees Fahrenheit. Because there is no absolute 0, a temperature of 20°f is not twice as hot as 10°f. A scale that has all three properties is called a ratio scale. The best examples include temperature measured in Kelvin and speed of travel in miles/kilometres per hour (k/mph). Another basic way to classify variables is as discrete or continuous. A continuous variable may take on any value within a defined range (for example, seconds taken to run 100 metres), whereas a discrete variable inherently has gaps between successive observable values (for example, religious categories).

Descriptive statistics

One of the most frequent questions in statistics is to identify whether given values are average or abnormal in any way. This sub-section presents methods for describing and summarising distributions of scores.

Two different summaries are central tendency (typicalness) and variability. In statistics, there are at least three different ways to determine whether a score is typical. The typical score usually occurs in the centre of distribution and indices of typicalness are usually called measures of central tendency. The three measures of central tendency explored here are the mean, median and mode. The mean is the arithmetic average, the median is the point representing the 50th percentile in the distribution of a set of data, or the point in the distribution where half of the cases fall above and where the other half fall below, while the mode is the most common score.

The simplest method for describing variability is the range. The range is simply the difference between the highest score and the lowest score. The most frequently used measure of variability is the standard deviation.

Inferential statistics

Many problems in statistics require us to estimate or make educated guesses on the basis of numerical information. For example, we might want to estimate the average ability of British managers. Since it is extremely unlikely that we will be able to administer a test of ability to every manager, we will instead administer the test to a small number, calculate the average and estimate what the score may have been for the entire group. These estimations are, of course, subject to error.

Inferential statistics are used to test hypotheses. An important concept here is the null hypothesis (H0). Essentially, this hypothesis states that there is 'nothing going on'. Thus, if we were investigating whether two or more groups differed in their job satisfaction the null hypothesis would be that they did not. If we were investigating whether age and job satisfaction were associated, the null hypothesis would be that they are not. That is, knowing someone's age would tell you nothing about their level of job satisfaction and vice versa.

In each case, we can also make an alternative or **experimental hypothesis** (H1). This can either be directional or non-directional. For example, directional alternative hypotheses would specify whether people undertaking machine-paced work would experience higher or lower job satisfaction than those undertaking self-paced work, or whether job satisfaction increases or decreases as age increases. Non-directional hypotheses would be less specific. They would simply state that there was a difference between groups in levels of job satisfaction (but not which group was higher), or that age and job satisfaction do go together (but not whether older people are more satisfied or less satisfied).

Hypotheses refer to the **population(s)** from which the **sample(s)** of people who participate in research are drawn. They do not refer to those samples alone. In essence then, when doing research, we are asking: 'given the data one has obtained from a research sample, is the null hypothesis or the alternative hypothesis more likely to be true for the population as a whole?' Note that 'population' does not mean everyone in the whole world, or even a particular country. It should refer to those people to whom we wish to generalise the results.

Researchers are sometimes less than specific concerning what population they wish to draw conclusions about. Also, they sometimes use 'samples of convenience', namely people they can get hold of most easily. Ideally, those who participate in the quantitative research should be a **random sample** of the population of interest, that is, everyone in the population should stand an equal chance of participating in the research. This is rarely, if ever, achieved. Surveys often involve questionnaires being sent to a random sample of people from a given population, but of course not everybody replies and one inevitably wonders whether responders differ in important ways from non-responders. It is, therefore, more common for researchers to try to show that their inevitably non-random sample is reasonably **representative** (for example, as regards age, sex, type of employment, location) of the population as a whole. Put another way, the proportions of people of each age, sex, and so on, among those participating in the research should not differ much from those in the wider population. But it is still possible that participants differ from non-participants in other respects, including those of interest for the research.

The statistical analysis of data in management studies most often involves an assessment of the **probability** of accepting the alternative hypothesis when the null hypothesis is true for the population. The lower this probability, the more confident we should be that the alternative hypothesis can be accepted, and the null hypothesis can be rejected. This probability is also called **statistical significance**, a crucial concept in behavioural science.

Typically, statisticians are prepared to accept the alternative hypothesis (thus rejecting the null hypothesis) only if there is a probability of 0.05 or less that the null hypothesis is true given the data we have collected. Erroneously rejecting the null hypothesis is sometimes called **type 1 error**. We are therefore saying: 'I must be at least 95 per cent sure that I can reject the null hypothesis before I am prepared actually to do so'. This might be considered rather conservative – perhaps too conservative. After all, how many of us wait until we are 95 per cent certain of something before we act on the basis of it in our day-to-day lives? There is also the other side of the coin considered less often by researchers: the probability of accepting the null hypothesis when the alternative hypothesis is in fact true. Erroneously accepting the null hypothesis is sometimes called **type 2 error**.

If we find that, on the basis of our data, there is less than a 0.05 (namely, 1 in 20) chance of mistakenly rejecting the null hypothesis, we will usually declare that the result is statistically significant at the 0.05 level. If the probability is less than 0.01 (namely, 1 in 100), the result is statistically significant at the 0.01 level. A similar rule applies for a probability of 0.001 (1 in 1000). These are of course arbitrary cut-off points. Basically, the lower the probability, the more confident we can be in rejecting the null hypothesis. Notice that the lower the probability, the more 'highly statistically significant' the result is said to be.

But how do we calculate statistical significance given our research questions and data? Methods for comparing two or more sets of observations are outlined below:

- **t-test – to evaluate the statistical significance of a difference between two sets of scores.**
- **chi-square – equivalent to a t-test using discrete categorical data.**
- **analysis of variance (ANOVA-tests) – to evaluate the statistical significance of a difference between more than two sets of scores.**
- **correlation – used to assess whether two sets of scores are related.**
- **Spearman rank correlation – a form of correlation used with only ordinal (rank order) data.**
- **multiple regression – used to assess whether more than two sets of scores are related.**

These tests and other related permutations are to be found in many mainstream textbooks on research methods. Indeed, many texts merely describe these statistical tests and measures and go no further. For our purposes in this book, however, we cannot leave the analysis there. We take issue with claims to objective mathematical measurement that do not outline or critically examine the conceptual foundations on which their claims rest. We propose a critical outlook on statistics, and to that end we wish to draw upon a new but promising approach called ethnostatistics (Gephart, 1988).

Ethnostatistics: putting statistics into context

According to Gephart (1986), the production and consumption of statistics is a social enterprise that must be understood in its historical, cultural and practical context. Ethnostatistics attempts to understand the actual reasons and ways in which professionals (researchers, statisticians, and so on) produce and use statistical evidence. Ethnostatistics, as developed by Gephart, shares certain tenets with enumerology, the study of the social processes by which lay people generate and use numbers and the effect this has on processes of thought and behaviour (Bogdan and Ksander, 1980: 302). Similarly, ethnostatistics is related to ethnomethodology: the study of the means by which individuals make sense of their everyday lives. Associated with the work of Garfinkel (1967), ethnomethodology advances the broad view that social order is generated in the minds of individuals as they make sense – and thus construct order – out of the melee of everyday impressions and experiences. The focal point in ethnostatistics, namely the social practices surrounding the creation and interpretation of statistics, arises out of the application of the theoretical insights into sense making derived from ethnomethodology. As such, ethnostatistics is one instance of a perceptible interest among scholars in using the postmodern turn to question the certitude of statistics in particular and economics more generally. Admittedly, such interdisciplinary discussions are rare (ethnostatistics is an exception). But Luker et al. (1998) also offer a provocative and short piece on the significance of postmodernism ('as a general way of thinking about the world') for reminding statisticians and the like that they do 'not possess privileged scientific means of analyzing the present or seeing the future' (p. 451).

Returning to the key aim of this chapter, the task of ethnostatistics is to understand how social scientists produce or select certain conventions or meanings that consequently create measures conceived to be true measures. Singling out the phenomena to be counted also changes the meaning of the phenomena and therefore it is crucial that we explore the rationale for choosing certain phenomena at the expense of others. Counting has a temporal dimension and, as such, the task of the researcher is to understand how meaning and judgement are used through time and in context by those persons who generate statistics.

Multiple parties, situated on different levels, are usually involved in 'counting'. As such counting becomes a political process reflecting the interests of the most powerful. Counting is affected by the existing structures and the ideologies in play at a particular point in time. Bogdan and Ksander (1980) suggest that the rationales for counting and the initiators of counting will affect the meaning of the count, the processes of quantification and the actual figures or numerals generated.

Quantification and the products of this practice are assumed to have strong affective qualities in contemporary society. If something can be measured, it could also be managed and controlled. Quantification perpetuates the myth of rational organisational practice where the most minute feelings and perceptions could be known, controlled and changed (see for example, surveys on employee satisfaction, customer satisfaction, organisational commitment, and so on). The production of statistics triggers other social processes in the setting in which counting is done, for it contributes to the process of decision making by which certain aspects are deemed essential for organisational success, while others could be ignored.

The boundaries between enumerology and ethnostatistics are blurred: quantification in social science research is based on and influences how and what organisational members quantify. Gephart (1986, 2006) introduces a three-level ethnostatistics framework to help figure out some of the complexity here. First-level ethnostatistics explores the actual production of statistics and the cultural worlds of quantitative data procedures and users. Second-level ethnostatistics explores the technical choices made during quantitative organisational research and tests assumptions made about subject's sense making and behaviour that are embedded in the measurement instruments and measures. Third-level ethnostatistics uses literary and textual analysis methodologies to understand how statistics are used in documents to make persuasive claims about organisational realities. We explore these three stages in more detail with the help of a case study by Kilduff and Oh (2006).

'Deconstructing diffusion': an ethnostatistics case study

In this section we summarise Kilduff and Oh's (2006) analysis. At the heart of Kilduff and Oh's piece is the ethnostatistical examination of a seminal quantitative work produced by Coleman et al. (1966) on the adoption of tetracycline by small, private, medical practices in four Illinois towns in the USA. The main finding of the study was that 'integrated doctors introduced tetracycline earlier than did isolated ones'. Coleman et al's research relies on extensive statistical analyses of data collected in the early 1950s, but excludes any references to the historical and cultural contexts in which data were collected and analysed. Indeed, the authors never saw the communities they researched, for other people were, in fact, entrusted with the actual collection of the data.

Four subsequent re-analyses of Coleman et al's set of quantitative data by other organisational network experts have provided diverse and contradictory results. This may come as no surprise given that some of these re-analyses were conducted from a 'structural equivalence' perspective that stressed competition between doctors while others embraced a 'cohesion' perspective stressing co-operation between doctors. Kilduff and Oh (2006) examined the chain of these linked articles to establish the missing historical context and uncover the processes by which statistical analyses were produced and interpreted. In so doing, they applied the three level framework developed by Gephart (1986).

First-level ethnostatistics invites the researcher to explore the context in which the data were collected and the statistics produced. Given that the work under scrutiny was a retrospective study, it was more difficult to reconstruct the social, economic and cultural situation of each physician. However, the task was not impossible. Kilduff and Oh found that Illinois physicians were self-employed owners of their general practices at a time when this status was increasingly under threat. Hence, outside threats served to increase physician group cohesion. They were also highly dependent on each other because of the uncertainties caused by the flood of new treatment and technologies appearing in the market. There was a shortage of physicians at the time so there was no reason as to why they should compete for resources that were abundant. In conclusion, the physicians working in these towns in the 1950s were swamped by work and relied on each other's help for keeping up with new technologies and medicines.

The second order of ethnostatistical analyses examines the adequacy of assumptions made in the statistical evidences together with a critique of potentially problematic assumptions. The first re-analysis of the data set by Burt (1987) adopts a structural equivalence perspective that emphasises the competition between physicians. As such, the decision to drop the friendship network data set appears appropriate because the focus is not on co-operation but on competitors jockeying for positions in professional networks. Moreover, this re-analysis required data concerning specialists' adoption of the tetracycline. As these data were not available, they were imputed by selecting surrogates among the generalists. Therefore the imputation of data was dictated by the particular statistical technique chosen and not by the historical context of the research.

In the second re-analysis, Marsden and Podolny (1990: 201) used an event history methodology that took into account the time-sensitive nature of the data. This permitted the consideration of how the process of adoption evolved over the 16-month period. They also dropped the friendship data, imputed prescription data for specialists, and used a psychophysics power function to exaggerate the effects of structural equivalence. The second re-analysis found that there were no effects of social networks on the physicians' decision making.

The third re-analysis by Strang and Tuma (1993) took into account individual level dynamics and went beyond assumptions concerning spatial and temporal homogeneity.

The authors made some attempt to recognise the possible validity of assumptions in the original work. They avoided the imputation of data and proposed an additive model to allow for influence to occur between physicians who adopted tetracycline in the same month as each other.

The fourth re-analysis by Van den Bulte and Lilien (2001) started from the assumption that any prior evidence of social cohesion is an artefact arising from omitting the effects of marketing efforts. More data on social context were added to the mix. Using the number of advertising pages in their medical journals as a measure of marketing effort, the researchers found that contagion effects disappeared once the marketing efforts during relevant months were controlled for. What was being tested was whether tetracycline adoption was affected by dyadic influence or whether adoptions were affected by the extent to which two physicians were both embedded in similar networks of contacts. Having analysed the reasons beyond the very different findings of each re-analysis, Kilduff and Oh (2006) suggested that numerical data, far from offering solid foundations for analysis, are always produced through a series of decisions that can be revoked or changed (Lakatos, 1970).

Kilduff and Oh's third-order ethnostatistics focused on the rhetorical implications of each of the re-analyses. Each re-analysis was positioned in the larger debate of quantitative methodology in its aim to overthrow the claims made by previous reanalyses rather than aiming to contribute to the knowledge of how tetracycline was diffused amongst physicians in the small towns of Illinois in the 1950s. The authors suggested that the assumptions may have been consistent with the theory being tested but they may have been discrepant with the social processes being studied. If data are abstracted from their historical and cultural context, researchers may be free to impose quite different meanings on the data. As such, only by focusing on the actual context of the production of quantitative data, could one use and enhance the suitability and usefulness of statistical data.

Queering statistics

To add to the criticality brought forth by the introduction of ethnostatistics into the examination of quantitative reasoning, we briefly consider the potential contribution of queer theory perspectives on understanding statistical data. There is little empirical evidence of queer theorists using quantitative research; ostensibly, queer theorists seem to display a natural affinity with lines of qualitative inquiry. But this is, as we suggest, a rather shortsighted view. Despite being heavily associated with qualitative forms of research, not least forms of deconstructive analysis (Seidman, 1996; Chapter 9), queer theory could be extremely valuable for helping management researchers to interrogate (and deconstruct) notions of 'normality' within quantitative research. For example, in

The Trouble with Normal (1999) queer theorist Michael Warner argues that definitions of normal tend to be expressed statistically. It is worth quoting Warner at length:

> **One reason why you won't find many eloquent quotations about the desire to be normal in Shakespeare, or in the Bible, or other common sources of moral wisdom, is that people didn't sweat much over being normal until the spread of statistics in the nineteenth century. Now they are surrounded by numbers that tell them what normal is: census figures, market demographics, opinion polls, social science studies, psychological surveys, clinical tests, sales figures, trends, the 'mainstream', the current generation, the common man, the man on the street, the 'heartland of America', etcetera. (p. 53)**

What the above excerpt gives emphasis to is the abundance and centrality of statistics in our everyday lives. As Warner goes on to argue, many of us are invited to make comparisons between ourselves and the people around us. To declare oneself as being 'normal' is reassuring. Statistical data that allow us to be labelled as 'normal' confer upon us a sense of being validated since we meet a set of normative standards. To be outside of the norm is, of course, to be declared 'abnormal' and thus to bear the stigma of deviancy.

What queer theory might help us to do, as Warner's text demonstrates, is to shake up the statistical foundations upon which definitions of 'normal' rest. As Warner's quote above shows, the statistical construction of normality is so strong in Western societies that certain people (in Warner's case non-heterosexuals) want to label themselves as 'normal'. However, queer theory alerts us to the precariousness of those senses of inclusion and belonging that statistical norms appear to afford. Warner again:

> **When you begin interacting with people in queer culture, by contrast, you unlearn that perspective. You learn that everyone deviates from the norm in some context or other, and that the statistical norm has no moral value. You begin to recognize how stultifying the faith in the norm can be. (p. 70)**

With the above quote in mind, and in relation to organisations, queer theorists might seek to expose the discourses of quantification that aim to normalise workers along the lines of certain aspects of individual difference. Thus, in much the same way as ethnostatistics has a concern for contextualising statistics, queer theory holds a concern for showing up the constructedness of statistical norms in order to destabilise them.

It is worth saying a little more here about the potential value of queering organisational statistical data. Many companies wish to account for the diversity of the workforce. In this case, statistics help organisations to identify and define discrete populations of minority groups. It is sometimes argued that by statistically organising the workforce into distinct groups companies can formulate diversity and equality initiatives (such as positive action policy instruments) to increase the presence of certain groups deemed to be underrepresented numerically. Indeed, one might argue that statistics have an important role to play in helping organisations address inequalities in, for example, the representation of women or certain ethnic minority groups in some workplaces. By painting in numbers a picture of workforce diversity, it might be said that an organisation can design initiatives to redress under-represented minority groups.

However, as Gastelaars (2002) points out, there are problems associated with using statistical aggregates in order to pigeonhole individuals into categories they might (not) wish to belong to. Indeed, the identification of certain aspects of individual difference through the construction of statistical classifications can have a major impact on how individuals perceive that aspect of the self deemed to be 'different', as much of the critical diversity and equalities literature shows (Foldy, 2002). Gastelaars writes: 'individuals may feel that they are either excluded or included because of this one attribute that happens to be explicitly labelled, and may even expect this to influence their future positioning as a part of an organization' (p. 16). It is hardly surprising that some individuals might resist these attempts made by organisations to dissect and classify the self in different formulations. Gastelaars argues that increasing numbers of organisational statisticians are finding that individuals are refusing to answer questions that require them to categorise aspects of the self according to a menu of identity categories. One explanation is that such systems of classification (and some of the initiatives used to overcome under-represented aspects of difference in the workforce) can actually work to reinforce them as 'abnormal'.

Like Warner, Gastelaars highlights the discourses of normalcy that surround the generation of statistical data. The creation of statistical norms within the realm of organisational diversity can establish what Gastelaars calls a '*range of acceptable diversity*' (p. 16, emphasis in original). Diversity itself becomes normalised. From a queer perspective, statistical classifications and normative standards are viewed as arbitrary but situated systems that aim to sift, split and fix the workforce in terms of diversity. In this way, by drawing attention to how statistical data can generate a disciplinary effect on diversity, queer theory interrogates the power effects of statistical data. In a typically Foucauldian move, discourses of statistics would be seen to be enmeshed within relations of power. The construction of such organisational norms can then be analysed in order to ascertain the impacts they might have on certain individuals or organisational groups of people, like gay men, lesbians, bisexuals, and so on. From Warner's and Gastelaar's insights into the relationship between statistics and normalcy it is clear that statistics ought not to be accepted at face value. Without doubt statistical forms of data play an important and often essential part of organisational life. But what is more, it is almost inconceivable that statistical norms and classifications will disappear in the foreseeable future (Gastelaars, 2002). Yet queer theory perspectives remind us that we need to cast a critical eye over statistics in order to think about the linkages to normality, difference, identity and belonging. As this section has demonstrated, albeit briefly, there is one powerful way in which statistics can work, in organisational contexts and otherwise, to (re)produce existing normative power relations.

Feminist perspectives on quantitative research processes and analysis

Feminism might not be seen to be in the business of quantification. After all, despite the fractured nature of feminist theory, feminist researchers are largely united in their suspicion of positivistic approaches and quantitative methods. As we note below, there is a great deal of validity to the major feminist objections to quantitative research.

Feminist objections to quantitative research

Jayaratne (1993), who has done much to document feminist unrest about quantitative research, outlines the main critical responses among feminists to quantitative research both as a process and as a form of analysis. It is useful to briefly summarise some of these objections. First, feminists of all theoretical persuasions have attacked quantitative researchers for not only excluding the experiences of women, but also producing research that is sexist because it privileges a white, middle-class, heterosexual, able-bodied standpoint. In some of the worst cases, all male samples have been constructed and used to yield data from which wider generalisations are made that claim to relate to men *and* women. In other instances, as Sprague (2005) illustrates, questions used in surveys have been constructed on the experiences and interests of men. Using the US Census as an example, Sprague demonstrates how questions about paid work have appeared to favour the supervisory and higher managerial roles where most men are located. Such questions leave little or no room to explore the diverse occupational locations and experiences of women within the labour market.

Second, Jayaratne (1993) also points out that much quantitative research leaves untouched the social structures that (re)produce gendered inequalities. Academic quantitative research that achieves publication has often arrived at its final destination. While some academic scholarship does leach out into the public domain, and can influence how people go about their daily lives, a vast number of scholarly activities cannot boast such a deep impact. Academic feminist research is not immune to this shortfall, leading some feminists to question whether academic feminism can help make a discernible difference in improving women's lives (Reinharz, 1979). We would add that much qualitative research does fall foul of this failing, but in the context of feminist ambitions to engage in gender politics in order to eradicate gendered inequalities in society, then quantitative research is roughly brought up short by feminists for not facilitating that endeavour.

Lastly, and perhaps most significant of all, Jayaratne notes that quantitative research processes offer little micro-level detail about the lives of study participants. Quantitative concerns with the standardisation of measurements, researcher control and maintaining objectivity do not always provide the conditions for generating rich, in-depth data about the lives of those under empirical examination. Of course, this is frequently taken to be one of the defining features of quantitative research: the capacity for making generalisations and for analysing relationships between numerous complex variables. It might be said, then, that in-depth data might stand in the way of the quantitative researcher's desire to generalise. But for countless feminists, the generalisations of quantitative researchers have drowned out women's voices, voices that have for many decades been silenced in research of this type (also see Jayaratne and Stewart, 1991).

Stanley and Wise (1983), both well-respected writers on feminism and methodology, show how the apparent disregard within quantitative research for understanding the context-specific and varied experiences of women is a direct effect of the pursuit of 'objective truth'. When viewed through a positivistic lens, quantitative research can be damaging for women because it upholds a subject/object dualism in the research process. By that, Stanley and Wise refer to the separation of the object (to be studied) and the subject (researcher) and the distance positivistic approaches fosters between the two, so as to procure impartiality and objectivity. Within this research process, the researcher is positioned as an 'expert' who is able to comment upon the object under study. As Stanley and Wise (1983) remark, many women have sought to reject positivistic interpretations of their lives because they attach no premium to the validity of women's personal experiences.

Feminist-inflected quantitative research practices

With the above criticisms in mind, it is not surprising that many feminists do not turn out quantitative research. Indeed, some feminists have appealed for the creation of qualitative analyses using specific research methods (such as the interview) that are considered to be better designed for gathering in-depth data about the different aspects of women's lives (for example, see Oakley, 1981). As feminists have responded favourably to such appeals over the years, discussions have also ensued as to whether feminists should abandon quantitative research altogether or, as Jayaratne (1993) adds, seek to reduce its sphere of influence within the social sciences. Crucially, however, not all feminists support these lines of reasoning.

At the risk of repeating ourselves, feminism is an extremely varied body of theory and it is important to acknowledge that not all feminists speak in unison. Over the past decade or so, the number of feminists who have challenged what they perceived to be an over-reliance among feminist scholars on qualitative research processes has grown. Prominent feminist theorists on methodological issues such as Reinharz (1979, 1992), Stanley and Wise (1993, 2000) and Oakley (1998, 2000) have all written about the possibilities of using quantitative research to aid the attainment of feminist goals. The most notable of these, perhaps, is Ann Oakley. In 1981, Oakley wrote about the masculine bias present in models of interviewing that (re)produced the conditions for asymmetrical power relations to flourish between interviewer and interviewee (we come back to this in Chapter 8). Oakley's essay, designed to expose the ways in which traditional approaches to interviewing are harmful to women, quickly gained seminal status. What Oakley forcefully argued for was the adoption of qualitative forms of research among feminist theorists to help craft analytical insights into women's experiences.

Nearly two decades later, Oakley (1998) published a paper in a UK sociological journal in which she offered a more measured view of the 'allegiance' feminist researchers (should) exhibit to qualitative research approaches. What is interesting about Oakley's essay is her assertion that the divide between qualitative and quantitative research is excessively sharp. Distinctions between quantitative and qualitative research paradigms might not actually be advantageous for feminist researchers. In a candid review of feminist sociological debates on methodology, Oakley modified her original 1981 argument, proposing that 'what feminism and social science both "need" is a more integrated approach' to researching the lives of women (1998: 725). More precisely, Oakley foregrounds the merit of integrating forms of quantitative and qualitative research, although she questions the value of using the terms 'quantitative' and 'qualitative' when speaking about research methods. Arguing for the use of quantitative research might, at first glance, appear to run counter to feminist critiques of quantitative research processes and analyses. But, as Oakley neatly sums up, shoddily constructed qualitative research will do women fewer favours than a robust, well-planned and transparent quantitative research process. Rigorous quantitative research conducted under a gender lens might prove to be useful for policy-making activities that concern the interests of women (Oakley, 2000).

Oakley (1998) and others (Jayaratne, 1993; Sprague, 2005) do much to problematise the quantitative/qualitative dichotomy because they shut down the possibility for feminism to develop quantitative data. According to Letherby (2004), informed by Oakley's (1998) appeal for more feminist quantitative research, the pressing issue for feminism is the interrogation of the relationship between 'doing and knowing: how the way we undertake research (the process) relates to the knowledge we present at the end (the product)' (2004: 176). Following Letherby here, we also argue for a critical approach to thinking about the relationship between research processes and their products by focusing on issues of appropriateness. By this, we mean assessing the methods that may be appropriately employed to generate data that will best address a specific research question. In this regard, methods traditionally associated with the quantitative and qualitative tradition may be used either separately or in combination.

Organisational feminist quantitative research

Despite having sketched out some recent debates in feminist methodological theorising that have prised open new opportunities for mobilising quantitative approaches to research within feminist scholarship, only a small number of feminist researchers have done so. Letherby (2003: 88) notes the unwavering dominance of qualitative-based, contemporary, feminist research, as well as her own difficulty in finding and writing about quantitative examples of feminist research. Yet, examples do exist, and appear to be increasing in number. We outline a number of these, directing attention to the helpful ways in which quantitative data have been pressed into the service of organisational feminist research.

Sprague (2005) offers up a rare, full-blown account of how feminists in the USA have used quantitative methods, which we recommend reading. Examples are drawn from feminist studies on why unpaid domestic labour remains 'women's work' (Brines, 1994), on how structural racism may create a correlation between race and perceived levels of stress in white and African American women's lives (LeClere et al., 1998), on identifying gender differences in speech patterns (Carli, 1990) and on the gendered dynamics of influence in work groups (Ridgeway, 1982). For Sprague, these studies are exemplars of the feminist mobilisation of quantitative data. In a similar way to how feminists use qualitative data, Sprague's feminist researchers analyse statistical data, conduct experiments and produce mathematical data to 'develop variables that identify and make visible the processes through which gender inequality operates in everyday life' (2005: 114). Viewed in this way, quantitative data are not organised in a traditional 'malestream' fashion. Rather, they are aligned with the perspectives of women.

Sprague's citation of Glass and Camarigg's (1992) study is a case in point. They sought to (re)examine the contention put forward by some neoclassical economists that women purposefully seek out lowly paid and poor status employment because it is more likely to fit in with their family responsibilities. Re-examining statistical data from the 1977 Quality of Employment Survey through a gender lens, Glass and Camarigg turned this argument on its head. They found that the people most likely to be employed in roles that were most compatible with family responsibilities were men without children. Gender was found to be a key predictor in the study, particularly when turning to the occupational positions of men. From a neoclassical economic theory perspective, senior jobs with high pay would be considered to be the least compatible with shouldering family responsibilities. Yet, as Glass and Camarigg show, these types of roles occupied by men were more compatible with parenting duties than those occupied by women. The study is an interesting example of how statistics can be reframed within a feminist paradigm in order to uncover the parochialism of traditional economic perspectives for explaining women's and men's positions in the labour market.

Elsewhere, research on gender inequalities in the workplace has used and/or developed statistical data to highlight gender pay differences between women and men in the UK

(Joshi et al., 2007), to assess how men and women combine paid work with family life in Sweden (Nordenmark, 2002) and to profile (in gendered terms) a new generation of female, small business owners in New Zealand (McGregor and Tweed, 2002). In contrast, Pugh's (1990) account on the feminist dilemmas associated with statistical data is striking for its discussion about whether statistics can be feminist. Using traditional procedures to produce statistics about young persons' usage of a small youth advice and counselling service in the UK, Pugh quickly became suspicious of the 'easy power [her] statistics commanded' (p. 109). One step in 'cutting statistics down to size', as Pugh puts it, is to consider them within their originating context. In so doing, Pugh examined what the statistics did and (more crucially) did not represent about the counselling and advice organisation and its users. Mobilising feminist perspectives allowed Pugh to unwrap her statistics and to underscore their contructedness and limitations, as well as their contextual contingency. In summary, statistics, according to Pugh, 'need chaperoning' (ibid.).

Other researchers have combined statistical data with qualitative forms of data. Here, we consider Brandth and Kvande's (2002) study on the fatherhood practices of men in response to the introduction of parental leave in Norway. The researchers posted 2194 questionnaires to all men who had become fathers in two Norwegian municipalities in order to gain an overview of work environment factors influencing how the men used the parental leave system. An overarching view of the factors that shaped the men's responses to parental leave is extremely valuable. In this case, the researchers were able to identify that level of education, sector of employment and seniority of position affected how the men used parental leave. However, this type of quantitative data is less able to permit an analysis of the localised differences in how the men negotiated their take up of the parental leave system. Brandth and Kvande interviewed 30 couples from the study's sample, and from these data were able to identify different types of parental leave practices and the choices made by the men (and their partners) as to how they should use the parental leave provision. The study is a fine example of how quantitative data can be used to establish a broad impression of gendered practices among and between different groups of people in varied locations. Combined with qualitative data that operate at the micro-level, the study's richly textured findings may contribute to wider public debates on policy matters, such as how the parental leave system in Norway affects the interests of men and women.

In Chapter 4 we referred to Judy Wajcman's (1998) UK study of women and men in corporate management as a postmodern-slanted study. Here we construct Wajcman's study as an exemplar of feminist research that develops and deploys quantitative and qualitative data to good effect. Wajcman combined questionnaire survey data gathered from 324 completed questionnaires with qualitative data collected from in-depth, face-to-face interviews with male and female managers. Throughout the text Wajcman expertly weaves quantitative and qualitative materials into her analysis. For example, apart from the obvious benefit of using the survey data to formulate comparisons between men and women managers in terms of age, managerial position, length of service, and so on, Wajcman also gained insight into men's and women's attitudes towards female managers. Crucially, she found 'no major differences between the views of women and men in response to more general questions about the role of women in management' (p. 63). By contrast, the study's qualitative components allowed Wajcman to elucidate how 'gender difference is the basis for the unequal distribution of power and resources' (p. 160). So put in another way, while men and women managers may share the same attitudes to women managers and female senior managers manage in the way as senior men within specific work locales, the experience of being a manager is not the same given the tensions and asymmetry in gendered power relations. Wajcman's study was innovative for being able, by virtue of its quantitative/qualitative approach to data collection, to make analytical comparisons between male and female senior managers. Prior research had tended to treat men and women managers in isolation.

Summary

In this chapter we have explored how quantitative research can be viewed critically. We have not followed a conventional approach in outlining the defining features of quantitative research by describing quantitative research methods. To do so, as we have argued in this chapter, would mistakenly assume that the methods make up a research tradition. Numerous factors, including those that stem from researchers' epistemological and ontological positioning, determine how certain research methods are put to use. In turn, these shape a quantitative (and qualitative) research process. In order to remain critical about these research processes, researchers must be aware of how they are situated in relation to matters of how they see the world around themselves, as well as how they see the relationship between researchers and the researched.

Within quantitative research processes we are, like many other academics, uneasy about how quantitative research has been heavily infused by conventional positivistic philosophy. This has often led quantitative researchers to adopt intractable positions on one side of the quantitative/qualitative divide. One of the main aims of this chapter has been to erode this dichotomous line of thinking by showing how certain critical theoretical perspectives steer attention towards the narrow thinking associated with positivistic quantitative research, as well as opening up new and helpful ways of developing and analysing quantitative data. Three illustrations have been provided: ethnostatistics, queer theory and feminist theorising. All these approaches force us, albeit in differing ways, to critically review the wider social, cultural, political and economic practices that surround the production of quantitative forms of data such as statistics. In summing up this chapter we draw out our own observations in relation to two of the examples provided above: ethnostatistics and feminism.

Regarding ethnostatistics, in a special issue of *Organizational Research Methods* dedicated to ethnostatistics, Gephart (2006) bemoans the relative lack of interest in this approach, but suggests that its future may be bright. Due to the contemporary obsession with quantification at all levels in our society, it becomes essential to focus our research efforts on the talk, activities and sense-making processes related to the production and consumption of statistics. To do so, one needs to develop new and innovative observational methods such as systematic self-observation to study specific features of quantitative discourse (discussions about university rankings, budgeting, and so on). Of course, observational techniques are tried and tested in the qualitative field and it may be that the difference between studying quantitative practices and numerals and the study of qualitative practices can only be surmounted by a good grasp of the technicalities of quantitative research when making such observations. Gephart's agenda calls for the use of computational models to compare and contrast different approaches to data analysis, with a view to examining how varying the underlying assumptions of statistics affects statistical outcomes and interpretations. Finally, he suggests that it is crucial to demystify statistical tests, to show what alternative tests could have been used to reflect the assumptions made by the subjects and to highlight alternative interpretations and outcomes that could be produced from a given set of data.

Similarly, a small but growing number of feminist theorists have been at pains to problematise the quantitative/qualitative dichotomy. Such debates are valuable in many ways, not least of all for rupturing a gendered paradigm that would have us believe that qualitative research methods make for feminist scholarship. That feminists are, perhaps, one of the least likely groups of theorists to display any sympathy for quantitative research processes is crucial here. By showing how feminists could engage and have engaged with quantitative research processes, we have revealed that the quantitative research tradition ought not to be regarded as a bundle of immutable assumptions and fixed meanings. We anticipate that such insights will encourage management researchers to challenge their own preconceived ideas about quantitative research processes as they might pertain to the critical study of management.

Lastly, this chapter provides a platform upon which we are able to explore the various critiques of and contributions to mainstream qualitative management research put forward by postmodernism, deconstruction, pragmatism, feminism and queer theory. It is to these matters that we now turn in Chapter 9.

Further reading

There is a wide selection of research method texts that deal with the mechanics of how to produce quantitative data. While some of our readers may find these particularly useful, we would urge reading those texts that are sympathetic to mixed (quantitative/

qualitative) methods procedures: see for example, Creswell (2003) *Research Design: Qualitative, Quantitative, and Mixed Methods Approaches* (Thousand Oaks, CA: Sage). Based on the material we have cited above, for a closer reading of ethnostatistics, try: Gephart (2006) 'Ethnostatistics and organizational research methodologies', in *Organizational Research Methods*, 9 (4): 417–431. For an introduction to the opportunities and limitations of quantitative research for feminist theorists, read Sprague's (2005) *Feminist Methodologies for Critical Researchers: Bridging Differences* (Lanham: AltaMira Press).

9

Critical Perspectives on Qualitative Research

Introduction

This chapter builds upon the ideas established in Chapter 8; specifically, that critical researchers should have an open mind towards constructing and deploying quantitative and qualitative forms of research. This brings us to a discussion of qualitative research. Again, we are keen to stress from the outset that critical theories do not have a natural affinity towards qualitative research, despite vociferations to the contrary. There is nothing *intrinsically* qualitative or quantitative about certain research methods or methodologies. Rather, the theoretical assumptions that underpin the approach taken to the study of certain phenomena provide an indication of qualitative (and quantitative) research activities. As such, the conceptual parameters of qualitative research are more blurred than some scholars might have us believe, making qualitative research a particularly eclectic and contentious academic domain. This is the impression of qualitative research that we hope to convey in this chapter.

Of course, we are not the first writers to argue this point. For example, Norman K. Denzin and Yvonna S. Lincoln are key examples of methodological theorists who precede us in that assertion. Following Denzin and Lincoln (2000), writing on the intricate history of qualitative research, we reason that qualitative research is a complex and evolving cluster of concepts and assumptions about the philosophical and empirical aspects of thinking about and carrying out research. Indeed, Denzin and Lincoln use the metaphors '*bricoleur*' and 'quilt maker' (2000: 4) to describe how qualitative researchers engage in multiple research and interpretive practices in order to gain a *deeper* understanding of the phenomena they seek to study. In our minds, these metaphors are apt both conceptually and literally, because they lead to a notion of qualitative research as a craft, as well as a science. Qualitative researchers often demonstrate great skill in responding to the limits and opportunities of any given research context and set of research questions, not least of all in how they design and use research methods associated with qualitative inquiry.

Qualitative researchers in organisational settings are no exception. There is a growing body of qualitative research that vividly illustrates the proficiency and experimentation among organisational researchers in their use of case studies (Brown and Eisenhardt, 1995; Gioia and Thomas, 1996, Lawrence and Hardy, 1999), interviews (Knights and McCabe, 1996, 1999), ethnographic forms of research (Kunda, 1992; Watson, 2001), focus groups (Deem, 2002), observation (Kelemen, 2000) and, in more recent times, written diaries (Symon, 2004), visual methods such as photography (Warren, 2002, 2005) and video diaries (Holliday, 2004), as well as quilt making (Rippin, 2006) and image/document analysis (Hancock, 2004).

One additional point we would extract from Denzin and Lincoln (2000) in order to cement the conceptual base to this chapter is that qualitative research does not singularly align itself to any specific theoretical paradigm. The refusal to abide by the traditional conventions of disciplinary self-enclosure means that qualitative research does not elevate one paradigm over another, allowing researchers to engage in multi-paradigm research in order to cast different rays of light onto any given research focus or foci. The aim then of this chapter is to show how the critical theories we discussed in Part II of this book articulate different concerns within the field of qualitative inquiry.

We do this in two ways. First, we indicate at various points where critical theory has provided perspectives that have resculptured the contours of methodological theory. Second, we explore how the same theoretical perspectives have shaped the use and design of a selection of research methods. However, in what follows next, we do not formulate a catalogue of 'qualitative research methods' (there are already many such publications that populate the academic market). As Morgan and Smircich (1980) argue, merely focusing on research methods can be at the expense of obscuring 'the link between the assumptions that the researcher holds and the overall research effort', thereby giving the false impression that 'it is the methods themselves, rather than the orientations of the human researcher, that generate particular forms of knowledge' (p. 499). It is how critical theory might inform the assumptions the researcher holds, and how these might then shape forms of qualitative inquiry in organisational locales, that are the main concerns here. Thus, we erect signposts that direct the reader to possible pathways of carrying out qualitative research using a range of empirical and theoretical work as examples.

The aim here is to inform the reader as to how the world of management and organisation may be critically researched and interpreted in different ways. In that respect, sections of discussion focus sharply on the interplay between a single paradigm and a specific research method. In other sections the commentary is more expansive, showing how critical theories have pushed the boundaries of qualitative research in relation to the approach taken by researchers to designing and using qualitative research methods. The examples should be read as indications of how forms of qualitative research could be given attention by critical management researchers.

Postmodernism and ethnography

Ever since the 'postmodern turn' within the social sciences, traditional ways of approaching the matters of interpretation and representation within research have been challenged. Positivistic approaches that assume neutrality and objectivity in the process of interpreting data and representing the lives and views of research subjects have been targeted by postmodern researchers, who have called into question the possibility and desirability of such assumptions. The explosion of postmodernism within the social sciences has, as we suggested in Chapter 4, created a rich assortment of postmodern perspectives that have been applied to the study of management and organisation. One further observation we wish to add here, is that postmodernism has brought into being a new way of thinking about the design and application of research methods. Indeed, postmodern theory has exerted an enormous influence on how we might consider using research methods to gather data, which for a long time previously had been dominated by positivistic modes of thought. Even a quick review of the body of postmodern research within the social sciences is enough to clearly discern not just the variety of research tools used by researchers working within the postmodern tradition, but also the advantages of drawing upon postmodern theories. What is clear from the postmodern research on organisation is that, by and large, they share a qualitative concern for exploring how subjects interpret and ascribe a multiplicity of meanings to aspects of their everyday lives. And, in turn, how such contextually-situated meanings can be described, and subjects' voices represented, as well as unravelling the knotty problem of asymmetrical power relations between the researcher and the subject.

With all of this in mind, in the remainder of this section we wish to consider ethnographic research as one particular form of qualitative research that has attracted much critical attention from postmodern theorists. Indeed, it is our intention to show how postmodern ideas have productively reshaped how researchers may use ethnography as a way of knowing, researching and writing about management and organisations.

To begin, then, it is useful to offer up a definition of ethnography. To be sure, definitions of ethnography vary widely, so we offer up two examples here. First, Brewer describes ethnography as a style – or approach – to research that may use multiple research methods to gather data:

> **The study of people in naturally occurring settings or 'fields' by means of methods which capture their social meanings and ordinary activities, involving the researcher participating directly in the setting, if not also the activities, in order to collect data in a systematic manner but without meaning being imposed on them externally. (2000: 10)**

The role of the researcher within ethnographic settings is pivotal, and many debates among ethnographers concern how ethnographic texts, as Lincoln and Denzin (1998: 413) put it, 'bear the traces of [their] author'. Flowing from this is a perspective that ethnography can be viewed as a quest for meaning from those who are being researched, as much as it can be a quest that involves the construction of the ethnographer's self-identity. Hammersley and Atkinson (1995) are also cognisant of this in their text on ethnographic research, in which they also provide a useful understanding of ethnography in practical terms. According to the writers, ethnography is a form of social research that has the following characteristics:

- **A strong emphasis on exploration and interpretation rather than testing.**
- **A tendency to collect data that are unstructured and difficult to quantify.**
- **The investigation of a small number of cases, and possibly only one case, in more depth.**

Ethnographic research has been carried out in a diverse array of social settings including numerous different types of work organisations (for examples, see Ahrens and Mollona, 2007; Burawoy, 1979; Dalton, 1959; Kanter, 1977; Kondo, 1990; Roper, 1994; Watson, 1994; Whyte, 1943). As a specific form of ethnography conducted in work locales, 'organisational ethnography' occupies a key position within the vast, scholarly canon of ethnographic research. It is important to appreciate the nature of the intellectual landscape that such types of ethnographic research are rooted within. In this regard, we may begin to appreciate that organisational ethnography is located within the larger disciplinary fields of sociology, ethnomethodology, phenomenology, critical theory, semiotics, anthropology and literary theory.

Against this wide-angled context, we may then consider organisational ethnography in three ways, as Bate (1997) suggests. First, as a way of knowing ethnography aims to cast light on, and disclose, the socially acquired and shared understandings necessary to be a member of a particular organisational or social culture. It invites the researcher to look at the world culturally, and to try and understand why and how people come to share certain ways of being and doing. Second, as a method, ethnography relies mainly on (participant) observation, a technique which presumes the presence of the researcher in the field over a considerable period of time, and an ability to make sense of the observed behaviour and language in use with a view to constructing a picture of what is going on in a particular culture. Typically, such observation data are then supplemented by data gathered from qualitative interviewing and document examination. Third, as a way of writing, contemporary ethnographic accounts will question the ways in which organisational reality is represented, the division between scientific and literary writing in organisation studies and the limits of both authorship and readership (Clifford and Marcus, 1986).

Understanding the impact of postmodern theories on ethnographic research as a way of knowing, researching and writing about management and organisation, is to come to acknowledge the history of ethnography, which reflects the tensions between positivist and interpretivist standpoints. Following Denzin (1997), a number of relatively distinct periods in the development of ethnography are identifiable. An early traditional period during which lone ethnographers (for example, Malinowski and Raddcliffe-Brown) studied remote and exotic places to write objective and colonising accounts of the cultures they encountered. Malinowski's detailed (1922) study of the habits and rituals of the people of the Trobriand Islands is a prime example of such early anthropological endeavours. This traditional period was followed by a modernist period (commencing after World War II) during which time the concern was to raise the scientific status of ethnography by developing reliable theories grounded in the immediate reality of subjects. Take, for instance, the Chicago School of Sociology, and in particular Robert Park and William Thomas, who although they employed qualitative methods, did so without questioning the relevance of natural science as a methodological model for social research.

The third ethnographic period is one that has witnessed the turn to meaning and 'thick description'. Clifford Geertz (1973, 1988) as its most prominent proponent viewed the ethnographer not as someone interested in discovering the truth about social reality, but as someone who inscribes it when writing it down. According to Geertz, ethnographic writings could be regarded as fiction in the same sense that they are crafted by authors with the help of literary devices. The fourth period, the so-called 'crisis of representation', was given impetus by Geertz's work, but became established in the 1980s when Clifford and Marcus (1986) published their seminal *Writing Culture* collection. Not only were they demystifying ethnography as a cultural product influenced by literary, rhetorical, historical and ideological discourses, they were also advocating new forms of writing to acknowledge multiple perspectives and allow for multiple voices to be heard. A tidal wave of criticism rose up (and still continues to flow in waves) against the postmodern injunction to question the capacity of ethnographers to accurately capture the reality of the researched. As we have mentioned in Chapter 2, scholars have attacked postmodern theories for apparently doing away with any notion of a universal truth and objective reality in favour of an ethically uncomfortable form of relativism where 'anything goes'. The use of postmodern theories within the field of ethnography has not been immune from such criticisms. Yet they have usefully brought to our attention important questions about what constitutes valid and reliable ethnographic data, which demands of the ethnographer a high degree of reflexivity in attempting to address such thorny issues.

It is not generally accepted that a fifth period has followed, but in recent years new forms of ethnographic writing have been questioned by standpoint epistemologies such as those articulated by Clough (1992) and Trinh (1989) who, by pointing to the essentially socially constructed nature of ethnographic research, argued that ethnographic texts cannot be separated from the social constituents of their producers. These authors experiment with literary criticism, new journalism, and performance arts in an attempt to highlight the conditions of possibility of ethnographic texts. What is proposed at present is a new mode of thinking, writing and researching that is more aesthetic and poetic than scientific (Linstead, 2000). Despite anxieties among some researchers within scholarly circles over what they perceive to be the excess and relativism of postmodernism, organisational researchers have crafted sophisticated, postmodern-inflected ethnographic accounts of workers' and managers' lives to brilliant effect. Two examples are provided here.

Kondo's (1990) study of work life in a family-owned confectionery company in Japan is a sensitively crafted ethnography that displays both poststructuralist and postmodern sensibilities. We do not deny or wish to foreclose the possibility of reading Kondo's study using different conceptual lenses (though much depends on how one conceptualises the relationship between postmodernism and poststructuralism), since Kondo's ethnography has been separately and productively read as poststructuralist and postmodern in terms of its theoretical scaffolding. Since Kondo sets out to de-essentialise a Westocentric notion of the totalising subject, her analysis of fractured and contradictory selfhood finds resonance with postmodernist critiques of totalising and universal theories of the self. Kondo's ethnography largely concerns itself with exploring how Japanese factory workers construct their identities and subjectivities in relation to other workers, managers and family members, as well as with people who live in the local community. Gender is a key factor here and Kondo spends much time analysing the gendered constructions of identity and work that help to (re)produce inequalities between male and female workers. In that regard, Kondo avoids presenting a simplistic account of gendered organisational inequalities. By explicitly engaging with poststructuralist notions of discourse and power, Kondo draws out the discursive spaces in which female workers are able to forge positive identities as workers, which in some cases enable female workers to resist the dominance of male, artisan, work colleagues.

In a move characteristic of the postmodern ethnographer, Kondo devotes much commentary to exploring the instability, ambiguity and contingency of her own and her participants' constructions of selfhood and identity. This serves as a major point of departure from what Emma Bell (1999: 22) describes as those organisational ethnographies that adopt a 'realist approach'. Unlike those organisational ethnographies that tend to quarantine the ethnographic self in the process of writing up (for example, see Kanter, 1977), Kondo steers our attention towards how her senses of self and identity percolate her ethnographic research. For instance, Kondo remarks at length upon the threats to her 'American' identity from those factory workers who, noting that

Kondo did not act like a 'real' Japanese woman, tried to reposition and fix her Japanese identity accordingly. At one point, in a startling (rather Lacanian) moment of (mis)recognition, Kondo fails to recognise her own reflection in a mirror. Her identity as an American-Japanese woman slides out of view as Kondo temporarily takes on the normative appearance, posture and mannerisms of a Japanese woman. While such an identity undoubtedly assists Kondo in generating incredibly rich ethnographic data, it also causes her to contemplate leaving the research field on more than one occasion. Such vivid and critical portraits of the trials of undertaking ethnographic fieldwork are one illustration of how Kondo's ethnography demonstrates a postmodern rejection of neat and tidy ethnographic accounts in which all traces of the ethnographer are brushed out.

Another organisational ethnography that exhibits postmodern characteristics is Kunda's (1992) *Engineering Culture: Control and Commitment in a High-Tech Corporation*. Like Kondo (1990), Kunda's ethnography explores the relationship between self and organisation, but within a high-tech organisation. In the company under study, the self is encouraged to become one and the same with the company. Having fun at work and working long hours are no longer seen as a dichotomy but part of a concerted effort to be dedicated to the organisation while, at the same time, retaining a sense of individuality. Even burnouts are read differently in the company, being no longer a sign of individual failure but an indicator of the individual's organisational commitment. A burnout individual who survives the experience and comes back to work is a hero rather than a loser, and is expected to work just as hard as before to demonstrate loyalty to the company. Managers do not seek recourse to traditional techniques of management because the engineers can be trusted to work on their own and in an innovative fashion. The internalisation of a company's demands and expectations by the employees is seen to be crucial for the effective working of organisational power and politics. As such, management practices within the firm result in 'a sort of creeping annexation of the workers' selves, an attempt to capture the norms of the workplace and embed control "inside" members' (1992: 12).

Kunda's ethnography cleverly challenges taken-for-granted assumptions about worker commitment, burnout, and forms of managerial control by demonstrating that meanings attributed to these concepts and phenomena are context specific and susceptible to change. In a similar move, redolent of postmodern perspectives elsewhere, identity is regarded as fractured and provisional, and identity construction as an ambiguous and unfinished project. Furthermore, the work realities of the engineers in Kunda's study are not simplistically interpreted so as they might misleadingly claim to expose a universal truth or knowledge about work life in a high-tech organisation. Instead, Kunda's ethnography invites strong scepticism about traditional ethnographic forms of research that have laid claim to the production of universal truths.

Deconstruction

While forms of deconstructive analysis have gained much interest among organisational researchers ever since the 1980s, their passage into organisational theory has not been smooth. As we have mentioned in Chapter 5, deconstruction has often been greeted with suspicion and apprehension among academics. Much in the same way that postmodernism has been forced onto the defensive in order to fend off its adversaries, so too has deconstruction theory. In a succinct review of deconstructive analysis, as it pertains to the domain of organisational studies, David Weitzner (2007) notes the negativity among academic audiences who have not been receptive to the wave of innovative, Derridean-styled deconstructive analyses that achieved publication in a select number of North American academic business journals in the early 1990s. Weitzner points out that the amount of space given over to deconstructive (and postmodern) analyses of organisational life in these journals was small, and has since evaporated in the heat of anti-postmodernism/deconstruction criticism.

By comparison, both postmodernism and deconstruction are thriving in many universities across Europe, for which explanations may be advanced that point out the greater scope afforded to academics for theoretical experimentation within European universities. As we already know, Derrida himself and his ideas have not always been afforded comfortable lodgings within European academic institutions. Weitzner documents the controversy that has courted Derrida and the outrage among some academics regarding the high premium other scholars have attached to his writings. Little surprise, perhaps, that the impact of Derrida's work on qualitative organisational analysis is in many ways both 'disturbing' and 'unsettling'. Our aim in this section is to provide examples of how Derrida's concept of deconstruction has been variously understood and put into the service of critiquing aspects of organisation and management.

For some academics deconstruction has been partly approached and thus partially conceived as a method, or relatedly, as a set of principles that constitute a deconstructive methodology (Boje, 1998; Calás, 1993; Martin, 1990). One example is considered here. Joanne Martin's much cited and lauded (1990) article 'Deconstructing organizational taboos' blends deconstruction with feminist theory. Martin deconstructs the story of a corporation president to reveal how organisational efforts to help women have in fact suppressed gender conflict and reified false dichotomies between the private and public spheres of activity. Martin's main deconstructive message is that if feminist perspectives were to be taken seriously in organisational critique, the usual emphasis on rationality, hierarchy, competition, efficiency and productivity would be exposed as simply one side of organisational life rather than being all encompassing and omniscient.

The article outlines some useful analytical strategies employed in deconstruction (p. 355):

- **Exposing and dismantling false dichotomies.**
- **The examination of what is not being said.**
- **Attending to disruptions and contradictions.**
- **The interpretation of metaphors.**
- **Concentrating on things that are out of place in the text.**
- **Identifying and interpreting metaphors as a source of multiple meanings.**
- **Analysing *double-entendres*.**
- **Identifying bias.**
- **Exploring the unexpected consequences of plots and policies.**
- **Highlighting the limitations of such 'reconstructed' scenarios to explain the persistence of the status quo and what might be needed in terms of reform.**

At first glance, such a list might appear to function much as a recipe has to: follow each step to achieve a successful deconstruction. This is not Martin's intention, as she argues that deconstruction is 'far more than a methodology' (p. 340). Rather like queer theory, deconstruction contains a set of destabilising impulses that can expose ambiguities and contradictions within the commonplace (often logical and rational) assumptions that underpin thinking about theory building itself. Instead, the inventory acts as a user-friendly introduction to deconstructive analysis – one that was certainly needed at the time of its publication when deconstruction had yet to be taken up by organisational researchers with any gusto, but still remains, in our view, just as useful today.

Jones (2004), writing on Derrida's influence within organisational studies, also notes the utility of Martin's strategies in that respect. However, he also contends that such 'lists' (despite the disclaimers attached to them by their authors) tend to falsely imply that deconstruction is purely a research method as well as an activity that can be undertaken from a 'position of safe exteriority, if not objectivity' (p. 41). Jones goes much further than Martin in his contemplation of deconstruction as a method. Citing Boje (1998: 462), who argued that 'Deconstruction is not meant by Derrida to be defined, lest it become a rational and token blueprint of analysis steps', and staking the assertions made by Martin (1990) and others (see Calás, 1993) that deconstruction is more than just a method and yet has the capacity to be used as such, Jones points up a paradox of Derridean proportions: 'the description of deconstruction as method is necessary but impossible … we *cannot* describe deconstruction as a method, at the same time as we grapple with the dangers of doing so' (ibid.). This is clearly a double bind – a bind that, as Jones remarks, is 'perhaps inescapable' (2004: 55).

Concerns such as these are important but should not deter or drown the ambitions of those seeking to apply deconstruction to the critical study of organisation and management. For one thing, Jones (2004) argues that the absence of any facile schema for deconstructive analysis forces the researcher to find new possibilities of comprehending and activating Derrida's ideas. After all, the spirit of deconstruction (if it can said to have just one) is necessarily restless, ever questioning and always challenging. We appreciate that such theoretical adventures may be for the more experienced (and Jones's essay is informative reading for this type of reader); for the uninitiated, Joanne Martin's essay is a helpful point of departure.

Not least of all because Martin's article also attests to the fruitfulness of how deconstruction can find points of connection with other critical theories, such as feminism. This is not to suggest that deconstruction has a *natural* affinity with feminism or even queer theory, even though dimensions of both share similar points of view regarding, for example, the pivotal role of language and power. Martin is not oblivious to the potential pitfalls of using various deconstructive analytic strategies in conjunction with feminist theory. Especially those objections from feminist critics who regard deconstruction as an apolitical 'language-game, played by intellectuals for intellectuals', and the penchant deconstructive theorists seem to show for selecting 'esoteric texts' as the objects of analysis (p. 341). As Chapter 5 demonstrated, deconstructive analysis (when used to deconstruct classic texts) presupposes a genuine and sympathetic reading of a text together with a view to unearthing its contradictions as well as opening up possibilities for alternative interpretations. Saying so begins to acknowledge that deconstruction does not *oppose* science itself, but aims to engender *critical* debate on the complexities and issues that have been either ignored or suppressed previously (Kilduff, 1993). This is a point that cannot be overstated given the ease with which deconstruction can be read as an entirely negative enterprise. As we have already shown, in management and organisations studies, commentators have clearly attempted to deconstruct classical management texts (Kilduff, 1993; Kilduff and Kelemen, 2004), as well as organisational texts and artefacts (Boje, 1995; Dick and Cassell, 2004; Martin, 1990). In what remains of this section then, we provide more detail about some of these studies, as well as other examples of deconstructive approaches, to demonstrate the diversity and vitality of deconstruction as a mode of critical analysis.

Kilduff (1993) is one example of how deconstruction has been used to deconstruct an organisational text. Kilduff's deconstructive reading of March and Simon's classic (1958) book, *Organizations*, suggests that this foundational text replicates the moves of the predecessors it condemns, and asserts an ideology of programming that justifies the inevitability of fractioned work. The text positions itself as scientific through the use of rhetorical devices such as standard propositions, operationalised variables and testable hypotheses. As such, the power of *Organizations* appears to reside in its embodiment of logic, rationality and truth rather than its literary qualities. Kilduff demonstrates how, in fact, the text's literary qualities contribute to its 'objectivity' and how the logic of the machine (so criticised in the book) is eventually upheld and legitimised as the most effective blueprint for the modern corporation.

David Boje's (1995) study of Walt Disney is another fine example of how deconstruction can be used to search for hidden stories and meanings within organisational 'texts'. Boje theorises Walt Disney enterprises as a story-telling organisation. Here he analyses official and unofficial texts, recordings, inscriptions and memorabilia related to Walt Disney and the so-called 'Magic Kingdom' in an attempt to demonstrate that there is more to Disney culture than meets the eye. His postmodernist deconstruction aims to re-situate the excluded/unofficial stories and voices and to analyse their relationship with the dominant legend of the official, happy and profitable Disney studio. Here *Tamara* – a play that is also a discursive metaphor – is used to demonstrate a plurivocal theory of competing organisational discourses.

It is worth dwelling a little longer on the value of using deconstruction to unearth the 'dark side' of organisational story telling, as Boje does so well in relation to Disney. Collecting narratives and stories has attracted much attention in recent times within the field of organisational studies, and there is now a growing volume of literature to delve into (see Boje, 1991; Czarniawska, 1998b; Gabriel, 2000). Organisational scholars have increasingly turned to narratives in search for an antidote to the perceived sterility and normative arrogance of much management writing. Some have started to collect organisational stories in an attempt to give voice to *marginalized individuals and collectives* (Boje, 1991). Here, storytelling is seen as a potent device for capturing people's (often resentful) feelings about an organisation, a culture or a society. As Gabriel (2000) puts it, stories grow out of misfortune and adversity and tend to problematise or laugh at the irrational and destructive side of organisational life, rather than upholding the dominant agenda of management as a scientifically storied endeavour.

Elsewhere, Dick and Cassell (2004) use Foucauldian theoretical insights in their deconstructive analysis of identities and managerial discourses in the police force in the UK. Concerned with exploring issues surrounding the position and experiences of policewomen, they aim to problematise the notion that women are difficult to retain because they are unable to meet the demands of police work once they have children. The article examines how policing is socially constructed, and why policewomen 'consent' to dominant, yet potentially 'oppressive', constructions of police work. In the article, the research interview is seen as an interactional context that predicates 'identity work'. In this sense, the interview is a crucial site for the generation of empirical texts that may then be analysed in terms of discourse – searching out and analysing competing and intersecting discourses that relate to police work, gender and so on. Using Foucauldian principles, the article argues that the power relations operating in both the interview and the broader socio-cultural context are productive of discourses through which individuals constitute their identities. It is this constitutive act that produces women's consent to dominant constructions of policing because, at the same time, this 'resists' broader ideological discourses that threaten their integrity.

American pragmatism

As we have already stated, American pragmatism has yet to make its mark on the field of organisational studies. Our aim here, then, is simple: in this section we wish to direct readers to an approach towards pragmatist-inspired organisational qualitative research.

In accordance with pragmatism's theoretical cornerstone, the pragmatist researcher is most likely to adopt research practices that will allow him/her to solve a practical problem in an efficient way. Abstract concepts and theories must thus be translated/understood with respect to practice. Pragmatist theorising means an acknowledgement of the full dialectics between knowledge and action. Hence, proper knowledge is knowledgeable action and proper action is actable knowledge. Moreover, the practicalities of knowledge help establish the difference between meaningful and non-meaningful knowledge. In line with the process-oriented participative research, the pragmatist researcher's closeness to the empirical world via observation and the triangulation of sources and methods is a way to counteract an over emphasis on what people say.

The pragmatist researcher tends to concentrate on human actions. By studying actions, he/she can better grasp how individuals and groups render the world meaningful. The pragmatist researcher will also tend to conflate the Habermasian distinction between material (instrumental) and social (discursive) actions. The sayings and doings of an individual are both regarded as actions and therefore worth studying. Moreover, actions must be placed in their practical context in order to avoid atomistic descriptions of individual actions. Practice is treated here as an holistic notion: 'the embodied, material mediated array of human activity centrally organised around shared practical understandings' (Schatzki, 2001: 2). Thus practice transcends individual human actions to include material artefacts, language conventions and other material and discursive props that determine which actions are adequate within the practice. Structuration theory (Giddens, 1986) is an attempt to reconcile theoretical dichotomies of social systems such as agency/structure, atomism/holism and subjective/objective perspectives. The approach does not focus on the individual actor or societal totality but on social practices ordered across space and time. Giddens's followers adopt this balanced position, attempting to treat the influences of structure and agency equally (see for example, Desanctis and Poole, 1994; Orlikowski, 1992; Sewell, 1992).

The focus here is on both successful and unsuccessful actions for learning from failure and mistakes are as fruitful as learning from successes. As our elaboration of a pragmatist ethnographic orientation to the study of management in Chapter 3 indicated, much insight can be gained from observing the successes and failures of managerial endeavours. In light of this, a number of research practices have found resonance with elements of pragmatist thought, for example action learning, action research and Mode 2 research (Gibbons et al., 1994). Action learning, for example, is purported to be a means of learning which focuses on reflecting on experience which in turn results in action to solve real problems within an individual's own environment (McGill and Beatty, 1995). It is therefore a practical approach based on reflecting on previous experience to help the practitioner/manager to solve current problems.

Thus, action learning is based on the need to find a solution to a real problem (Inglis, 1994). Participants are brought together in a small learning group (learning set), typically with four to eight members. This group can be made up of members from the same organisation or from different organisations. The group will then hold intermittent meetings over a fixed programme cycle, typically 6 to 12 months in length. The focus of the set can be either on one problem that is relevant to all the participants, or can tackle a different problem for each member. Whichever approach is taken, it is important that the problem at hand should be an issue of major importance to the manager(s) and their day-to-day work (for details, see Wallace, 1990) and the participant(s) should have the power to take action on any of the strategies developed (Marquardt and Waddill, 2004).

As Marquardt and Waddill (2004) argue, the main aim of such meetings is to provide the members of a forum with the opportunity to discuss problems and to enable the participants to gain different perspectives and insights on how to approach such problems. The intention is that through the questioning offered by the other members, individuals will understand issues more fully and be able to reflect on their own experience with a view to stimulating new ideas for action (Davey et al., 2004).

Farmer (2007) points out that asking questions is a vital part of learning. To pose a question invites a response and, in so doing, allows for modification in response to findings. As Farmer suggests, asking questions aids comprehension, it stimulates thinking and invites conversation. It is claimed that, through the action learning process, participants learn to question taken-for-granted assumptions and that people will then ask new questions, thereby generating a fuller picture of the problem and context before attempting to solve it (Marquardt, 2000). Participants in action learning programmes are made to focus most of all on asking questions and are discouraged from giving advice (which is seen as a form of programmed knowledge) (Farmer, 2007). The aim of questioning in action learning is not to seek answers but to help each participant to explore and understand their situation better. The idea is that the questions will uncover what participants do not know about any given problem.

However, in any group there will be elements of power play and social practices that will influence the way that the group operates. There is a risk that these social norms and group pressures will impact on the types of questions asked by members, which could lead to the important/difficult questions remaining unasked. For example, minorities or people with different cultural backgrounds may find it difficult to get their voices heard within such a group. Similarly, people with less experience may be less likely to ask questions (for fear of ridicule) than those perceived to be more experienced or knowledgeable on the subject. While action learning programmes have ground rules which exclude such behaviours – deterring judgement, barring questioners from showing how clever or knowledgeable they are, and stressing the importance of being supportive at the same time as challenging (for details, see Weinstein, 1995) – it can be difficult in practice to ensure that the rules are maintained, as many of these issues manifest themselves covertly.

Furthermore, research by Oultram (2007) questions some of the practices of action learning that are often taken-for-granted as being beneficial and unproblematic. It uncovers some of the embedded struggles and conflicts underpinning the process of action learning that may reduce the effectiveness of the learning in action learning sets. By taking such a stance, the researcher subscribes to a pragmatist paradigm which sees action learning as providing an informed basis for practitioners in micro business to decide whether action learning has something to offer them. And for policy makers and project co-ordinators, as a guide to some of the possible reasons why action learning does not always achieve its intended outcomes.

Finally, Mode 2 research requires researchers to adopt a transdisciplinary approach by attempting to go beyond any single discipline and utilise well-established collaborative links with organisational practitioners to ensure validity in the collection and codification of data. Mode 2 methods of research are not bound by a certain discipline or paradigmatic orientation and it develops its own distinct theoretical structures, research methods and modes of practice, which may not be positioned on a single disciplinary map. Thus, reflexivity becomes crucial in the process of designing and conducting research, being redefined away from a mere reflection upon the weaknesses of established research methods to account for the point of view of all stakeholders involved in research. Consequently, research excellence cannot be simply defined by academic peers (usually in terms of abiding to the conventions of a certain academic community), but it is defined in terms of the contribution the research has made to the overall solution of transdisciplinary problems and the way in which this reflects the broader social composition of the review system (Kelemen and Bansal, 2002).

Feminism and qualitative research

In Chapter 6 we considered the distinct appeal of poststructuralist feminist perspectives for exposing the multiple and contradictory discourses drawn upon by men and women in organisations in order to construct gendered work identities. Because poststructuralist feminists set such great store on notions of discourse, power and knowledge, their contributions to qualitative-based inquiry have raised crucial questions about the limits of representing the lived experiences of men and women. In that respect, poststructuralist feminist offerings hold specific value, but in terms of conveying something of the deeper impact of feminism on the field of qualitative research, we aim in the following discussion to explore the relationship between feminisms and qualitative research more broadly.

In what ways some forms of research might be understood as 'feminist' has given rise to a complex and rather capacious set of debates among feminists (for examples, see Harding, 1987; Reinharz, 1992; Stanley and Wise, 1990, 2000) and non-feminists (Hammersley, 1992, 1994). Indeed, high voltage discussions over whether feminist research has its own distinctive set of ethics, political values and research methods have spanned the past few decades or so, and have in some quarters become breathless. It is not our intention to (re)trace the detail here. One point of view we may usefully harvest from these discussions is a widespread (though by no means consensual) view that the search for a unique set of feminist research methods is futile. Research methods such as interviews, diaries and forms of observation, though commonly used by feminist researchers, are not intrinsically feminist. As we have argued across the pages of this text, while boundary making has been customary within the field of research methodologies and methods for many years (Alvesson and Sköldberg, 2000), the resulting compartmentalisation of research methodologies and methods is often unproductive. Thus on the matter of distinctiveness in feminist research, we follow Ramazanoglu and Holland (2002) who reject the notion that feminism inheres in certain research methodologies or methods. They argue instead that any claim to distinctiveness in this theoretical field is better seen as arising from the interplay between feminist epistemologies and politics. In other words, *how* research methodologies and methods are used is a determinant of whether they might be considered feminist or otherwise (also see Reinharz, 1992).

As such, the line of reasoning promulgated by some feminist theorists that a feminist consciousness can only occupy a female body has, in our minds, reached a state of collapse. As we outlined in Chapter 5, the study of gender relations in management and organisation is not the exclusive intellectual property right of women. Men, too, play an important part in producing analyses of gender relations that help dismantle normative gender regimes that disadvantage women, and also constitute alongside women an important foci of critical analyses in feminist research. Nonetheless, we do not wish to imply that men's relationship to feminism is unproblematic, as numerous books written by male (pro)feminists and female feminists attest (Gardiner, 2002; Segal, 1990; Stoltenberg, 1990; Whitehead, 2002). With Ramazanoglu and Holland's (2002) assertion in mind, feminist research is regarded here as research that is informed by feminist theories that may be about, and undertaken (in various ways) by, men and women, in which gender is a key epistemic category of analysis. Feminist research is also political, not least in the sense that it can be a powerful intervention in addressing and dismantling gender inequalities in a range of sites including organisations (see Hearn, 2000).

Arguably, it is not surprising that a great deal of feminist research is qualitative. After all, one of the major contributions within methodological theory in the closing decades of the twentieth century is the view put forward by feminists that knowledge is not objective. Indeed, feminist perspectives have fuelled a closely related set of debates regarding the limitations of quantitative research methods. In addition, how we might understand knowledge as political and power-ridden has been amply demonstrated by feminist scholars of all theoretical persuasions, but especially by poststructuralist feminists, as we argued in Chapter 6. In summary, Donna Haraway (2004) articulates the implications of positivistic claims to objective knowledge succinctly: knowledge is 'never a disembodied set of ideas' waiting to be discovered by a subject. Rather, knowledge is contextually situated and always produced 'for some things and not others' (p. 200).

Such feminist concerns are important here because they have greatly influenced how feminist researchers conceptualise and use research methods to gather data. The point is, of course, that research methods are never simply neutral tools that may be used objectively by researchers to extract data and produce value-free knowledge. But it is unsound to presume that qualitative research is a problem-free antidote to positivism's failings in that respect. For one thing, as the history of qualitative research has shown, feminists have not always been sensitive to women's experiences (see Denzin and Lincoln, 2000). Also Reinharz and Chase (2003) inform us, some of the classic works on the interview (they cite as an example Merton et al., 1956) are silent on the impact of gender on the shape and content of the interview. They also point out that women have routinely been excluded from interview-based studies. One result of this neglect is that for many decades women's experiences have been encased in silence, and worse still, in some cases men have spoken on behalf of women. Thus feminists have for the past few decades or so, sought to overcome the masculine bias clearly present in methodological theory and its associated techniques and methods.

For example, feminist researchers have capsized conventional views about structuring the dynamics of the interview based on a model in which the interviewer is detached from the interviewee. Feminists have critically scrutinised the hierarchical dynamics of the interview, in which the interviewer is assumed to have control of the event, and as such the interviewee is constituted as an object that, through the application of structured interviewing techniques, is opened up during the interview for examination (Reinharz, 1984). Suspicious of this protocol, feminists have argued that it reflects a positivistic approach that aims to separate the subject (the interviewer) from the object (the interviewee) of scrutiny. According to Oakley (1998), this type of objective detachment strikes at the very heart of emancipatory feminist ideals. This objection is a widely shared starting point among countless feminist researchers when considering how to move beyond the mainstream/'malestream' model of interviewing.

For inspiration and guidance, many feminists have turned to Ann Oakley's classic essay 'Interviewing women: a contradiction in terms', in which she proclaims:

> **... in most cases, the goal of finding out about people through interviewing is best achieved when the relationship of interviewer and interviewee is non-hierarchical and when the interviewer is prepared to invest his or her own personal identity in the relationship.** (1981: 41)

Oakley's now familiar assertion motivated countless feminist researchers to foster non-hierarchical relationships between the researcher and the researched. While the interview in qualitative research is typically regarded as a tool to help researchers gain a deep level of understanding about interviewees' perspectives in relation to a specific topic, or set of issues (King, 2004; Kvale, 1996), feminist theorists have gone much further in trying to equalise the relationship between interviewer and interviewee.

To that end, unstructured or lightly structured interviews are typically used, whereby the agency of the interviewee is given primacy, or is in some cases privileged over that of the interviewer's. The interviewee may largely determine topics for discussion, and the interviewer usually plays a minimal role in directing the flow of conversation. Feminists have also tried to overcome the assumed instrumental nature of research interviewing, where female interviewees are said to be vulnerable and powerless in comparison to the interviewer (see Finch, 1984; Oakley, 1981). A range of techniques has been applied among feminists to overcome the stark instrumentality of some interview formats by, for example, remaining in contact with interviewees after the interview, sharing interview transcriptions with interviewees and involving them in the data analysis process (see Chase, 1996). Elsewhere, some feminist researchers have explored the opportunities and limitations of cultivating intimacy, friendliness and even friendship with interviewees to the same end (Birch and Miller, 2000; Cotterill, 1992; Kirsch, 2005; Neal and Gordon, 2001).

Many of these strategies are now regarded as synonymous with feminist research (as Oakley later pointed out in a published article in 1998), or as we would add, have unthinkingly been taken to *be* feminist research techniques. However, all of these approaches to interviewing have influenced, and can be deployed in, non-feminist qualitative studies (Gubrium and Holstein, 2001). Furthermore, animated debates have ensued among feminists regarding the merits and drawbacks of, for example, fostering intimacy and friendliness with interviewees as a means of quashing hierarchies of power between the researcher and the researched. And rightly in this case, Oakley

(1998) reminds us that such problems are also encountered in non-feminist qualitative research more generally. What feminist theorising does offer is another turn of emphasis on how issues of gender are considered in the context of the research interview. Since the interview remains the most widely applied qualitative method used by both feminist and non-feminist researchers alike, feminists have been highly critical of the impact of gender on interviewing women and men. Especially where gender intersects with other identity categories associated with race, ethnicity, sexuality, disability, and so on.

With the above discussion in hand, how does feminist inflected qualitative research help researchers to produce critical qualitative research on management and organisation? In one respect, feminist researchers can explore how the interview itself is an important site for exploring senses of identity that relate to work and gender. For example, Aaltio's (2002) account of how senior female managers in Finland construct their gendered and professional identities in the research interview is made possible because Aaltio conceptualises the interview not merely as a research tool, but as a 'socially constructed, localized interactional process' (p. 213). When viewed as such, the interview may be regarded as a crucial site in which interviewees and the interviewer collaboratively engage in identity artistry. In Aaltio's study, female managers were noted as placing less emphasis on their gendered identities and more on the presentation of their professional selves. Such presentations of self reveal much about the local discursive arrangements within these female managers' work contexts that help and/or hinder them in their efforts to position themselves as professional representatives of female management.

A strong parallel is visible here with the poststructuralist feminist, interview-based research of Linstead and Thomas (2002), Leonard (2003), and Thomas and Davies (2005) discussed in Chapter 6. In these studies, the interviewees' talk is treated as a series of empirical texts in which the researchers search for traces of competing and intersecting discourses. One challenge for researchers is to try and grasp a sense of the gendered identity of the interviewee in the interview. Doing so is to be acutely mindful, as Aaltio (2002) suggests, that the 'gendered self is processed in the interaction between the researcher and the interviewed' (p. 213). Indeed, this point is emphasised by Schwalbe and Wolkomir (2001) in relation to the interview as a site for signifying masculinity, as well as by Alison Pullen (2006) in her discussion of how the researcher's identity is also subject to (re)construction during the research process.

In another respect, feminist attentiveness to the power relations that undergird the interview help us to appreciate that in some organisational contexts, interviewees may exercise power over the aspiring interviewer. Puwar's (1997) account of interviewing female MPs in the UK is a clear example of how gender and other identity categories such as ethnicity helped Purwar to associate more closely with her interviewees. Yet gender alone could not be relied upon to generate the type of collegial 'female rapport' that feminist Ann Oakley alludes to. As Puwar explains: 'So even though I was, in Ann Oakley's terms, an insider, because we were both women, I was often considered an outsider, because I did not share the occupational identity of my interviewees' (1997: 8). In such organisational contexts other factors 'count', as Purwar suggests, which are themselves revealing of how interviewees present the self as gendered and otherwise in interview situations.

Organisational feminists have also used other research methods and approaches to gather qualitative data. For example, spurred on by the 'crisis of representation' within ethnographic research, the subsequent weight invested in self-reflexivity by feminist ethnographers has aided the interrogation of power relationships in ethnographic research locales. One result of these feminist analyses is the destabilising of conventional masculine approaches to the study and representation of those who are marginalised (for a comprehensive overview, see Skeggs, 2001). A rich tapestry of 'fieldwork tales', as Fletcher (2002: 398) describes them, is now evident in ethnographic research carried out by organisational feminists. Some are highly revealing of the problems female ethnographers face when conducting qualitative research in organisations dominated by men. For example, Fletcher (2002: 399) recalls how she 'felt female and alien' soon after entering a small factory in the UK where the walls were decorated with 'pornographic images of women'. Here, the experience of the ethnographer as stranger (even an impostor) in the field is mediated by gender (see also Salzinger, 2000). Conspicuous both as a female and as an organisational 'outsider', Fletcher details how such aspects of difference can impede access routes into studying certain facets of factory life.

Fletcher also describes, in a similar fashion to Kondo (1990), the transitional and temporal state of the ethnographic self. Both Kondo and Fletcher recall how they negotiated the acquisition of a subject position and identity that allowed them to penetrate what Bell (1999: 33) dubs the 'backstage regions' of their research settings. As Fletcher observes, only by conforming to a female sexual stereotype to meet the men's expectations of her as a 'listener', carer and emotional nurturer, did the men agree to participate. One outcome of adopting the 'passive organisational-researcher identity' is that such gendered identity work (re)produces existing heteronormative gender relations in the workplace. The implications of taking up or being marshalled by participants into such subject positions may elicit an ethnographic pay-off in terms of deeper empirical insight, but there are costs to this as Fletcher's work illustrates. Such tales from the field lend support to a line of reasoning that suggests that ethnographers do not vacate the field unmoved by their gendered identities. Yet despite the problems encountered by women in the field of qualitative research, the reflexivity that characterises these accounts (and of feminist research more broadly) and allows women to verbalise the challenges they face, gives rise to a number of critical perspectives on the management and organisational dynamics they study.

Queering qualitative research

Given the high profile of queer theory within other scholarly domains such as cultural studies and the adoption of queer theory by a cadre of organisational researchers, it is now possible to make out more clearly the horizon of possibilities queer theory affords for generating critical perspectives on management and organisational studies. More broadly, queer theory is one of many new theoretical directions within the social sciences that have robustly challenged and significantly weakened the stranglehold of positivist approaches.

It is useful here to recap briefly several key points made previously in Chapter 6. For Dilley (1999: 462), queer theory is 'more *transdisciplinary* than *interdisciplinary*'. While the results of one queer analysis constructed in one scholarly domain might not hold much relevance for queer analyses being conducted in another academic sphere, the research methods and theoretical approaches used by researchers in one academic discipline to craft certain queer analyses might well find a clear resonance elsewhere. This is an important observation, one that formed a base argument in our discussion of queer theory in Chapter 7. What is happening with queer theory in the humanities more broadly, especially the specific techniques and conceptual resources used by queer theorists, provides a significant impetus for researchers wishing to apply queer's critical resistant theory in the world of management and organisation. The aim of this section then is to provide a range of insights into queering qualitative research so researchers of management and organisation may be stimulated into integrating qualitative inquiry with queer theory's critical analysis of normativity.

What then might it mean to queer qualitative research? A useful starting point is to consider the concept of 'queer methodology'. Because in one sense this represents a turn towards addressing a set of debates that concern destabilising what researchers have traditionally conceived as 'natural' within the social world. As discussed in the section above, and elsewhere in the book, positivists have invoked and valorised the notion of objectivity and neutrality. Certainly, feminist and postmodern critiques have shown the folly of upholding such positivistic ideals, and queer theory is no exception in that respect. More specifically, however, queer is, perhaps, more ambitious in its designs to destabilise what appears to be 'normal' in everyday life, and to rupture disciplinary boundaries in order to do so. In a well-cited passage from the introduction to *Fear of a Queer Planet*, Michael Warner (1993) remonstrates that queer theory disrupts the 'normal business in the academy' (p. 25) and, as we add, this includes the 'normal business' of methodological inquiry and theory. Becoming equally conspicuous in its level of citation is a definition of 'queer methodology' from Judith Halberstam's *Female Masculinity*, which may be usefully read as putting flesh on the bones of Warner's bold assertion:

> **Queer methodology is a scavenger methodology that uses different methods to collect and produce information on subjects who have been deliberately or accidentally excluded from traditional studies of human behavior. The queer methodology attempts to combine methods that are often cast as being at odds with each other, and it refuses the academic compulsion towards disciplinary coherence. (1998: 13)**

As previously discussed, to some, queer theory is the *enfant terrible* of certain bodies of feminist and postmodern theory. Like Halberstam, we find queer theory's disregard for disciplinary boundaries and orderly paradigmatic classification an exciting feature that can be productively pressed into the service of critical analysis. Given queer theory's amorphous form, it is more useful to talk of queer methodology as a set of methodolog*ies* that defy neat and tidy cataloguing.

However, as with feminist methodological theory, some commonalities are evident among the applications of queer theory in empirical and conceptual terms. For instance, it is not altogether remarkable that queer theory has a close relationship with qualitative research. As Warner (2004) points out, the reason why queer theorists adopt qualitative research methods is not simply because of 'an implicit phobia of numbers, but because any attempt to quantify homosexuals, heterosexuals, etc., assumes a commonality between the individual's desires and lives that is suspect' (p. 334). By comparison, qualitative research offers a 'better chance of accounting for queer experiences in the same terms as the actual people living these experiences. This is the most liberationary knowledge of all, because it speaks directly to the experience of the oppressed' (pp. 334–335). Elsewhere Gamson (2000), writing on queer theory and qualitative research, asserts that queer theorists are 'particularly comfortable with the strategies of qualitative research – which at least appear to be less objectifying of their subjects, to be more concerned with cultural and political meaning creation, and to make more room for voices and experiences that have been suppressed' (p. 347).

It should still be borne in mind here that the above quotations should not be read to show that queer theory exempts the traditions of qualitative research from its anti-normative critique: far from it. As a number of recent and important publications demonstrate, queer theory has made advances into how researchers may approach traditional research methods such as the interview. In an essay entitled 'Queering the interview', Kong et al. (2001) explore how queer theory has changed the way gay men and lesbians are invited to speak within the context of the research interview. Like some feminist perspectives, queer theory reminds us that the interview is an historically and culturally specific method that is susceptible to change in both its form and content. As Kong et al. note, traditional standardised interviews used in the greater part of the twentieth century aimed to study 'homosexuals … initially as perverted, then as sick, and finally as different persons' (p. 240). During this time researchers, especially within the discipline of psychology, approached the interview as an instrument of diagnosis, the effect of which was to pathologise homosexuality and the homosexuals they interviewed. In the light of this history of interviewing 'homosexuals' it is obvious, as Kong et al. assert, that the interview is a 'moral and political intervention through and through' (p. 245).

As Kong et al. go on to say, it was not until the rise of social constructionist perspectives that suggested 'homosexuality' was a cultural phenomenon rather than a biological or psychological defect that such approaches to interviewing members of sexual minority groups changed. In parallel with the emergence of feminist and gay liberation movements, and a sociology of sexuality, so interviewers used the interview as an opportunity to explore and validate the identificatory practices by which gay men and lesbians constructed and managed a sexual identity in different aspects of their everyday lives. As feminism made deeper in-roads into challenging the traditional tenets of methodological theory, and as the ideas of postmodernism gained more traction within the social sciences, so queer theory broke through and pushed interviewing in a new direction.

Approaching the matter of sexual identity categories, queer theorists have asked a different set of questions that seek to deconstruct the efforts made by subjects to construct sexual identities, as well as what might be at stake in such identity claims. Indeed, queer theory may well throw the researcher onto the horns of a dilemma regarding who exactly 'fits' certain sexual categories such as 'gay', and whether interviewing simply those subjects who claim a 'gay' identity is in effect to miss out on interviewing others who, as Kong et al. put it, 'experience same-sexedness' (2001: 247). Indeed, another way in which we might draw on some of the classic queer deconstructive analyses of identity (see Fuss, 1991) is as a series of prompts about the difficulties of representation when subjects claim certain identity categories over others. A challenge faced by the researcher during the analysis of interview data, and when identity category membership is used to invite individuals to participate in interviews (for a fuller exploration of these issues in relation to sexual minority groups, see Meezan and Martin, 2003). As in other qualitative fields such as ethnography, who is being represented, by whom and how, are vital questions that seldom find easy solutions. Additionally, such questions are equally weighted for 'queer' researchers who self-identify as heterosexual and gay/lesbian/bisexual and so on, even though the paths they take to dealing with issues of how to represent the voices of interviewees may diverge at some points.

Kong et al. (2001) sketch out possible ways in which queer theory has been innovatively applied by researchers to handle some of these thorny issues. One example provided by the authors regards one of the writers' preferred style of interviewing. Rather than simply selecting interviewees on the basis of a shared sexual identity alone, a more participative approach is favoured whereby the researcher participates in gay social groups before asking individuals if they would like to become interviewees.

Adopting such an approach is fruitful not least because it allows the researcher to build an 'ethical identity', which is considered by Kong et al. to be equally, if not more, effective at establishing mutual trust than trying to generate interview opportunities by disclosing that the interviewer shares the same sexual identity as the potential interviewee.

In regards to queering the field of management and organisation, researchers have so far approached interviewing in the manner Kong et al. outline to gain insights into the cacophony of ways in which, for example, gay men may experience workplace friendships (see Rumens, 2008a, 2008b). Lee (2004) also uses the interview to explore the multiplicity of identity dilemmas associated with becoming 'gay', 'masculine' and 'manager' among gay, male, senior managers in the field of men's sexual health promotion (ibid.). However, much more work has yet to be done that experiments with fresh alternatives to interviewing (for example, using video or even video diaries, as Holliday's [2004] work explores) in order to explore the queer dynamics of organisational life.

In ethnography, we may find similar changes afoot. Susan Talburt (1999, 2000) and James King (1999) both integrate queer theory into ethnographic research conducted in educational work contexts. Writing on the shortfalls in ethnographic studies of gay and lesbian subjects, Talburt (1999) argues that 'ethnographic inquiry ... has been limited by its disciplinary and sociocultural locations and must move beyond the production of realist representations that voice and make visible identity and experience' (p. 529). In her own ethnographic work, Talburt displays this sense of direction by analysing the 'enactment of *practices*' (ibid.), a crucial theoretical manoeuvre that makes possible a critical examination of what is at stake in terms of identity and subjectivity when subjects engage with cultural and organisational discourses. Exploring the work practices of a small number of lesbian university academics in the USA, Talburt (2000) depicts in rich detail the intersections between cultural and organisational discourses that position the women as 'academic' and 'lesbian'. Drawing upon poststructuralist theories, Talburt's ethnography exhibits a queer approach to the ethnographic exploration of marginalised voices and identities because one of its main concerns is the critical interrogation of organisational and cultural norms, and the effects such norms have on subjects' constructions of identity and subjectivity. It is clear from Talburt's research that academic and lesbian selves are context-specific fictions that contain many incoherencies because they are shaped by the constitutive opportunities and constraints of localised discourses.

As such, and in not a dissimilar way to Tierney's (1997) productive mixture of autobiography, life history and case study methods to analyse the queer dynamics of the work lives of US academics, Talburt reveals that lesbian subjects are not necessarily 'powerless, voiceless, or without privilege' (2000: 221). Queering ethnography is then crucially (though not solely) about venturing beyond a liberal remit of merely acknowledging the presence of sexual minority groups and giving their members 'voices'. Tierney (2000), writing on the life history as a research method, captures this concern well. On the one hand, giving non-heterosexuals a 'voice' has been an important act within the social sciences that acknowledges both their presence and the validity of their existence. On the other hand, as Tierney warns, the 'naming of silenced lives' is not singularly sufficient to 'break the stranglehold of metanarratives that establishes rules of truth, legitimacy, and identity' (p. 546).

Moving towards a deeper analysis of how sexual minority identities and subjectivities are continuously reinvented and attributed culturally specific meanings, other researchers have employed storytelling as a research tool to that end. Storytelling is certainly compatible with some of the tenets of queer theory, as Ward and Winstanley's (2003, 2004, 2005, 2006) research into the work experiences of gay men and lesbians employed in a variety of public and public sector UK organisations reveals. Using storytelling as a research tool, Ward and Winstanley explored how organisational discourses shape minority sexual identities and subjectivities. In keeping with queer theory's delight in paradox, uncertainty and ambiguity, so Ward and Winstanley's storied data bear testimony to the provisionality and incongruency of identities that relate to work and sexuality. Of particular interest is how collecting stories, despite its associated frustrations and difficulties as described by the authors (see Ward and Winstanley, 2004), can bring to the fore queer resistances that might otherwise be lost or obscured using other research methods. While Ward and Winstanley's research handsomely contributes to a rich seam of literature on sexual minority identities, and to the 'coming out' narratives of gay men and lesbians especially (Ward and Winstanley, 2005), further advances into queering management and organisation are needed, as both the authors acknowledge. As we reason, this includes the diverse stories of heterosexuals alongside sexual minority individuals. Such a proposition has yet to find empirical articulation. This provides a tantalising research agenda that might enrich our knowledge of 'queer' organisational narratives.

Summary

In this chapter we have sought to provide a number of insights into how the critical theories that formed the object of our discussion in Part I of the book have influenced the field of qualitative inquiry. Throughout, we have highlighted how aspects of these critical theories have modified the types of assumptions researchers may hold when carrying out organisational research. Qualitative researchers must be explicit about (and should reflect upon) the conceptual assumptions they hold if they are not to fall foul of casting an illusion of objectivity. How researchers draw upon critical theory will shape how they articulate the organisational worlds which they study in general, as well as the organisational experiences of those who participate in their research activities in particular.

It is clear from the empirical examples we have provided in each section of discussion that significant variation exists in how researchers mobilise the conceptual resources that belong to certain groups of theories. Certainly, there are disagreements and points of divergence among organisational scholars over the strengths and limitations of using, for example, a specific strand of feminist theorising over another. Conflict of this sort is highly revealing not only of the methodological and theoretical advancements that have taken place in relatively recent times, but also of the potential points of connection that one body of theory may find with another. As we have stated in Chapter 2, multi-paradigm research should not be read as a 'cherry picking' activity. The decision to engage with more than one paradigm is governed by the theoretical assumptions that relate to each field of theory which qualitative researchers – given that qualitative research is a reflexive project – are compelled to attend to. This chapter offers an impression of the possible openings in the fault lines running between and across certain critical theories and the progressive shifts each theory has instigated in relation to (re)specifying the focus of qualitative inquiry. Thus, examples of empirical and theoretical research are given to encourage the reader to reappraise existing and consider new approaches to critical qualitative inquiry within organisational settings.

This chapter is the last one in Part III. Having established a number of insights into how critical theories can influence research methodologies, the book now proceeds to consider the consequences of doing critical management research. As the next chapter shows, two key issues that critical researchers must address are ethics and reflexivity.

Further reading

The field of qualitative research is populated by numerous texts. For teaching and research purposes, we have found the following three texts to be useful for conceptualising the field of qualitative research in a critical fashion: Denzin and Lincoln (eds) (2005) *The SAGE Handbook of Qualitative Research*, 3rd edition (Thousand Oaks, CA: Sage); Denzin and Lincoln (eds) (2003) *The Landscape of Qualitative Research: Theories and Issues*, 2nd edition (Thousand Oaks, CA: Sage); Lincoln and Guba (1985) *Naturalistic Inquiry* (Newbury Park, CA: Sage). For a stimulating text on qualitative research methods in organisational research try Cassell and Symon's (2004) *Essential Guide to Qualitative Methods in Organization Research* (London: Sage). Given the diverse array of materials we have cited in relation to the critical theories covered in this chapter, we advise readers to follow up any particular references they find interesting.

Part IV

Consequences of Management Research

10

Ethics and Reflexivity

Introduction

In the previous two chapters we have illustrated how the critical theoretical perspectives introduced in Part II have influenced on the qualitative and quantitative research traditions. Part IV of this book examines two issues that critical researchers need to address in order to think deeply about the impact critical forms of research may have on those involved in their formation. Ethics and reflexivity are important notions lodged at the heart of any attempt to explore how critical theory has shaped qualitative and quantitative inquiry. Our main concern in this chapter is to introduce the concept of ethics and then discuss the influence of the postmodernist, feminist, pragmatist and queer theory approaches to debates on ethics in management research. All these bodies of theoretical perspectives throw light on, albeit in varying ways, the ethical dilemmas that arise throughout the entire research process: from the early stage of research design through to data gathering, data analysis and reporting findings to an audience. Put differently, the process of doing critical management research is an ethically charged project. In this chapter we argue that the researcher's epistemological positioning has a heavy bearing on the actual course of action for engaging in and eventually solving ethical dilemmas. Here, reflexivity is a critical concept. Adopting a reflexive stance is a fundamental step in acknowledging the existence of ethical dilemmas and considering the implications they may have on the process and outcomes of doing critical management research.

The chapter is structured as follows. We begin by providing a short overview of the models of ethics that have dominated thinking within organisational studies. With these frameworks in mind, we then proceed to establish why ethics is an important matter for scholars within the CMS community. To illustrate this, we draw upon an important article by Wray-Bliss (2003) regarding the tendency within CMS to duck out of a finer-grained analysis of the ethical issues surrounding the construction of the relationship between the researcher and the researched. One major source of vexation here is the way in which research participants can be (un)wittingly ascribed a subordinate status in relation to the researcher, with the latter standing above the researched as 'expert'. For Wray-Bliss, Foucault's commentary on power relations is key for helping scholars to enact the anti-oppressive/emancipatory spirit of CMS.

In the light of Wray-Bliss' concerns on ethics, we turn to examine the principal contribution made by some of the critical theories reviewed in the first part of this book (postmodernism, feminism, American pragmatism and queer theory). The approach taken here is to provide an indication of the potential within each theory for helping researchers to redirect their thoughts on the notion of ethics. As such, we do not assemble fully formed theoretical propositions – arguably, an endeavour that requires more space and, undoubtedly, deeper exploration into existing bodies of theory. Finally, we offer up a number of insights into the notion of reflexivity. Closely tethered to ethics and thus crucial to any project of critical analysis, 'reflexivity' is a contested term, understood in many different ways. Some of this conceptual diversity is conveyed in the last section of the chapter before we round off our discussion in the conclusion.

An overview of ethics

The term 'ethics' is not an easy one to define. There is some general consensus among academics that it refers to the study of morality, specifically the attempts to construct frameworks of thinking that govern morals. Crudely put, a system of moral codes helps us to make moral choices between what is 'right' and 'wrong'. Viewed as such, 'ethics' refers to the systems of morality that govern how people ought to go about their everyday lives. Not surprisingly, the subject of ethics has long been debated by commentators, especially within the realm of philosophy. The work of philosophers such as Aristotle and Kant has furnished us with moral codes that serve as signposts – or guidebooks – to which people can defer to modify their own behaviours in order to be 'good'. For example, the Kantian version of ethics asserts that people must treat others with respect. Here, we must regard others as ends in themselves rather than the means to accomplish instrumental goals. Such a code of morality might be seen by some to be located at the very centre of what it is to be 'good' within society. Indeed, at first glance the basic principles of Kantian ethics have an appeal that is hard to resist. They offer us a utopian model of how people should conduct their daily affairs not just in their private life but also at work. However, this is where the matter of ethics quickly becomes very complex. As Woodall and Winstanley (2001) demonstrate in relation to human resource management, the idea of treating people as ends in themselves is obfuscated by some of the methods and practices of HRM that accord with treating people as the means to achieving instrumental business outcomes. In this example much depends on how HRM is defined, since such conceptions have a bearing on whether its practices are seen to violate, for example, the central tenets of Kantian ethics (Legge, 1998).

We do not have the space here to offer a close reading of the philosophy of ethics (or an arm of that scholarship now called 'business ethics'), but suffice it to say that some of the most well known models include Kantian, Stakeholder/Rawlsian, Utilitarianism and Aristotelian ethics. The logics of these ethical frameworks have informed debates about business ethics within organisational studies for some considerable time. For our purposes in this chapter, it is worth briefly mentioning some of the most well known models of ethics. In relation to the field of management research, numerous commentators on ethics bring to the fore two models of ethics. The first of these frameworks – a normative/utilitarian model – assesses the morality of any given action by evaluating its consequences. Simply put, these teleological theories of ethics encourage the individual to adjudicate on the consequences of one action over another; in other words, by which avenue of action is the greater good (for the greater number of people) achieved? See for instance the empirical work of Fritsche and Becker (1984), who explored how individual managers thought about ethical behaviour in terms of social consequences. They found that most managers followed a utilitarian orientation. There are some obvious difficulties with the utilitarian approach, not least over the boundaries and criteria of defining what counts as 'best consequences'.

Other writers on business ethics adopt the second framework – a deontological frame (stressing intentions rather than consequences). Subscribers to deontological theories of ethics embrace the idea that the moral worth of an action is dependent on the intentions of the person taking the action and not on the consequences. Within this model the ends justify the means. Some authors suggest that ethical decisions are those based on a consistent pattern of moral values (Smedes, 1991), while others would put forward that individuals' decisions about what is right or what is wrong are influenced by their level of cognitive moral development (Trevino, 1986). These Kantian reverberations suffer, however, from a number of shortcomings: first, moral principles are viewed as general rules, which apply universally and impartially to all individuals. Second, the individual is seen to possess the ability to decide what is right or wrong by the application of reason. Finally, the goal of ethics is to recognise and maximise each individual's absolute freedom, a practically unworkable formula (Pearson, 1995).

Running counter to these models, Mauthner et al. (2002) direct attention to the emergence of a virtue ethics of skills framework. Critical of frameworks that follow universal principles, the virtue ethics of skills model places the emphasis on context and on the 'researchers' moral values and ethical skills in reflexively negotiating ethical dilemmas' (p. 20). Additionally, a value-based model of ethics complements the virtue skills model, calling for an analysis of power relations between those involved in the research and society. This model is suffused with insights derived from feminist theories: for example, it is a framework that admits emotion into the ethical process as well as acknowledging that ethics do not stand in isolation to issues of power. We now turn to examine the place of ethics in critical management research.

Ethics and critical management research

Debates on the possibilities of forging links between different ethical frameworks are fractious. However, the diversity of competing perspectives on ethics should not dissuade us from considering ethics as a crucial part of the critical management research process. There are good reasons as to why management researchers should want to engage with ethical issues beyond the reason that they are an inescapable part of the research process. In one respect, as we have hinted at above, dominant ethical theories are obviously flawed. The drawbacks to each model can have serious repercussions for how research processes are constructed and experienced by those involved. In another respect, if doing critical management research is partly seen as an effort to defamiliarise phenomena within organisations that appear to be self-evident and a natural feature of corporate landscapes, then developing critical sensitivity is key (Alvesson and Deetz, 2000). As Alvesson and Deetz note, 'many students of management and organization could benefit by viewing their objects of study with fresh eyes' (p. 167). We agree, but adopting critical sensitivity to facilitate the emergence of fresh perspectives on what seems familiar also involves interrogating the dynamics of the relationship between the researcher and the 'objects of study', to coin Alvesson and Deetz's words. Put differently, the research process itself must be subject to critical scrutiny.

For example, in an important article on the ethics and politics of critical management research, Edward Wray-Bliss (2003) argues that critical management researchers do not always reflect upon the power relations within which they and their study participants are embedded. Wray-Bliss regards this as a vexing matter. After all, many within CMS claim to take as a central concern the importance of laying bare power relations within organisational settings (see for example, much of the labour process theory studies). Yet, as Wray-Bliss avers (also see Wray-Bliss, 2002), a good deal of this research constructs the researcher and the researched as independent entities rather than considering them as interdependent (2003: 307–310). As such, CMS tends towards an unreflexive stance, especially on methodological ethical matters such as the configuration of participants as 'objects' of study juxtaposed against researchers as 'experts' in their field. For Wray-Bliss, the net result of this impoverished reflexivity is reflected in the characteristics of much methodological debate within CMS:

> **'Methodology' in empirical CMS texts tends … to be limited to minimal, technical, descriptions, which rarely extend beyond listing formal methods, duration of the researcher's stay in the field and brief backgrounds to the organization within which the research was conducted. (2003: 310)**

We are generally supportive of Wray-Bliss's observations. We do not advocate the construction of research participants as mere 'objects' of study that confers onto them a subordinate status (feminist methodological theory and practice have taught us that much at least). Drawing upon Foucault's (1976) methodological precautions for analysing power, Wray-Bliss (2003) advances a number of ethical issues that could form the focus of study within CMS research:

> **In the context of an analysis of the power of CMS research, numerous practices could be explored, including: the effects of including/excluding certain lives as worthy of CMS research; the language used to describe the researched; the theoretical resources drawn upon or ignored; the selective validation of certain acts of 'resistance'; the choice of where to publish and who is likely to access the research. (p. 312)**

The above ideas for future research resonate well with the spirit of CMS as an anti-oppressive political movement, although Wray-Bliss's article is a very poignant reminder that such matters are easily and (un)wittingly eschewed. In our view, engaging with issues of power, resistance and language in the research process goes a long way in furthering the anti-oppressive craft of critical management research. After all, one key point that should now be plain is that critical management researchers (like any management researchers) do not work within a power-free zone. In that regard, Wray-Bliss's proposal also finds accord with each of the theoretical approaches we have outlined in the first part of this book. Each one of the theories we have reviewed places much emphasis on the researcher to engage in research ethics in ways that might help them to, as Wray-Bliss puts it, 'better understand, and avoid, the painful puzzle of how an academic discipline with strong anti-oppressive/emancipatory commitments can textually reproduce its superiority over and distance from those whom it purports to represent' (2003: 321).

In the following section we outline some of the contributions of critical theory, specifically some of those outlined in the first part of this book (postmodernism, feminism, queer theory and American pragmatism), on (re)directing thinking about research ethics. It is our aim to provide a number of insights into how certain critical theories might help critical management studies researchers to address thorny ethical dilemmas, not least of all those identified by Wray-Bliss (2003).

The impact of critical theory on ethics

The contribution of postmodernism

As we have stated in Chapter 4, postmodernist theories view the self as decentred, fragmented and only partially accessible or knowable to him/herself or the outside world.

Ethics is seen to be one of the many practices in which individuals engage in order to constitute themselves into subjects. However, the knowledge one can have about the self is limited, contextual and temporal. In that regard, there are no universal codes of ethics that could be enacted on this basis. With these ideas in mind, we briefly map out the contribution of two writers (Zigmunt Bauman and Michel Foucault) whose work has infused postmodern debates on ethics in management research. In so doing, we draw from Kelemen's (2003) commentary on ethics in business and Kelemen and Peltonen's (2001) article on a postmodern alternative to business ethics formulated in light of the work of Bauman and Foucault. In particular, we dwell on the Foucauldian concern for the day-to-day practices and discourses that go into the making of subjectivity, and on the Baumanian concern for studying the conditions that make possible the 'being-for' form of togetherness.

We start with Bauman. In the main, Bauman is credited for his nuanced and compelling analysis of modernisation and its effects on the possibilities for the self. In regard to ethics, Bauman's argument is that ethics is essentially a modernist project, a project that aims to construct a world free of moral ambiguity. Two institutions appear to be central to this endeavour: bureaucracy and business. Both institutions draw upon the logic of rationality and view emotion as an intruder. Bureaucracy is grounded in impersonal rules and in the following of scientific procedures, considered to be fair and true. Providing that individuals adhere to the rules faithfully and do what their superiors tell them to do, it is the rules that bear the responsibility for the effects individual actions might occasion. Bureaucracy helps people escape from moral evaluation, but in return they are requested to obey the rules. It is the deviation from scientific procedures that is open to challenge, not the procedures themselves. However, Bauman (1989) contests the assumption that scientific procedures are automatically fair or moral in his analysis of the conditions that made possible such atrocities as the Holocaust. As Parker (1998) also notes of Bauman, the Holocaust could not have been possible if not for the efficiency of bureaucratic processes.

According to Bauman (1995), neither the market nor the state can decide morality, for morality is primarily a personal pursuit that implies taking responsibility for the Other. This has relevance for understanding the relationship between the researcher and the researched. What Bauman means by taking responsibility for the Other is that the Other is not treated like an abstract category, but like an individual, with sympathy and emotion. The Other becomes the self's responsibility and this is where morality begins. But to be responsible for the Other is also to have power over him/her and be free vis-à-vis him/her. Taking responsibility for the Other presupposes safeguarding the uniqueness of the Other. Bauman coins this sort of relation as 'being for the other' and suggests it can only exist as a project, on its way to being completed but never quite accomplished.

For Bauman, this is a disturbing and lonely project as there are no rules by which to judge whether our acts will have positive consequences upon others or not. The occurrence of the state of 'being for the other' cannot be predicted in any deterministic or probabilistic way, as it has nothing to do with reason, but with passion, sentiment and emotion (Bauman, 1995). It is only through trial and error that the individual can pursue his/her moral project. While inspiring, Bauman's position may be difficult to attain within the realm of organisation and management research: if there are no criteria by which to judge values, conduct and behaviour, there is no way of knowing if the interests of all stakeholders have been accounted for within the research process, for example.

As we have already indicated, Michel Foucault's work has not merely provided the intellectual stimulus for feminist and queer theorists. Foucault's ideas have been enormously influential in management studies, providing the conceptual resources for theorising power and subjectivity in work organisations more fluidly than Marxist theories (Townley, 1993a). Elsewhere, Foucault's legacy has been evaluated from the viewpoint of moral philosophy and ethics (see Bernauer, 1992; Bernauer and Mahon, 1994; Davidson, 1994). As Brewis (1998) notes, Foucault uses the concepts of ethics and morality in a different way to Bauman. For Foucault (1983b, 1984), ethics refers to an explicit attempt to shape oneself into a moral subject whereas morality is understood as a hidden normativity of seemingly neutral human scientific knowledge.

Foucault's ethics is directed at the primary dialogue or relation of forces. As Falzon (1998) observes, ethics is for Foucault a secondary concept, just like domination and discipline. We are engaged in the active structuring of the field in which we operate. Here we meet the Other – not only as a concrete, different actor, but also in a more general sense as something that resists our active 'powering'. Due to Otherness, difference and resistance, the one who is touched by this encounter is altered. S/he realises that his or her truths are not the only possible ways to interpret and approach the world. There is also something else: an excess that cannot be incorporated into the order proposed. 'Ethics' is an attitude of keeping oneself open to Otherness in our worldly (including our research) activities. It is not a negative orientation but a positive exposure by oneself to the experiences of resistance. One of the terms Foucault used to describe this attitude was 'curiosity'. By that he wanted to engender courage in order to experience what is odd or rare in our way of life, helping us to find new orientations for our conduct and self. In summary, an ethics of curiosity refers to a mode of engaging in the on-going, power-laden activities, a project that cherishes open-ended play and constant friction in organisational relations rather than accepting ideals of complete order and pre-social subjects.

In summary, what Bauman and Foucault are concerned about is the idea of the ethical individual as a rule-following subject. Their 'postmodern' alternative is not to invent new meta-rules, but to release moral instincts and feelings that are currently domesticated by modern institutions. At the heart of moral experiences is the meeting with the Other: the unknown or alien. By stressing this, it is not claimed that current organisational practices do not at all arouse ethical sensitivity in individuals. Rather, the taken-for-granted way of thinking about the self in organisations marginalises destabilising encounters that take place all the time. Finding out that, even as an appointed, educated and valued manager, one still possesses desires that can harm the Other is often an experience to be pushed aside. The same may be said within some management research situations (see Wray-Bliss, 2003). Management theory also finds it hard to acknowledge that, despite all the efforts to ensure that individuals are 'good', unwanted outcomes (for example, harassment, exclusion, inequality) sometimes occur (Kelemen and Peltonen, 2001).

The postmodern approach to ethics is keen to affirm what is strange in the self, thus promoting continued preparation for the dangers of strict ideas about what is right and wrong, about who to like and who to dislike, in an a priori fashion. If there is nothing to hate, there is no ground to turn one's actions against those who are somehow different; the Other is, in a way, already met in the way individuals experience worldly interaction. In this vein, ethics is incorporated into the very way action is taken, as opposed to being offered up as a set of abstract rules or subject positions. Individuals are constantly created, and are creating themselves, as agents of some sort, and it is the task of the postmodern perspective to remind us of the possibility of the pre-social self refusing to use identity for unethical projects.

The postmodernist approach to organisational and research ethics has been viewed in a largely negative fashion. One major line of criticism is that it does not provide clear guidance as to how one could build an ethical subjectivity, and not as to how one could be 'for and with the Other'. Our understanding of postmodern ethics articulates an alternative politics and ethics of managing, one that sustains on-going dialogue and interaction between individuals, rather than denying and concealing these. This is not an all-or-nothing attitude towards ethical codes, but a marker for a pathway to a heightened sensitivity towards the location of moralities in the concrete practices in which they are used or enacted in research relationships and organisations. Detaching ethical dialogue from absolutist and rationalist projects, however this is implemented, could enhance our capacity to live an ethical life. Actively creating oneself as an ethical subject extends rather than narrows the coverage of ideas about what is right and wrong. As Weber (1930/1992) notes, the mundane methods people used to craft a life avoiding excesses and balancing the self with moral values were subsumed with the rise of organised capitalism. Davidson (1994) in turn bemoans the lost techniques of ethical moderation, commenting that constructing a moral philosophy on the basis of such practices is, unfortunately, very strange for prevailing modern thought. The main task of postmodern ethics could be to restore and revitalise that ordinary art of life and to not confuse it with the purification programmes of contemporary bureaucracy and modernism.

The contribution of feminism

Another form of critique comes from the feminist tradition. A good deal of the feminist theory of ethics has argued that in the Western philosophical tradition what is understood and articulated as 'ethics' is marked by gender. More precisely, feminists such as Lloyd (1984) have suggested that the intellectual frameworks for producing codes of moral conduct are part and parcel of a wider system of (re)producing male privilege. It is true that men have been the main progenitors of ethical theory in the West. For some feminist theorists, this has led to the proliferation of moral theory that has served the interests of men. For that reason, the issue of developing an ethics that is able to articulate women's experiences has been regarded as a very important project. Early work in this field includes the development of an ethics of care (Gilligan, 1977). However, a radical feminist critique has forcefully questioned the need and purpose of ethical theory itself. Walker (1992) sums up the thrust of this arm of feminist theorising:

> **... moral theories code the viewpoint and preoccupations of a very particular group of privileged people. Further, moral reasoning itself is a specific practice of intellectual authority that legitimises and reproduces the systematic relations, including hierarchical ones, that the theories reflect. (p. 25)**

Interestingly, radical feminists such as Marilyn Frye (1990) criticise the motivations of those feminists who produce moral theory. As she pithily states, moral theory is a project for 'those people who must have a foundation for assuming the direction and administration of everything' (cited in Walker, 1992: 27). Such sentiments echo questions raised elsewhere by scholars who have pondered the vexed question: what is ethics for? Within feminist circles the responses to this question are mixed and polemical. As stimulating as these debates are, for our purposes here we broadly outline the legacy of some of the early and influential feminist theorising on ethics, indicating how this has shaped the approach taken to conducting empirical research.

In contrast to deontological and teleological models of ethics, a feminist ethics of care gives primacy to care and responsibility, rather than, as Edwards and Mauthner (2002) point out, 'outcomes, justice or rights' (p. 20). The key principles that guide an ethics of care originate from early feminist theories. One feminist in particular is associated with developing the moral theory that underpins the ethics of care or 'care perspective', as it is sometimes referred to. The work of feminist psychologist Carol Gilligan (1977, 1982, 1987) is cited heavily in that respect. One key finding of Gilligan's empirical research was that women mobilised a specific set of criteria when solving ethical dilemmas. These included that individuals are viewed relationally: that is, seen in relation to others through the relationship ties that connect people across a multitude of contexts. As well, women were found to readily acknowledge the differences in how other people construct realities. Allied with a demonstrable commitment to preserving the emotional, physical and psychological welfare of others, Gilligan's work had a far-reaching impact on feminist theorising. As Drakopoulou (2000) notes of Gilligan's earlier work, while her critique on mainstream/malestream psychology was well received at the time, it was the potential contained in Gilligan's care perspective that attracted wider attention from feminists as an approach for valorising the values and characteristics negatively associated with feminity and women. For Gilligan, reciprocal compassion and care, empathetic values, co-operation and mutuality in human relationships such as friendship, function as the cornerstones of an ethics of care. All these constituents of the ethics of care help to resolve the ethical dilemmas and conflicts that arise between people.

The ethics of care, as articulated by Gilligan and others (Elshtain, 1983; Noddings, 1984; Ruddick, 1980; Whitbeck, 1983), has offered feminists an ethical framework for resisting patriarchal values and practices. For example, the primacy given to the role of nurturing relationships finds a clear resonance in the politics of feminist friendship. As radical feminist Janice Raymond (1986) argues, the 'culture of female friendship has a distinctive purpose, passions and politics' (p. 38). Through a passion for friendship women can 'provide women with a sense of difference, importance, autonomy, and affection' (ibid.). In other words, an ethics of care operating within a radical feminist politics of friendship can revalorise female values as a way of resisting patriarchal hetero-relations.

More recently, Judith White (1999) advocated the synthesis of an ethics of care with a Buddhist ethic of compassion for governing ethical comportment within work organisations. In her provocative article, White outlined her vision of ethical comportment, a form of 'interpersonal behavior, including thoughts, intentions, and effort, that has both the means and purpose of extending kindness, caring, and compassion to all others affected in every situation' (p. 120). The implications of such a theory of ethical standards stretch beyond the power of the care perspective for enabling women to relate to other women, as White shows in her outline of the promise of ethical comportment for improving human resource management practice and management development/education.

Undoubtedly, the notion of an ethics of care has greatly influenced academic understanding (far beyond feminist circles) about the relationship between the researcher and the researched. Be that as it may, the ethics of care model has drawn scathing criticism from feminists dissatisfied with the relational morality concept upon which the model hinges. For example, Martha Nussbaum (1999) chides the ethics of care model for reinforcing the idea that women are naturally predisposed towards caring and nurturing. Nussbaum points to the essentialism in which femininity and female values are grounded. Further to this, while there might be some gains from arguing that caring principles have a place within the public realm, it does not automatically follow that an ethics of care will help resolve conflicts and promote egalitarian practices. Indeed, the claim that feminism is grounded in caring, trust and reciprocity, and that feminist inflected research relationships ought to be constructed along these lines, is problematic (see Chapter 9). From Nussbaum's point of view, there is nothing intrinsically feminist in concepts of care, some of which have served to (re)produce women's subordinate status within patriarchal societies.

Trying to overcome the impasse in feminist debates about an ethics of care, Charlene Haddock Seigfried (1996, 2002) has explored the possible points of connection between American pragmatism and feminist theorising. One interesting observation made by Seigfried (1996) is that some strands of pragmatist theory chime with the core principles of the ethics of care. Unlike Gilligan's version of maternalist feminism, one that falls into the essentialist trap of reifying caring characteristics as 'feminine', Seigfried claims that an ethics of care model within American pragmatist theory avoids the essentialism of this type of feminist theorising. This assertion is partly based on an understanding of John Dewey's notion of democratic community in which a cacophony of feminist and pragmatist voices may coalesce. As stated in Chapter 3, Dewey's argument for polyvocality can operate well as a means for sustaining open-ended and unfinished discussion. In this light, Thayer-Bacon (2003) observes that Dewey in particular offers feminists a notion of experience (for example, that may relate to gender) as an 'unanalyzable totality' (p. 436). Thus, from a pragmatist's point of view, the process of thinking about an ethics of care is marked by social negotiation, fluidity and openness, by which tentative (non-essentialist) conclusions may be reached. As Mottier (2007) also notes of a potential fusion of feminist and pragmatist perspectives, the likely outcomes of such a project remain largely speculative, although Seigfried is one of a small handful of scholars who attempt to offer insight here. It is clear that such debates have made little, if any, impact on the field of critical management research.

In relation to doing critical management research, the ethics of care model or, as Denzin (1997) calls it, the 'communitarian' model, has radically influenced how feminists have approached the study of women's lives. As we have mentioned in Chapter 9, feminists have adopted specific approaches to overcoming the asymmetry in power relations between the researcher and the researched. For example, Oakley's famous (1981) appeal to friendliness when interviewing women is now eclipsed by more sophisticated feminist debates on research ethics. Feminists such as Cotterill (1992) have quickly pointed out that striking up friendships with research participants may not be ethically sound, insofar as they do not always counter asymmetrical power relations between researchers and the researched. Elsewhere, Edwards and Mauthner (2002) valuably use the work of Iris Young (1997) as a counter-point to the notion of symmetry between the self and the Other within the research relationship. As they argue, Young rightly underlines the impossibility of symmetry between self and Other, for individuals have 'particular histories and occupy social positions that make their relations asymmetrical' (p. 26). In this way, the strategy of 'stepping into the shoes of the Other' that some scholars (like Denzin, 1997) advocate becomes highly problematic (if not impossible). Somewhat similarly, the notion of 'being with and for the Other' is appraised by some feminists as too flimsy a concept for building ethics because it does not capture the concrete relations of dependency and connection that are central to an ethics of care

(Sevenhuijsen, 1998). As Edwards and Mauthner (2002) note of Sevenhuijsen's stance on ethics, it is 'fundamentally contingent practice-based' (p. 27) and, as we add, embraces to a large extent postmodernist and pragmatist ideals alongside a feminist agenda.

Finally, Stanley and Wise (1993) also push the debate on feminist ethics beyond narrow conceptions of research ethics and morality that centre on the quality of research relationships. They highlight the 'epistemological issues that concern '*whose* knowledge, seen in *what* terms, around *whose* definitions and standards, and judged by *whose* as well as *what* criteria, should count as "knowledge itself"' (p. 202, emphasis in original). Like Wray-Bliss's (2003) call for CMS scholars to pay attention to context-specific epistemological questions regarding the type of academic service into which knowledge is pressed, so Stanley and Wise's (1993) perspective on the ethics of knowledge production is usefully considered in a contextual manner. This might well hold much value for management researchers because guidelines for conducting research ethically need not be abandoned altogether; rather, ethical frameworks may be modified and adapted to the 'relational parameters of different situations' (p. 203).

The contribution of pragmatism to ethics

Pragmatism challenges the dualistic relationship between knowledge and experience by suggesting that reality can and should be changed through reason and action. As discussed in Chapter 3, pragmatism equates action to change and knowledge is given a central status in achieving this change. Put differently, researchers have a moral responsibility in presenting knowledge that has consequences for future applications. Such future applications must make a difference to the lived world and should contribute to enhanced and more enlightening social practice. For the pragmatists, theories can never be neutral (namely, value-free) for they have ethical and political implications. A pragmatist ethics counsels tolerance towards ambiguity and calls for personal responsibility on the part of the researcher. Personal effort in one's immediate community of practice is more important than following universal codes of ethics, for 'every moral situation is a unique situation' (Dewey, 1927/1950: 132–133).

Judging whether researchers' abilities to engage with the world have resulted in a piece of writing that not only advances scholarly debate, but has a positive impact on the life experiences of the people studied and on the researcher's identity, should become the red thread of doing management research. Some of the pragmatic questions to address while designing, doing and writing up the research findings are listed below (adapted from Mauthner et al., 2002). The list is by no means comprehensive but it does represent a useful starting point for attempting to handle the ethical dilemmas of management research and life in a pragmatic fashion.

- **Who are the people involved in and affected by the ethical dilemmas raised in the research?**
- **What are the specific social and personal locations of the people involved in relation to each other?**
- **What are the needs of those involved in the research and how do they inter-relate?**
- **Whom is the researcher identifying with, and why?**
- **What is the balance of social and personal power between those involved in the research?**
- **How can the researcher best communicate the ethical dilemmas to those involved and give them an opportunity to have a say?**
- **How will the researcher's actions affect the relationships between the subjects of research?**
- **To what extent will the end product help the reader make more moral choices in their day-to-day life?**

In keeping with some pragmatist lines of thought, the answers to such questions will always be incomplete and tentative. Nonetheless, it remains important that these questions form part of the research agenda along with the key topics to be studied. Engaging with such a line of questioning will help researchers decide what works, what does not work and the reasons as to why this is the case. The result of this process is the sort of knowledge that is anti-foundational and directed towards problem solving, by using the data and understandings available at the time.

The contribution of queer theory

As we may deduce from the above discussion on feminism, feminists, like queer theorists, understand that research is a politically and ethically charged process. The matter of ethics is brought to the fore especially when researchers have an interest in studying organisational Others: that is, those who remain shadowy figures within the world of work, who are sometimes marginalised, whose voices tend to be unheard. Sara Ahmed (2002), writing on the dilemmas associated with approaching and thinking about Others, asserts that much violence can be done when having an encounter with the Other, especially when differences are unwittingly assimilated or contained. To acknowledge the risks inherent here is to be cognisant that the researcher does not leave the field of research 'unmarked'. The researcher is an active agent in the construction of research relationships and how they might be experienced by those involved. In thinking about how we might sustain a research ethics that is sensitive to difference, we may do no better than to turn to queer theory.

Read any mainstream book on ethics and you will be hard pushed to find a reference to queer theory. Indeed, it is highly likely that any such search will be unfruitful. Somewhat similarly, scour much of the critical management studies literature on ethics and it is doubtful that you will find any mention of queer theory (for example, see Parker, 1998). In contrast, references to feminist, postmodern and poststructuralist perspectives on ethics are much easier to locate. This state of affairs is hardly surprising. As we stated in Chapter 7, queer theory has not particularly troubled the minds of organisational studies scholars. To reiterate a previous point, queer theory is likely to be conceived of as a trespasser in the day-to-day running of organisations given that it is in the business of questioning its normative constituents. Following on from this, it is hardly surprising that queer theory has yet to permeate debates on business ethics.

In unpacking this state of neglect a fundamental question needs to be addressed. As Donald Hall puts it, from one vantage point queer theory might not hold any particular concern for the matter of ethics. Hall explains:

> **So is there a 'queer' ethics or is that phrase an oxymoron? In other words, when we challenge the 'norm' and confront its advocates, when we repudiate 'essential' values and definitions, are we led inevitably to wholesale chaos, murder, and mayhem? (2003: 145)**

What Hall is referring to here is the criticism often levelled at queer theory for an impulse to place and detonate a bomb under the structures and cultural norms that seemingly provide us with social order. In a similar way to how deconstruction is said by its harshest critics to amount to a form of destruction, so the opponents of queer theory will often construct its apparent irreverence for normativity as being something of a scandal. It is worth teasing out the parallel between the two bodies of theory. Willmott (1998) advances a poststructuralist form of ethics that takes it cue from the work of Derrida. As Willmott suggests, Derridean poststructuralism (with its emphasis on deconstruction) does not have a specific normative purpose in mind. This is not to say that a Derridean ethics is rudderless or without 'normative effects'. Willmott explains:

> **... by deconstructing the distinction between 'descriptive' and 'normative' ethics, thereby questioning whether the former can ever be generated through a relationship of externality to what it purports to describe, poststructuralist analysis stresses the normative character of avowedly descriptive ethics. (p. 93)**

Poststructuralist ethics does not offer an alternative set of moral codes. Moreover, as Willmott rightly points out, the contribution of poststructuralist ethics lies in its 'subversion of closure' rather than its offering up another 'authoritative means of resolving ethical dilemmas' (ibid.). This brief glimpse into a poststructuralist ethics strikes a chord with an ethics suffused with queer theory perspectives. Both have a concern for critiquing normativity rather than harbouring a grand ambition to impose a new order of moral theory amidst the rubble of its predecessor's.

To recap an earlier point, queer theory is not a dead hand on the life of dominant cultural norms and values that help to provide us with senses of familiarity and order in our lives. Such a viewpoint is far too brittle to be of any practical use here. Rather, as Hall goes on to say, queer theory may open up possibilities for a 'supple, interpersonal sense of responsibility that at once minimizes "normalization" and at the same time allows for continued exploration and various enactments of desire and selfhood' (2003: 145). Expressed differently, a queer ethics may allow researchers to challenge and resist the normative aspects of people's life worlds without reproducing the same normalising tendencies and practices they seek to critique. From this angle, queer ethics is generative and creative, enabling people (especially researchers) to explore new ways of relating, understanding and becoming.

However, in seeking to mobilise a queer ethics many researchers might be disappointed to find that no universal model exists. More in the manner of postmodernist approaches to ethics, queer theory is suspicious of the certitudes that seemingly surround tightly designed frameworks and models. Instead, what we have to hand is a plurality of ideas and impulses that formulate a number of queer positionalities. Viewed in this way, queer ethics may be informed by a number of its theoretical bloodlines: for example, poststructuralism, feminism and psychoanalysis. We might best see queer ethics as existing in a perpetual state of becoming, always on the move, operating in the spirit of incisive critique. As we suggested in Chapter 7, one of the strongest muscles in queer theory's conceptual repertoire is its drive to critique what is familiar and seemingly 'known' to us – in other words, queer theory's capacity for denaturalising social phenomena that are reassuringly recognisable and natural. This impulse is conducted within two broad veins: towards others (be they ideas, theories, behaviours, policies, laws, documents and norms, to mention but a few), as well as towards the self. What this means is that queer theory itself is not immune from its own line of critical sight. Handling a form of queer ethics requires a heightened level of sensitivity towards the risks of marginalising others and eliding differences by pursuing an overly forceful practice of critique.

By way of summing up (but not closing off) what has been said so far, we turn to the proposition of a queer ethics made by Elisabeth D. Däumer:

> **A queer ethics ... would support and nurture the queer in all of us – both by questioning all notions of fixed, immutable identities and by articulating a plurality of differences among us in the hope of forging new bonds and allegiances. (1992: 103)**

Importantly, Däumer's version of a queer ethics is applicable to all of us, irrespective of whether our sexual identity is heterosexual, gay, lesbian, bisexual, and so on. A queer ethics may operate as an ethics of difference, forcing all of us to question the heteronormative confines in which our identities and subjectivities are shaped. In that regard, a queer ethics is about generating critical distance around the terms 'gay', 'lesbian', 'bisexual', 'heterosexual', and so forth (Warner, 1993). To do so is to put a block on the calcification of identity and to resist rigid responses to issues about gender and sexuality, and, equally importantly, to stretch the relationship between queer theory to incorporate theories of economy, management, work, and so on.

The role of reflexivity in advancing an ethical agenda

What the above discussion indicates is that care in attending to and formulating ethics in research settings requires reflexivity. Like Alvesson and Deetz (2000), we broadly propose a concept of reflexivity that turns on critical reflection, not just of individual assumptions and values, but also an awareness of alternative research paradigms (we return to the matter of reflexivity in more detail in the conclusion to this book). That being said, calls for reflexivity in organisational research have become a commonplace, if not fashionable, move in the critical management tradition. In this final section we make a short incursion into the history of reflexivity to outline some of the major debates and existing controversies.

While the roots of this concept have been traced back to Socrates and the associated 'know thyself' practices of the ancient Greeks, one of the first social scientists to put reflexivity on a pedestal was Gouldner (1970). In a nutshell, reflexivity is a way of problematising what we know and how we know it, by revealing some of the assumptions on which knowledge is based, for example, the author's background or theoretical standpoint, as well as the social and political relations in which these are located that cannot be transcended easily (Foucault, 1980; Wray-Bliss, 2002). However, reflexivity remains a concept fraught with ambiguity (Johnson and Duberley, 2003) and any attempt to provide a widely accepted definition or a definitive position on how to pursue reflexivity remains a chimera.

There are numerous conceptualisations of reflexivity. Lynch (2000) has identified six genres: mechanical, substantive, methodological, meta-theoretical, interpretative and ethnomethodological, with each of these having sub-genres. Thus, reflexivity has been defined, inter alia, as: an habitual response to stimulus; the property of feedback systems; a hall of mirrors; the organising principle of late modernity; a property of intersubjective relations; self-knowledge; an aid to correct bias; communal or individual self-reflection; an existential engagement with marginalised standpoints; the questioning of taken-for-granted reality; a device of sociological exegesis; the problematisation of representation and objectification; and an everyday property of networks of individuals, practices, and interactions.

A cursory glance at the literature on reflexivity suggests that there are as many critics as there are supporters of the concept (Booth, 2000). For the supporters, reflexivity is something to be cherished and strongly pursued (Chia, 1996; Weick, 1999). For the critics, reflexivity is a 'monster: the abyss, the spectre, the infinite regress' (Ashmore, 1989: 234), as they bemoan the self-referentiality of the social sciences and the textual character of social reality (Woolgar, 1988). Even supporters of reflexivity warn of the dangers lurking behind its promising façade: Karl Weick suggested that reflexivity for its own sake, as an end rather than a means, could have narcissistic consequences to the point where the author becomes obsessed with their own voice and forgets about others (Antonacopolou and Tsoukas, 2002). Lynch (2000), in turn, argues that it is important to question the premises and assumptions of any form of reflexivity rather than merely representing it as a source of authenticity for the writing of social text.

In the enterprise of critical management research, one needs to understand how different versions (genres) of reflexivity come about and how they co-exist with each other, as well as to what extent one can assess and judge a particular version of reflexivity outside the paradigmatic assumptions that allow its creation in the first place (Johnson and Duberley, 2003). We argued in Chapter 2 that paradigmatic assumptions shape our communities of practice. However, certain forms of reflexivity do downplay or, more likely, ignore, the role of paradigmatic assumptions in shaping scholarly practice. Researchers then merely question whether they have rigorously applied appropriate techniques to get closer to the 'truth' or to capture meaning within a certain context. This mechanistic form of reflexivity is dangerous because 'it is only by constantly re-examining and questioning the foundational assumptions of various theories and practices that the discipline can avoid becoming trapped within a limited range of conceptual possibilities' (Brocklesby, 1997: 192).

In a more advanced form of reflexivity, researchers will learn to identify their own and others' viewpoints, scrutinising their underpinnings and influence on research (Flood and Romm, 1997). The view is then taken that we can never expand our understandings unless we constantly examine our own assumptions in light of insights made available by other paradigms. As Chapter 2 suggested, multi-paradigm research extends this thinking by encouraging researchers to travel across paradigms to appreciate different languages and methodologies (Holland, 1999). In this way, research appears as a continuous process of self-discovery, and reflexivity arises out of experimentation with new research practices. Holland (1999) takes this notion further, suggesting that a form of intense reflexivity should not be bound by paradigmatic constraints. This form transcends personal and political concerns, as researchers explore intricate differences in identity between researchers, the subjects of research and the audiences for the text (Herts, 1997).

This is not to say that reflexivity is the ultimate goal, as it may, if taken to its extreme, encourage the formation of 'navel-gazing' within scholarly communities, which could become excessively introspective and egotistical. Given such precautions, however, one of the greatest values of reflexivity is the potential for personal learning and for opening new doors for cognition. As Weick (2002) suggests, perception and conception are two sides of the same reflective coin, hence an embodied reflexivity is key to a more nuanced comprehension of the self and our social surroundings. Weick's version of 'disciplined reflexivity' bridges reflexivity lived forward with one that is understood backwards. Developing 'disciplined reflexivity' may be an effective mode of reflexivity for critical management researchers, as we suggest in the book's concluding remarks.

Summary

To briefly recapitulate this chapter's main concern, we have outlined some of the knotty issues surrounding ethics and reflexivity in management research. Such an exploration has necessarily entailed a rather brief accounting approach to the theories of ethics and reflexivity and the contributions of some of the theories used in this chapter to illustrate how critical theory has contributed to (re)thinking through ethics. All in all, we hope to have provided a fairly general flavour of some of the key issues and contrasting perspectives on ethics and reflexivity.

In regard to the examples of critical theories documented above, in each case it is clear that each one displays a sensitivity, albeit in differing ways, to the conditions of possibility for the creation of ethical frameworks, as well as questioning why we need ethics, interrogating previous models of ethics, and (re)directing analysis onto the application of ethics within research settings. What each of these theories demonstrates is that the ethical field can be altered. Overall, the theories presented above are inclined to move away from the universalistic and normative frameworks of ethics that have until recently dominated the social sciences. Some of these theories (like queer theory) do not seek to install new models of ethics to replace frameworks now considered by some scholars to be intellectually (or morally) bankrupt. Rather, taking the example of queer theory further, the contribution of queer theory to ethics may be understood to hold open such debates, preventing them from petrifying within prescriptive and normative frameworks.

Indeed, queer theory and, to a lesser or greater extent, postmodernism, poststructuralism and some forms of feminist theorising, intentionally offer little in the way of tangible support to researchers looking to formulate new standards of ethical conduct (also see Willmott, 1998). There is much less of a concern within these theories for imposing rules and ideals that researchers must strive towards achieving and more of a concern for thinking about the possibilities of alternatives (see also Brewis, 1998). In so doing, to our minds at least, discursive spaces are opened up for researchers to reflect on the ethical issues surrounding power and politics that are not easily resolved, not least of all within the project of actually doing 'well-intentioned' critical management research (Wray-Bliss, 2003). Thus, by working in a more subversive fashion, these theories operate more imaginatively and promisingly to assist CMS researchers in maintaining openness and critical reflection on ethical issues, keeping them from turning towards a more conventional (normative) path of ethical thought. Such sentiments are captured in the book's Concluding Reflections, which offer a thematic account of the book's perspectives on critical management research.

Further reading

There are numerous texts on ethics and reflexivity that may be consulted for further details regarding many of the issues we have outlined above. Readers are advised to follow up some of the references that have supported our coverage of how critical theory has impacted on ethics and reflexivity. However, we have found several articles extremely thought provoking when exploring ethics and reflexivity within CMS and organisational studies more broadly. For an account of ethics within CMS research then Wray-Bliss's (2003) 'Research subjects/research subjections: exploring the ethics and politics of critical research', in *Organization*, 10 (2): 307–325, is invaluable. For an overview of the approaches taken to reflexivity and a gloss on 'disciplined reflexivity', read Weick (2002) 'Essai: real-time reflexivity: prods to reflection', in *Organization Studies*, 23 (6): 893–898.

Concluding Reflections

There is a plethora of books written on how to be a critical researcher in the world of organisation and management studies. But this book is different. On the one hand, it marshals together traditions that apparently have little in common with or indeed appear to have little relevance to organising, arguing that these traditions are in fact 'critical' because they share a common concern for disrupting orthodox logic and inscribing actors with resistive capacities. On the other hand, this book's uniqueness stems from the attempt to show that these traditions (American pragmatism, postmodernism, deconstruction, post-structuralist feminism and queer theory) have to a lesser or greater degree changed management research methodologies. Although this is ostensibly a book on critical theory it is not a theory book that merely speaks to theorists. One major theme connecting all the chapters is the emphasis we place on the empirical dimension to doing critical management research. Informed, empirical, analyses are crucial to furthering the CMS project.

We do not wish to conclude this book by simply re-iterating its contents chapter by chapter. Suffice it to say that it advances a challenging yet do-able agenda for critical management research/ers: one that focuses on an ethical, reflexive, pragmatic and emancipatory type of management science. On this matter we wish to say something more here because part of our ambition in this book has been to acknowledge, as fully as we can, some of the major opportunities and problems with generating management research modelled along these lines. For some readers, the challenges might seem insurmountable, but then doing critical management research is not an easy endeavour. This is not to say that some of the most vexing issues we have accounted for over the course of the book cannot be overcome. While we have refused to offer up simple solutions or shopping lists of prescriptions to resolve some of these problems, we have also encouraged researchers to view some of the trickier aspects of doing research from different perspectives. This is one way to face up to the challenges that confront critical management researchers. In doing this, we hope to have engaged our readers in ways that galvanise them to (re)consider existing (perhaps conventional) approaches to management research from alternative positions – although, as we quickly add, forms of critical management research are not exempt from a high level of scrutiny. One way to imagine what alternative perspectives might bring forth in terms of new insights or changes is to connect with others. In our view, central to the generation of stimulating critical management research is an openness towards and a willingness to enter into dialogue with others (including the Other). This might pertain to those whom we involve in our research, those who fund research projects, managers, business school students and the theoretical paradigms we do/not utilise (the list goes on).

We believe that by having a handle on these issues that critical management can progress in ways that, as Wray-Bliss (2003) reminds us, avoid falling foul of (re)producing the very hierarchical and oppressive relations that it might target for critique. Considering this, what we want to offer by way of our concluding remarks is a set of key themes that have served as the red threads of the book. Collectively, they formulate the beginnings of a programmatic (but non-prescriptive) agenda for the future of management research. For some, the themes presented below might read as a (re)assertion of what has already gone before in CMS though, as we argue, the signposting of the hazards associated with research ethics, reflexivity and anti-oppressive research practices has not always been heeded. As such, these themes may serve at once as reminders or new signposts pointing towards bundles of ideas that critical management researchers need to unpack. On that note, we acknowledge that what we offer up here is by no means exhaustive; rather, it is our own summation of a number of possibilities to that end (there are others). Nonetheless, we regard them as exciting and compelling. These are as follows.

Embodied rationality

For the critical management researcher, rationality must remain embodied in order to be able to cope effectively with the perennial indeterminacy and contingency which actors have to struggle with in organisations. As we established in relation to early American pragmatist theories, to think means to experience the world in one way or another, and not accounting for this experience means escaping into abstract and useless theory. Experience means not only turning to what has happened in the past but more importantly, accounting for our visceral and embodied response to the immediate context. In an obvious way, embodied rationality runs counter to a Cartesian split of the mind and body. Yet in another way, embodied rationality demands of the researcher a heightened self-awareness of the multiple aspects of experience. Specifically, the experiences of those they wish to involve in management research as well as their own. Some important issues here concern how the researcher interacts with research participants, concepts, theories, the material aspects of research settings, and so on. Above all, the researcher is located *within* (rather than detached from) the research context and enters into the process of meaning making neither as an 'expert' nor a single voice but as, what Ann Cunliffe

(2003) calls, 'many participant-expert voices'. Cunliffe suggests that meaning making then becomes a dialogical relationship as we seek to understand the views of others. Extending Pollner's (1991) notion of questioning what is considered to be 'natural' through the use of 'radical reflexivity', we draw upon Cunliffe to suggest that we need to 'go further than questioning the truth claims of others, to question how we as researchers (and practitioners) also make truth claims and construct meaning' (2003: 985). This allows consideration of an embodied rationality that demands attention not only to why and how we respond but also to how our situated physical presence, 'monstrous' or otherwise (Thanem, 2006), is itself worthy of analysis.

Denaturalisation

If there is one theme that underpins critical management research more than some of the others listed here, then it is denaturalisation. From the outset we have put forward a concept of management research as a knowledge-making enterprise that is embedded within power relations. Serendipitous as research findings might appear to be at times, we should not forget that knowledge is constructed. Equally and relatedly, knowledge acquisition is mediated by innumerable factors and choices that all shape the form it eventually acquires, as well as the legitimacy and status granted it by the researcher and others. This view accords closely with the theories we have presented in the second part of the book. As such, postmodern, deconstructive, pragmatist, feminist and queer theorists would feel very queasy at any claim that the production of management research can be a power- and value-free accomplishment. Both as a concept and as a set of practices, denaturalisation has an interest in the power-knowledge nexus. More specifically, any effort to denaturalise aspects of the worlds in which we live would entail questioning knowledge that is taken-for-granted. Since values permeate and are carried within knowledge, so knowledge is political. Denaturalisation does not simply show up the constructedness of knowledge in that regard, it also has an ambition to legitimise forms of knowledge that are marginal.

Furthermore, denaturalisation is not too far removed from what Alvesson and Deetz (2000) call 'de-familiarisation'. De-familiarisation is a powerful conceptual resource by virtue of how it can (re)orientate researchers to (re)look at the worlds they wish to research. The process of viewing what is familiar to us with a fresh pair of eyes is not always easy and sometimes (hopefully) the effect is disorientating. Alvesson and Deetz (2000) advance a set of suggestions for practically assisting researchers to make 'familiar' phenomena within organisational worlds 'strange' or 'exotic'. We endorse the emphasis they place on imagination, creativity, avoiding cultural parochialisms, working with others and activating theory. Denaturalisation can work well to that end, revealing the 'familiar' to us in the (tacit) assumptions that underpin organisational theory and practice. Of course, the processes of denaturalisation and de-familiarisation may overlap. In the context of this book, many of the theories we present as 'critical' warmly embrace the aim to denaturalise the discursive arrangements that constitute (managerial) knowledge as fact or 'common (business) sense'. Flowing from this, forms of critical management research that contain the impulse to denaturalise (and de-familiarise) can help researchers to see the possibilities for and the barriers to change in organisations, which are crucial to anti-oppressive/emancipatory research projects.

Emancipation

Within the Critical Management Studies arena the debate has traditionally centred on whether an emancipatory agenda could ever be consistent with relativist epistemology and ontology (see Fournier and Grey, 2000). Rather than 'settling' such debate, either through the modified, limited concept of 'micro-emancipation' (Alvesson and Willmott, 1992; Parker, 1995) or through the re-location of critical management studies within critical realism rather than post-modernism more broadly, our aim is much less grand. Our interest lies more in how emancipation (and we could add here resistance) could remain a site for debate and disturbance permeating organisational studies despite attempts from many sides to write it out of analysis. We see the emancipation of workers, managers, and other organisational and societal stakeholders as crucial to the edification of a more democratic, empowering world.

Yet in making such a bold assertion we appreciate the ball of questions that may tumble out of such a high-spirited statement. Not least of all those tricky questions that require researchers to address the ethical issues relating to: whom they should emancipate; how they should go about it; what do people need emancipating from; the effects of emancipatory management research on those involved; and fundamentally, the need to embark upon an emancipatory quest. One fear is that by generating more reflexive managers, we might pave the way for more managers to manipulate and exploit their various staff in more ingenuous and fiendish ways. In an obvious sense, this presupposes that managers are fundamentally minded to oppress those workers who fall within their span of control. We are highly suspicious of such bald depictions (and implicit assumptions) constructed by some scholarly perspectives. Managers are a highly diverse occupational group and we should avoid the tendency to homogenise their interests, desires, ambitions and needs. Conversely, as Wray-Bliss writes with much poignancy, we should not assume that all workers are waiting to be emancipated from oppressive work regimes and organisations by the efforts of well-intentioned CMS researchers. Importantly, we should not duck out of tackling the issues that surround the endeavour to generate emancipatory research, lest we run the risk of (re)producing the oppressive relationships that emancipatory management research aims to dismantle.

In light of this, the task of management science is to equip the various individuals and groups with sufficient intellectual and cultural resources for them to make the most adequate choices and understand their consequences for themselves and other people. In furthering that project each one of the critical theories dealt with in Part II of this book is extremely helpful for positioning researchers in different ways to address these matters. This is a particularly crucial point. If one of the current challenges facing CMS concerns the pressing need for CMS to enter into new (non) academic contexts, in order to increase its exposure to new (non) academic audiences, then one hope for advancing an emancipatory agenda is this:

> **In a sense, the most obvious strategy for CMS is to address its clients, mostly managers and managers in training, in order to educate them more broadly and use whatever rhetoric tools academics have to dethrone market managerial common sense. This is the obvious constituency, the group that arrive regularly at the [business] School and have some investment in the knowledges that it produces ... making managers 'critical' through providing them with the tools that CMS uses is the most obvious way to do it. (Parker, 2002a: 131)**

It is worth quoting Parker at length because it brings to the fore a rather practical (obvious?) possibility for generating emancipatory forms of critical management research. Problems remain in regard to how managers (and others) might be positioned: as needing 'assistance and enlightenment', as Parker goes on to say. However, the use of critical theory might not only help us to avoid getting snagged on the horns of such ethical dilemmas, but also may help to convince CMS clients that they have something to offer them in the design of anti-oppressive/emancipatory research. Parker's ideas virtually echo Fournier and Grey's (2000) observation that an obvious channel for the dissemination of CMS research is within management education.

Multi-paradigm research

One of the motivations for writing this book was to point up the possible points of connection that might be made across the theoretical paradigms we have presented in Part II. Since these theories have a correspondence with postmodernism in various ways, finding resonance between and across each of the theories is easier than searching for points of reference with, for example, more positivistic paradigms. We have already indicated some areas of overlap but there are many others, and we hereby invite readers to continue making such linkages. The critical management researcher must remain comfortable with indeterminate truth-values in the attempt to handle situational indeterminacy. Fuzziness, multiple realities, paradox and ambiguity can be accommodated via an eclectic *bricolage* of methods and paradigms. This approach adheres to Kilduff and Mehra's conviction that 'the practice of research should never be a timid adventure' (1997: 476). Critical researchers will value multiple methodological lenses, while at the same time recognising their blinkers. It is also entails rehearsing different perspectives, not discounting those considered to be 'normative' or 'conventional'. As we view it, critical management research is a dialogical enterprise: it does not dispense with the past or what might be considered 'normative', 'conventional' or 'unfashionable'. But instead connects with alternative and competing perspectives and sometimes denudes them of their normative appearance while at other times reconstituting them into the new modes of seeing. Mobilising divergent lenses may enable insights into the varied facets of organisations, potentially enhancing understandings of how dramatic transformations can intensify ambiguity, complexity, and conflict. Multiple strategies of research may guide explorations of pluralism and paradox, fostering the development of a more relevant and comprehensive theory.

On that last point, contemplating multi-paradigm research involves finding out about alternative theories that one might not ordinarily favour. It might be the case that the theories presented in Part II of this book are new to some readers: for example, American pragmatism and queer theory. We hope that some readers will have derived benefit from exposure to such theories that, at first sight, might not seem to be the most obvious or relevant theoretical paradigms for developing forms of critical management research. Of course, this book begs to differ. Still, as we have stated in our introduction, what we have offered up by way of critical theory is just one small window overlooking a diverse theoretical landscape. Accepting that multi-paradigm research is about weighing up alternatives, researchers must therefore delve more deeply into different theoretical currents. Outside of the book's main theoretical focal points other conceptual resources are gaining ascendancy within organisational theory. For instance, postcolonial theories that explore differences, diaspora, Otherness and hybridity offer much scope for exploring identities and subjectivities within organisational settings (see Prasad and Prasad, 2002). Not surprisingly, some of postcolonialism's concerns are shared by postmodernism, feminisms and queer theory. However, the argument that colonialism represents the most significant influence on how people's differences are understood in the West is a provocative and intriguing argument that has the potential for exploring the effects of postcolonial discourses within the workplace (ibid.). Postcolonial writings have fallen outside the central focus of this book; nonetheless, we feel that such theories are worth mentioning here as an example of alternative theoretical explorations that some of the book's readers might find appealing.

To conclude, we posit multi-paradigm research as *one* approach to generating a multiplicity of dialogues that enrols allies by engendering the formation of connections between groups, individuals and sets of ideas. After all, management research can lay claim to being 'critical' without needing to engage several paradigms. Nor does critical management research necessarily rely upon a paradigmatic approach in order to be critical or interesting (Rhodes, 2000). However, the skilled handling of multi-paradigm research has great potential. To recap Koot et al. (1996), 'the whimsicality of reality can only be grasped with a multi-perspective approach that combines various methods of data collection, multi-level analysis and the in-built view of paradoxes in the research plan' (p. 211). We tend to agree.

The centrality of ethics

Critical management researchers have a moral responsibility in presenting knowledge that has consequences for future applications. Drawing on Chia (1996), Cunliffe and Jun (2005) have argued that critical reflexivity (the questioning and complicating of our thinking and experience) involves not only the examination of taken-for-granted assumptions but also of 'who may be excluded or marginalised by policy and practice, and the responsibility for ethical action at the organizational and societal levels' (p. 228). Ideally, the research endeavour should be geared towards knowledge that makes a positive difference and contributes to enlightened practice. This is no small matter. As we have already stated, theories on management (or otherwise) cannot be neutral for they have ethical and political implications. This much at least queer and feminist theorising tells us. A critical position counsels tolerance towards ambiguity and calls for personal responsibility on the part of the researcher. Personal effort in one's immediate community of practice is more important than following universal codes of ethics, for every moral situation is a unique situation. Indeed, while we do not wish to construct another rulebook on research ethics, we do wish to advocate an open-ended questioning of ethical codes so that researchers remain vigilant and sensitive to their own impact on the field of relations within any given research setting.

Disciplined reflexivity

Critical management research must be a reflexive enterprise. In Chapter 10 we touched upon some of the swirling debates on reflexivity. Rather like the discussions on research ethics, there is much consternation among scholars about the consequences of adopting certain forms of reflexivity. Reflexivity is certainly a key feature of CMS (Fournier and Grey, 2000), but arising from this is the question as to which brand of reflexivity critical management scholars should bother with? Perhaps unsurprisingly, there are no easy answers. Although there is perhaps one obvious style of reflexivity that is to be avoided: the form of reflexivity that is engaged in for its own sake. This is the type of reflexivity regarded by Karl Weick (1999) as merging into narcissism. Here, the researcher's voice is elevated above all others, potentially silencing the voices of those that CMS aims to amplify (Fournier and Grey, 2000). Relatedly, Weick also mentions a crippling form of reflexivity that makes us fearful about making mistakes and induces us to heap self-doubt on top of self-doubt – equal to an intellectual blackout. In each scenario, reflexivity effectively becomes a paralysis.

How reflexivity is understood and engaged by researchers in relation to ontological, epistemological and methodological issues varies tremendously, depending in no small part on what critical theory the concept of reflexivity is mediated by. For example, we have mentioned some feminist perspectives on reflexivity to articulate the dilemmas surrounding the construction of egalitarian research relationships. But there are limits to this (and any other) form of reflexivity. As Gillies and Alldred (2002) note, considerably less attention is paid to reflecting on the intentions of doing research – or, as Gillies and Alldred (2002) describe it, engaging in 'forward reflexivity'. This is a more elastic concept of reflexivity that finds some resonance in Weick's (2002) notion of disciplined reflexivity in which forwards and backwards reflexivity co-exist. We suggest that Weick's conceptualisation of disciplined reflexivity is a productive point of departure for reflecting holistically: that is, as Weick avers, to become aware of the world as a 'network of interrelated projects rather than as an arrangement of discrete physical objects and events' (2002: 895). In such a world there is no separation between subjects and objects as the tendency is when, for example, a researcher (subject) reflects backwards on an interview (object) in the past. Reflecting forward permits a more nuanced and context-specific understanding of how research processes and relationships are constituted. What is more, shifting reflexive gears might help researchers handle multiple perspectives with greater dexterity, and perhaps more imaginatively. Of course Weick's take on reflexivity is not the only useful starting position but it is one that potentially encourages critical dialogues within and between diverse individuals, groups of people and organisations. As we see it, such dialogues are the arteries of critical management research.

With all the above themes in mind, the question then arises as to whether this is an overly ambitious agenda – our view is that we cannot envisage a future for critical management research unless such challenges become central to our research efforts.

Bibliography

Aaltio, I. (2002) Interviewing female managers: presentation of the gendered selves in contexts. In I. Aaltio and A. J. Mills (eds), *Gender, Identity and the Culture of Organizations*, pp. 201–218. London: Routledge.

Ahmed, S. (2002) 'This other and other others', *Economy and Society*, 31 (4): 558–572.

Ahrens, T. and Mollona, M. (2007) 'Organisational control as cultural practice – a shop floor ethnography of a Sheffield steel mill', *Accounting, Organizations and Society*, 32 (4-5): 305–331.

Alcoff, L. (1992) Feminist politics and Foucault: the limits to a collaboration. In A. B. Dallery and C. E. Scott (eds), *Crises in Continental Philosophy*. Albany, NY: SUNY.

Altman, D. (1982) *The Homosexualization of America, The Amercanization of the Homosexual*. New York: St Martin's Press.

Alvesson, M. (1987) *Consensus, Control, and Critique*. Brookfield, VT: Avebury.

Alvesson, M. and Deetz, S. (2000) *Doing Critical Management Research*. London: Sage.

Alvesson, M. and Karreman, D. (2000) 'Varieties of discourse: on the study of organizations through discourse analysis', *Human Relations*, 53 (9): 1125–1149.

Alvesson, M. and Sköldberg, K. (2000) *Reflexive Methodology: New Vistas for Qualitative Research*. London: Sage.

Alvesson, M. and Willmott, H. (1996) *Making Sense of Management: A Critical Introduction*. London: Sage.

Alvesson, M. and Willmott, H. (eds) (1992) *Critical Management Studies*. London: Sage.

Antonacopoulou, E. and Tsoukas, H. (2002) 'Time and reflexivity in organization studies: an introduction', *Organization Studies*, 23 (6): 857–862.

Antonio R. J. (2000) 'After postmodernism: reactionary tribalism', *American Journal of Sociology*, 106 (2): 40–87.

Archer, M. (2003) *Structure, Agency and the Internal Conversation*. Cambridge: Cambridge University Press.

Argyris, C. and Schön, D. (1978) *Organizational Learning: A Theory of Action Perspective*. Reading, MA: Addison Wesley.

Ashmore, M. (1989) *The Reflexive Thesis: Wrighting Sociology of Scientific Knowledge*. Chicago: University of Chicago Press.

Astley, R. and Zammuto, R. F. (1992) 'Organization science, managers, and language games', *Organization Science*, 3 (4): 443–460.

Bansal, P. and Clelland, I. (2004) 'Talking trash: legitimacy, impression management and unsystematic risk in the context of the natural environment', *Academy of Management Journal*, 47 (1): 93–103.

Barnard, C. (1938) *The Functions of the Executive*. Cambridge, MA: Harvard University Press.

Bartky, S. L. (1988) Foucault, femininity, and the modernization of patriarchal power. In I. Diamond and L. Quinby (eds), *Feminism and Foucault: Reflections on Resistance*, pp. 61–86. Boston, MA: Northeastern University Press.

Bats, S. P. (1997) 'Whatever happened to organizational anthropology? A review of the field of organizational ethnography and anthropological studies', *Human Relations*, 50 (9): 1147–1175.

Bauman, Z. (1989) *Modernity and the Holocaust*. Cambridge: Polity.

Bauman, Z. (1991) *Identity and Ambivalence*. Ithaca, NY: Cornell University Press.

Bauman, Z. (1995) *Life in Fragments: Essays in Postmodern Morality*. Oxford: Blackwell.

Beasley, C. (2005) *Gender & Sexuality: Critical Theories, Critical Thinkers*, London: Sage.

Bell, E. (1999) 'The negotiation of a working role in organizational ethnography', *International Journal of Social Research Methodology*, 2 (1): 17–37.

Benhabib, S. (1992) *Situating the Self: Gender, Community and Postmodernism in Contemporary Ethics*. London: Routledge.

Berger, P. and Luckmann, T. (1966) *The Social Construction of Reality: A Treatise in the Sociology of Knowledge*. Harmondsworth: Penguin.

Bernauer, J. (1992) Beyond life and death: Foucault's post-Auschwitz ethic. In *Michel Foucault Philosopher: Essays translated from the French and German by Timothy J. Armstrong*, pp. 159–66. Hemel Hempstead: Harvester Wheatsheaf.

Bernauer, J. and Mahon, M. (1994) The ethics of Michel Foucault. In G. Gutting (ed.), *The Cambridge Companion to Foucault*. Cambridge: Cambridge University Press.

Binnie, J. (2004) *The Globalization of Sexuality*. London: Sage.

Birch, M. and Miller, T. (2000) 'Inviting intimacy: the interview as therapeutic opportunity', *International Journal of Social Research Methodology*, 3 (3): 189–202.

Bogdan, R. and Ksander, M. (1980) 'Policy data as social process: a qualitative approach to quantitative data', *Human Organization*, 39: 302–309.

Boje, D. M. (1991) 'The storytelling organization: a study of story performance in an office-supply firm', *Administrative Science Quarterly*, 36: 106–126.

Boje, D. M. (1995) 'Stories of the storytelling organization: a postmodern analysis of Disney as "Tamara-Land"', *Academy of Management Journal*, 38 (4): 997–1035.

Boje, D. M. (1998) 'Nike, Greek goddess of victory or cruelty? Women's stories of Asian factory life', *Journal of Organizational Change Management*, 11 (6): 461–480.

Boje, D. M. (2006) 'What happened on the way to postmodern?', *Qualitative Research in Organizations and Management: An International Journal*, 1 (1): 22–40.

Boje, D. M. and Dennehy, R. F. (1993) *Managing in the Postmodern World: America's Revolution against Exploitation*. Dubuque, IO: Kendal-Hunt.

Boje, D. M. and Rosile, G. A. (1994) 'Diversities, differences and authors' voices', *Journal of Organizational Change Management*, 7 (6): 8–17.

Booth, C. (2000) 'The problems and possibilities of reflexivity in strategy', *Electronic Journal of Radical Organization Theory*, 4 (1).

Borgerson, J. L. (2005) 'Judith Butler: on organizing subjectivities', *The Sociological Review*, 53 (1): 63–79.
Bouchikhi, H. (1998) 'Living with and building on complexity: a constructivist perspective on organizations', *Organization*, 5 (2): 217–232.
Brandth, B. and Kvande, E. (2002) 'Reflexive fathers: negotiating parental leave and working life', *Gender, Work and Organisation*, 9 (2): 186–203.
Brewer, J. D. (2000) *Ethnography*. Buckingham: Open University Press.
Brewis, J. (1998) Who do you think you are? Feminism, work, ethics and Foucault. In M. Parker (ed.), *Ethics and Organizations*, pp. 53–75. London: Sage.
Brewis, J. and Linstead, S. (2004) Gender and management. In S. Linstead, L. Fulop and S. Lilley (eds), *Management and Organization: A Critical Text*, pp. 56–92. Basingstoke: Palgrave/Macmillan.
Brewis, J., Linstead, S., Boje, D. and O'Shea, T. (eds) (2006) *The Passion of Organizing*. Copenhagen: Copenhagen Business School Press.
Brines, J. (1994) 'Economic dependency and the division of labor', *American Journal of Sociology*, 100 (3): 652-688.
Brocklesby, J. (1997) Becoming multimethodology literate: an assessment of the cognitive difficulties of working across paradigms. In J. Mingers and A. Gills (eds), *Multimethodology*, pp. 189–216. New York: Wiley.
Brown, S. L. and Eisenhardt, K. M. (1995) 'Product development: past research, present findings, and future directions', *Academy of Management Review*, 20 (2): 343–379.
Bryman, A. (1984) 'The debate about quantitative and qualitative research: a question of method or epistemology?', *The British Journal of Sociology*, 35 (1): 75–92.
Burawoy, M. (1979) *Manufacturing Consent: Changes in the Labor Process Under Monopoly Capitalism*. Chicago: Chicago University Press.
Burrell, G. (1996) Paradigms, metaphors, discourses, genealogies. In S. Clegg, C. Hardy and W. Nord (eds), *Handbook of Organization Studies*, pp. 642–658. Thousand Oaks, CA: Sage.
Burrell, G. and Morgan, G. (1979) *Sociological Paradigms and Organizational Analysis: Elements of the Analysis of Corporate Life*. London: Heinemann.
Burt, R. S. (1987) 'Social contagion and innovation: cohesion versus structural equivalence', *American Journal of Sociology*, 92: 1287–1335.
Butler, J. (1990) *Gender Trouble: Feminism and the Subversion of Identity*. London: Routledge.
Butler, J. (1993) *Bodies That Matter: On the Discursive Limits of "Sex"*. New York: Routledge.
Butler, J. (2004) *Undoing Gender*. London: Routledge.
Calás, M. B. (1993) 'Deconstructing charismatic leadership: re-reading Weber from the darker side', *Leadership Quarterly*, 4: 305–328.
Calás, M. B. and Smircich, L. (1991) 'Voicing seduction to silence leadership', *Organization Studies*, 12 (40): 567–601.
Calás, M. B. and Smircich, L. (1999) 'Past postmodernism? Reflections and tentative directions', *Academy of Management Review*, 24 (4): 649–671.
Campbell, J. (1995) *Understanding John Dewey: Nature and Cooperative Intelligence*. Chicago: Open Court.
Carli, L. (1990) 'Gender, language and influence', *Journal of Personality and Social Psychology*, 59: 941–951.

Carr, A. N. (2005) 'The challenge of critical theory for those in organization theory and behavior: an overview', *International Journal of Organization Theory and Behavior*, 8 (4): 466–494.

Cassell, C. and Symon, G. (2004) *Essential Guide to Qualitative Methods in Organization Research*. London: Sage.

Chase, S. E. (1996) Personal vulnerability and interpretive authority in narrative research. In R. Josselson (ed.), *Ethics and Process in The Narrative Study of Lives*, pp. 45–59. Thousand Oaks, CA: Sage.

Chia, R. (1996) *Organizational Analysis as Deconstructive Practice*. Berlin: de Gruyter.

Cixous, H. and Clément, C. (1986) *The Newly Born Woman (*trans. Betsy Wing). Minneapolis: University of Minnesota Press.

Clegg, S. (1990) *Modern Organizations: Organization Studies in the Postmodern World*. London: Sage.

Clegg, S. and Hardy, C. (1996) Conclusion: representations. In S. Clegg, C. Hardy and W. Nord (eds), *Handbook of Organization Studies*, pp. 676–708. Thousand Oaks, CA: Sage.

Clegg, S., Kornberger, M., Carter, M. and Rhodes, C. (2006) 'For management?', *Management Learning*, 37 (1): 7–27.

Clifford, J. and Marcus, G. E. (eds) (1986) *Writing Culture: The Poetics and Politics of Ethnography*. Berkeley: University of California Press.

Clough, P. T. (1992) *The End(s) of Ethnography: From Realism to Social Criticism*. Newbury Park, CA: Sage.

Cohen, M. D., March, J. G. and Olsen, J. P. (1972) 'A garbage can model of organizational choice', *Administrative Science Quarterly*, 17 (1): 1–25.

Coleman, J. S., Katz, E. and Menzel, H. (1966) *Medical Innovation: A Diffusion Study*. Indianapolis IN: Bobbs-Merrill.

Collinson, D. and Hearn, J. (eds) (1996) *Men as Managers, Managers as Men: Critical Perspectives on Men, Masculinities and Managements*. London: Sage.

Cooper, R. and Burrell, G. (1988) 'Modernism, postmodernism and organizational analysis: an introduction', *Organization Studies*, 9 (1): 91–112.

Cooper, R. and Law, J. (1995) 'Organization: distal and proximal views', *Research in the Sociology of Organizations*, 13: 237–274.

Cotterill, P. (1992) 'Interviewing women: issues of friendship, vulnerability, and power', *Women's Studies International*, 15 (5–6): 593–606.

Creswell, J. W. (2003) *Research Design: Qualitative, Quantitative, and Mixed Methods Approaches*. Thousand Oaks, CA: Sage.

Cunliffe, A. L. (2003) 'Intersubjective voices: the role of the "theorist"', *Administrative Theory & Praxis*, 25 (4): 481–498.

Cunliffe, A. L. and Jun, J. S. (2005) 'The need for reflexivity in public administration', *Administration and Society*, 37 (2): 225–242.

Czarniawska, B. (1998a) 'Who is afraid of incommensurability?', *Organization*, 5: 273–275.

Czarniawska, B. (1998b) *A Narrative Approach to Organization Studies*. Thousand Oaks, CA: Sage.

de Lauretis, T. (1991) 'Queer theory: lesbian and gay sexualities', *Differences: a Journal of Feminist Cultural Studies*, 3 (2): iii–xviii.

Dalton, M. (1959) *Men Who Manage*. New York: Wiley.

Darryl, J. (1998) 'Postmodernism: a critical typology', *Politics and Society*, 26 (2): 95–143.

Däumer, E. (1992) 'Queer ethics, or the challenge of bisexuality to lesbian ethics', *Hypatia*, 17 (4): 91–106.

Davey, C., Powell, J. A., Cooper, I. and Powell, J. E. (2004) 'Innovation, construction SMEs and action learning', *Engineering, Construction and Architectural Management,* 11 (4): 230–237.

Davidson, A. (1994) Ethics as ascetics: Foucault, the history of ethics, and ancient thought. In G. Gutting (ed) *The Cambridge Companion to Foucault*, pp.115–140. Cambridge: Cambridge University Press.

Deem, R. (2002) 'Talking to manager-academics: methodological dilemmas and feminist research strategies', *Sociology*, 36 (4): 835–855.

Deetz, S. (1996) 'Describing differences in approaches to organization science: rethinking Burrell and Morgan and their legacy', *Organization Science*, 7 (2): 191–207.

Denzin, N. K. (1997) *Interpretive Ethnography: Ethnographic Practices for the 21st Century*. Thousand Oaks, CA: Sage.

Denzin, N. K. and Lincoln, Y. S. (2000) Introduction: the discipline and practice of qualitative research. In N. K. Denzin and Y. S. Lincoln (eds), *The SAGE Handbook of Qualitative Research*. Thousand Oaks, CA: Sage.

Denzin, N. K. and Lincoln, Y. S. (2003) (eds) *The Landscape of Qualitative Research: Theories and Issues*, 2nd edition. Thousand Oaks, CA: Sage.

Denzin, N. K. and Lincoln, Y. S. (2005) (eds) *The SAGE Handbook of Qualitative Research*, 3rd edition. Thousand Oaks, CA: Sage.

Derrida, J. (1976) *Of Grammatology*. Baltimore, IL: The Johns Hopkins University Press.

Derrida, J. (1978) *Writing and Difference*. Chicago: University of Chicago Press.

Derrida, J. (1988) *Limited Inc*. Evanston, IL: Northwestern University Press.

Derrida, J. (1996) Remarks on deconstruction and pragmatism. In C. Mouffe (ed.), *Deconstruction and Pragmatism*, pp. 77–88. London: Routledge.

Desanctis, G. and Poole, M.S. (1994) 'Capturing the complexity in advanced technology use: adaptive structuration theory', *Organization Science,* 5 (2): 121–147.

Dewey, J. (1910) *How We Think*. Boston, MA: D. C. Heath & Co.

Dewey, J. (1916) *Democracy and Education*. New York: Macmillan.

Dewey, J. (1920) *Reconstruction in Philosophy*. New York: Holt.

Dewey, J. (1925/1958) *Experience and Nature*. New York: Dover.

Dewey, J. (1927/1950) *The Public and its Problems*. New York: Holt.

Dewey, J. (1929) *The Quest for Certainty: A Study of the Relation of Knowledge and Action*. New York: Minton Blach & Co.

Dewey, J. (1938/1998) *Logic: The Theory of Inquiry*. New York: Holt.

Dick, P. and Cassell, C. (2004) 'The position of policewomen: a discourse analytic study', *Work, Employment & Society*, 18 (1): 51–72.

Dilley, P. (1999) 'Queer theory: under construction', *International Journal of Qualitative Studies in Education,* 12 (5): 457–472.

DiMaggio, P. J. and Powell, W. W. (1983) 'The iron cage revisited: institutional isomorphism and collective rationality in organizational fields', *American Sociological Review,* 48 (2): 147–160.

Donaldson, L. (1996) *For Positivist Organization Theory*. London: Sage.

Donaldson, L. (1998) 'The myth of paradigm incommensurability in management studies: comments by an integrationist', *Organization*, 5 (2): 267–272.

Donaldson, L. (2003) Position statement for positivism. In R. Westwood and S. Clegg (eds), *Debating Organization: Point-Counterpoint in Organization Studies*, pp. 116–127. Oxford: Blackwell.

Drakopoulou, M. (2000) 'The ethic of care, female subjectivity and feminist legal scholarship', *Feminist Legal Studies*, 8 (2): 199–226.

Earley, P. C. and Singh, H. (1995) 'International and intercultural management research: what's next?', *Academy of Management Journal*, 38 (2): 327–340.

Edwards, R. and Mauthner, M. (2002) Ethics and feminist research: theory and practice. In M. Mauthner, M. Birch, J. Jessop and T. Miller (eds), *Ethics in Qualitative Research*, pp. 1–31. London: Sage.

Eisenhardt, K. M. (1989) 'Building theories from case study research', *Academy of Management Review*, 14 (4): 532–550.

Elkins D. J. (1995) *Beyond Sovereignty: Territory and Political Economy in the 21st Century*. Toronto: University of Toronto Press.

Elshtain, J. B. (1983) *Antigone's Daughters: Reflections on Female Identity and the State*. New York: Longman.

Epstein, S. (1996) A queer encounter: sociology and the study of sexuality. In S. Seidman (ed.), *Queer Theory/Sociology*, pp. 145–167. Oxford: Blackwell.

Esping-Andersen, G. (2000) 'Two societies, one sociology, and no theory', *British Journal of Sociology*, 51 (1): 59–77.

Evans K. (2000) 'Reclaiming John Dewey: democracy, inquiry, pragmatism and public management', *Administration and Society*, 32 (3): 308–328.

Faderman, L. (1997) Afterword. In D. Heller (ed.), *Cross Purposes: Lesbians, Feminists and the Limits of Alliance*, pp. 221–229. Bloomington: Indiana University Press.

Falzon, C. (1998) *Foucault and Social Dialogue*. London: Routledge.

Farmer, L. S. J. (2007) 'What is the question?', *IFLA Journal*, 33 (10): 41–49.

Fayol, H. (1949) *General and Industrial Management*. London: Pitman.

Feldman, S. P. (1996) 'Incorporating the contrary: the politics of dichotomy in Chester Barnard's organizational sociology', *Journal of Management History*, 2 (2): 26–40.

Finch, J. (1984) It's great to have someone to talk to: the ethics and politics of interviewing women. In C. Bell and H. Roberts (eds), *Social Researching: Politics, Problems, Practice*, pp. 70–87. London: Routledge and Kegan Paul.

Fletcher, D. (2002) '"In the company of men": a reflexive tale of cultural organizing in a small organization', *Gender, Work and Organization*, 9 (4): 398–419.

Flood, R. and Romm, N. (1997) From metatheory to 'multimethodology'. In J. Mingers and A. Gills (eds), *Multimethodology*, pp. 291–322. New York: Wiley.

Foldy, E. G. (2002) Managing diversity: identity and power in organizations. In I. Aaltio and A. J. Mills (eds), *Gender, Identity and the Culture of Organizations*, pp. 92–112. London: Routledge.

Foucault, M. (1970) *The Order of Things: An Archaeology of the Human Sciences*. London: Tavistock.

Foucault, M. (1973) *Birth of the Clinic: An Archaeology of Medical Perception*. London: Tavistock.

Foucault, M. (1976) Two lectures. In M. Foucualt (ed.) (1980) *Power/Knowledge*, pp. 79–108. New York: Pantheon.

Foucault, M. (1977) *Discipline and Punish: The Birth of the Prison*. London: Allen Lane.

Foucault, M. (1978) *The History of Sexuality, Vol. I: An Introduction*. London: Allen Lane.

Focuault, M. (1980) *Power/Knowledge: Selected Interviews and Other Writings 1972–1977*. New York: Pantheon.

Foucault, M. (1983a) 'Structuralism and post-structuralism: an interview with Michel Foucault', *Telos*, 55: 195–211.

Foucault, M. (1983b) On the genealogy of ethics: an overview of work in progress. In H. L. Dreyfus and P. Rabinow (eds), *Michel Foucault: Beyond Structuralism and Hermeneutics* (2nd edn), pp. 229–252. Chicago: University of Chicago Press.

Foucault, M. (1984) Preface to *The History of Sexuality, Volume II*, in P. Rabinow (ed.), *The Foucault Reader*, pp. 333–339. London: Penguin.

Foucault, M. (1985) *The Use of Pleasure: The History of Sexuality, Vol. II*. Pantheon: New York.

Foucault, M. (1986) *The Care of the Self: The History of Sexuality, Vol. III*. Pantheon: New York.

Fournier, V. and Grey, C. (2000) 'At the critical moment: conditions and prospects for critical management studies', *Human Relations*, 53 (1): 7–32.

Fournier, V. and Kelemen, M. (2001) 'The crafting of community: recoupling discourses of management and womanhood', *Gender, Work and Organisation*, 8 (3): 267–290.

Fritsche, D. J. and Becker, H. (1984) 'Linking management behavior to ethical philosophy – an empirical investigation', *Academy of Management Journal*, 27: 166–175.

Frye, M. (1990) 'A response to lesbian ethics', *Hypatia*, 5 (3): 132–137.

Fuss, D. (1989) *Essentially Speaking: Feminism, Nature, and Difference*. New York: Routledge.

Fuss, D. (1991) *Inside/Out: Lesbian Theories, Gay Theories*. New York: Routledge.

Gabriel, Y. (2000) *Storytelling in Organizations: Facts, Fictions, and Fantasies*. New York: Oxford University Press.

Gamson, J. (1996) Must identity movements self-destruct? In S. Seidman (ed.), *Queer Theory/Sociology*, pp. 395–420. Oxford: Blackwell.

Gamson, J. (2000) Sexualities, queer theory and qualitative research. In N. K. Denzin and Y. Lincoln (eds), *The SAGE Handbook of Qualitative Research*, pp. 347–365. Thousand Oaks, CA: Sage.

Gardiner, J. K. (ed) (2002) *Masculinity Studies and Feminist Theory: New Directions*. New York: Columbia University Press.

Garfinkel, H. (1967) *Studies in Ethnomethodology*. Englewood Cliffs, NJ: Prentice Hall.

Gastelaars, M. (2002) How do statistical aggregates work? About the individual and organizational effects of general classifications. In B. Czarniawska and H. Höpfl (eds), *Casting the Other: The Production and Maintenance of Inequalities in Work Organizations*, pp. 7–22. London: Routledge.

Geertz, C. (1973) *The Interpretation of Cultures: Selected Essays*. New York: Basic.

Geertz, C. (1988) *Works and Lives: An Anthropologist as Author*. Cambridge: Polity.

Gephart, R. P. Jr (1986) 'Deconstructing the defense for quantification in social science: a content analysis of journal articles on the parametric strategy', *Qualitative Sociology*, 9 (2): 126–144.

Gephart, R. P. Jr (1988) *Ethnostatistics: Qualitative Foundations for Quantitative Research*. Thousand Oaks, CA: Sage.

Gephart, R. P. Jr (2004) Ethnostatistics. In M. Lewis-Beck, A. Bryman and T. Futing Liao (eds), *Encyclopaedia for Research Methods for the Social Sciences*. Thousand Oaks, CA: Sage.

Gephart, R. P. Jr (2006) 'Ethnostatistics and organizational research methodologies: an introduction', *Organizational Research Methods*, 9 (4): 417–431.

Gherardi, S. (1994) 'The gender we think, the gender we do in our everyday organizational lives', *Human Relations*, 47 (6): 591–610.

Gherardi, S. (1995) *Gender, Symbolism and Organizational Cultures*. London: Sage.

Gherardi, S. (1996) 'Gendered organizational cultures: narratives of women travellers in a male world', *Gender, Work and Organization*, 3 (4): 187–201.

Gherardi, S. and Nicolini, D. (2000) 'To transfer is to transform: the circulation of safety knowledge', *Organization*, 7 (2): 329–348.

Gibbons, M., Limoges, C., Nowotny, H., Schwartzman, S., Scott, P. and Trow, M. (1994) *The New Production of Knowledge: The Dynamics of Science and Research in Contemporary Societies*. London: Sage.

Giddens, A. (1986) *The Constitution of Society: Outline of the Theory of Structuration*. Berkeley: University of California Press.

Giddens, A. (1987) *Social Theory and Modern Sociology*. Stanford: Stanford University Press.

Giddens, A. (1991) *The Consequences of Modernity*. Stanford: Stanford University Press.

Gill, J. and Johnson, P. (2002) *Research Methods for Managers*. London: Sage.

Gillies, V. and Alldred, P. (2002) The ethics of intention: research as a political tool. In M. Mauthner, M. Birch, J. Jessop and T. Miller (eds), *Ethics in Qualitative Research*, pp. 32–52. London: Sage.

Gilligan, C. (1977) 'In a different voice: women's conception of the self and of morality', *Harvard Educational Review*, 47 (4): 481–517.

Gilligan, C. (1982) *In a Different Voice: Psychological Theory and Women's Development*. Cambridge, MA: Harvard University Press.

Gilligan, C. (1987) Moral orientation and moral development. In E. F. Kutay and D. T. Mayers (eds), *Women and Moral Theory*. London: Rowan & Littlefield.

Gioia, D. A. and Thomas, J. B. (1996) 'Institutional identity, image, and issue interpretation: sensemaking during strategic change in academia', *Administrative Science Quarterly*, 41 (3): 370–403.

Gioia, D. A. and Pitre, E. (1990) 'Multiparadigm perspectives on theory building', *Academy of Management Review*, 15: 584–602.

Glaser, B. and Strauss, A. L. (1967) *The Discovery of Grounded Theory: Strategies for Qualitative Research*. Chicago, IL: Aldine De Gruyter.

Glass, J. and Camarigg, V. (1992) 'Gender, parenthood, and job-family compatibility', *American Journal of Sociology*, 98: 131–151.

Goldman, R. and Papson, S. (1994) The postmodernism that failed. In D. R. Dickens and A. Fontana (eds), *Postmodernism and Social Inquiry*. New York: Guilford.

Goles, T. and Hirschheim, R. (2000) 'The paradigm is dead, the paradigm is dead ... long live the paradigm: the legacy of Burell and Morgan', *Omega*, 28: 249–268.

Gouldner, A. W. (1970) *The Coming Crisis of Western Sociology*. New York: Basic.

Grey, C. and Mitev, N. (1995) 'Management education: a polemic', *Management Learning*, 26 (1): 73–90.

Grey, C. and Sturdy, A. (2007) 'Friendship and organizational analysis: towards a research agenda', *Journal of Management Inquiry*, 16 (2): 157–172.

Guba, E. G. and Lincoln, Y. S. (1994) Competing paradigms in qualitative research. In N. K. Denzin and Y. S. Lincoln (eds), *Handbook of Qualitative Research*, pp. 105–117. Thousand Oaks, CA: Sage.

Gubrium, J. F. and. Holstein, J. A. (eds) (2001) *The Handbook of Interview Research: Context and Method*. London: Sage.

Hackman, J. R. and Oldham, G. R. (1976) 'Motivation through the design of work: test of a theory', *Organizational Behavior and Human Performance*, 16: 250–279.

Halberstam, J. (1998) *Female Masculinity*. London: Duke University Press.

Hales, C. (1993) *Managing Through Organisation*. London: Routledge.

Hall, D. E. (2003) *Queer Theories*. Basingstoke: Palgrave/Macmillan.

Hall, M. (1989) Private experiences in the public domain: lesbians in organizations. In J. Hearn, D.L. Sheppard, P. Tancred-Sheriff and G. Burrell (eds), *The Sexuality of Organization*. London: Sage.

Halperin, D. M. (1995) *Saint Foucault: Towards a Gay Hagiography*. Oxford: Oxford University Press.

Hammer, M. (1990) 'Re-engineering work: don't automate, obliterate', *Harvard Business Review*, July–August: 104–112.

Hammer, M. and Champy, J. (1993) *Re-engineering the Corporation: A Manifesto for Business Revolution*. New York: Harper Business.

Hammersley, M. (1992) 'On feminist methodology', *Sociology*, 26 (2): 187–206.

Hammersley, M. (1994) 'On feminist methodology: a response', *Sociology*, 28 (1): 293–300.

Hammersley, M. and Atkinson, P. (1995) *Ethnography: Principles in Practice*, 2nd edition. New York: Routledge.

Hancock, P. (2004) *On Aesthetics and Organization: A Critical Engagement*. Unpublished PhD thesis, Keele University.

Hancock, P. and Taylor, M. (2004) 'MOT your life: critical management studies and the management of everyday life', *Human Relations*, 57 (5): 619–645.

Haraway, D. (2004) *The Haraway Reader*. New York: Routledge.

Harding, S. G. (ed) (1987) *Feminism and Methodology: Social Science Issues*. Bloomington: Indiana University Press.

Hardy, C. and Leiba-O'Sullivan, S. (1998) 'The power behind empowerment: implications for research and practice', *Human Relations*, 51 (4): 451–483.

Hartsock, N. (1983) The feminist standpoint: developing the ground for a specifically feminist historical materialism. In S. Harding and M. B. Hintikka (eds), *Discovering Reality*. Dordrecht: Reidel.

Hartsock, N. (1987) 'Rethinking modernism: minority vs. majority theories', *Cultural Critique*, 7: 187–206.

Hartsock, N. (1990) Foucault on power: a theory for women? In L. Nicholson (ed.), *Feminism/ Postmodernism*, pp. 157–175. New York and London: Routledge.

Hassard, J. (1991) 'Multiple paradigms and organizational analysis: a case study', *Organisation Studies*, 12 (2): 279–299.

Hassard, J. (1993) *Sociology and Organization Theory: Positivism, Paradigms and Postmodernity*. Cambridge: Cambridge University Press.

Hassard, J. (1995) *Sociology and Organization Theory*. Cambridge: Cambridge University Press.

Hassard, J. and Kelemen, M. L. (2002) 'Production and consumption in organizational knowledge: the case of the "paradigms debate"', *Organization*, 9 (2): 331–355.

Hassard, J. and Parker, M. (eds) (1993) *Postmodernism and Organization*. Newbury Park, CA: Sage.

Hassard, J., McCann, L. and Morris, J. (2007) 'At the sharp end of new organizational ideologies: ethnography and the study of multinationals', *Ethnography*, 9 (8): 324–344.

Hearn, J. (2000) 'On the complexity of feminist intervention in organizations', *Organization*, 7 (4): 609–624.

Hearn, J., Sheppard, D. L., Tancred-Sheriff, P. and Burrell, G. (eds) (1989) *The Sexuality of Organization*. London: Sage.

Herts, R. (ed.) (1997) *Reflexivity and Voice*. Thousand Oaks, CA: Sage.

Hodgson, D. (2005) 'Putting on a professional performance: performativity, subversion and project management', *Organization* 12 (1): 51–68.

Holland, R. (1999) 'Reflexivity', *Human Relations*, 52 (4): 463–90.

Holliday, R. (2004) 'Filming the closet: the role of video diaries in researching sexualities', *American Behavioral Scientist*, 47 (12): 1597–1616.

Horsted, J. and Doherty, N. (1994) 'Poles apart?: integrating business process redesign and human resource management', *Business Change and Re-engineering*, 1 (4): 49–56.

Hotho, S. and Pollard, D. (2007) 'Management as negotiation at the interface: moving beyond the critical—practice impasse', *Organization*, 14 (4): 583–603.

Huff, A. S. (2000) '1999 presidential address: changes in organizational knowledge production', *Academy of Management Review*, 25 (2): 288–293.

Huselid, M. A. (1995) 'The impact of human resource management practices on turnover, productivity, and corporate financial performance', *Academy of Management Journal*, 38: 635–672.

Huselid, M. A., Jackson, S. E. and Schuler, R. S. (1997) 'Technical and strategic human resource management effectiveness as determinants of firm performance', *Academy of Management Journal*, 40 (1): 171–188.

Hutcheon, L. (1989) *The Politics of Postmodernism*. London: Routledge.

Huyssen, A. (1984) 'Mapping the postmodern', *New German Critique*, 33: 5–52.

Ichniowski, C., Kochan, T., Levin, D., Olson, C. and Strauss, G. (1996) 'What works at work: overview and assessment', *Industrial Relations*, 35 (3): 299–333.

Inglis, S. (1994) *Making the Most of Action Learning*. Brookfield, VT: Gower.

Jagose, A. (1996) *Queer Theory: An Introduction*. Melbourne: Melbourne University Press.

James, W. (1907) *Pragmatism: A New Way for Some Old Ways of Thinking*. Cambridge, MA: Riverside.

James, W. (1897/1956) *The Will to Believe*. New York: Dover.

Jayaratne, T. (1993) Quantitative methodology and feminist research. In M. Hammersley (ed.), *Social Research: Philosophy, Politics and Practice*, pp. 109–123. London: Sage.

Jayaratne, T. and Stewart, A. (1991) Quantitative and qualitative methods in the social sciences: current feminist issues and practical strategies. In M. Fonow and J. Cook (eds), *Beyond Methodology: Feminist Scholarship as Lived Research*, pp. 85–106. Bloomington: Indiana University Press.

Jeffreys, S. (2003) *Unpacking Queer Politics: A Lesbian Feminist Perspective*. Cambridge: Polity.

Johnson, P. and Duberley, J. (2003) 'Reflexivity in Management Research', *Journal of Management Studies* 40 (6): 1279–1303.

Jones, C. (2003) 'As if business ethics were possible, "within Such Limits"...', *Organization*, 10 (2): 223–248.

Jones, C. (2004) Jacques Derrida. In S. Linstead (ed.), *Organization Theory and Postmodern Thought*, pp. 34–63. London: Sage.

Joshi, H., Makepeace, G. and Dolton, P. (2007) 'More or less unequal? Evidence on the pay of men and women from the British Birth Cohort Studies', *Gender, Work and Organization*, 14 (1): 37–55.

Kanter, R. M. (1977) *Men and Women of the Corporation*. New York: Basic.

Katz, D. and Kahn, R. L. (1978) *The Social Psychology of Organizations* (2nd edn). New York: Wiley.

Kelemen, M. (2000) 'Too much or too little ambiguity: the language of total quality management', *Journal of Management Studies*, 37 (4): 483–498.

Kelemen, M. (2003) *Managing Quality: Managerial and Critical Perspectives*. London: Sage.

Kelemen, M. and Bansal, P. (2002) 'The conventions of management research and their relevance to management practice', *British Journal of Management* 13 (2): 97–108.

Kelemen, M. and Peltonen, T. (2001) 'Ethics, morality and the subject: the contribution of Zygmunt Bauman and Michel Foucault to "postmodern" business ethics', *Scandinavian Journal of Management*, 17 (2): 151–166.

Kerfoot, D. and Whitehead, S. (1998) '"Boys own" stuff: masculinity and the management of further education', *The Sociological Review*, 46 (3): 436–457.

Kerfoot, D. and Whitehead, S. (2000) 'Keeping all the balls in the air: further education and the masculine/managerial subject', *Journal of Further and Higher Education*, 24 (2): 183–201.

Kilduff, M. (1993) 'Deconstructing Organizations', *The Academy of Management Review*, 18(1): 13–31.

Kilduff, M. and Kelemen, M. (2004) Deconstructing discourse. In D. Grant, C. Hardy, C. Oswick, N. Phillips and L. Putnam (eds), *The SAGE Handbook of Organizational Discourse*, pp. 259–272. London: Sage.

Kilduff, M. and Mehra, A. (1997) 'Postmodernism and organizational research', *Academy of Management Review*, 22 (2): 453–481.

Kilduff, M. and Oh, H. (2006) 'Deconstruction diffusion: an ethnostatistical examination of medical innovation network data reanalyses', *Organizational Research Methods*, 9 (4): 432–455.

King, J. R. (1999) 'Am not! Are too! Using queer standpoint in postmodern critical ethnography', *International Journal of Qualitative Studies in Education*, 12 (5): 473–490.

King, N. (2004) Using interviews in qualitative research. In C. Cassell and G. Symon (eds), *Essential Guide to Qualitative Methods in Organizational Research*, pp. 11–22. London: Sage.

Kirsch, G. E. (2005) 'Friendship, friendliness, and feminist fieldwork', *Signs: Journal of Women in Culture and Society*, 30 (4): 2163–2172.

Kirsch, M. H. (2001) *Queer Theory and Social Change*. London: Routledge.

Knights, D. and McCabe, D. (1996) 'An evaluation of quality in financial services: problems and prospects', *Managing Service Quality*, 6 (1): 18–21.

Knights, D. and McCabe, D. (1998) 'What happens when the phone goes wild?: staff, stress and spaces for escape in a BPR telephone banking work regime', *Journal of Management Studies*, 35 (2): 163–194.

Knights, D. and McCabe, D. (1999) 'There are no limits to authority? TQM and organizational power relations', *Organization Studies*, 20 (2): 197–224.

Knights, D. and Morgan, G. (1995) 'Strategy under the microscope: strategic management and IT in financial services', *Journal of Management Studies*, 32 (2): 191–214.

Knorr-Cetina, K. D. (1983) The ethnographic study of scientific work: towards a constructivist interpretation of science. In K. D. Knorr-Cetina and M. Mulkay (eds), *Science Observed: Perspectives on the Social Study of Science*. Beverley Hills, CA: Sage.

Kolb, D. A., Rubin, I. M. and McIntyre, J. (eds) (1971) *Organizational Psychology: An Experiential Approach*. Englewood Cliffs, NJ: Prentice Hall.

Kondo, D. K. (1990) *Crafting Selves: Power, Gender and Discourses of Identity in a Japanese Workplace*. Chicago: Chicago University Press.

Kong, T. S. K., Mahoney, D. and Plummer, K. (2001) Queering the interview. In J. F. Gubrium and. J. A. Holstein (eds), *The Handbook of Interview Research: Context and Method*, pp. 239–58. London: Sage.

Koot, W., Sabelis, I. and Ybema, S. (1996) Global identity-local oddity? Paradoxical processes in contemporary organizations. In W. Koot, I. Sabelis and S. Ybema (eds), *Contradictions in Context*, pp. 1–16. Amsterdam: VU University Press.

Kuhn, T. S. (1962) *The Structure of Scientific Revolutions*. Chicago: Chicago University Press.

Kunda, G. (1992) *Engineering Culture: Control and Commitment in a High Tech Corporation*. Philadelphia, PA: Temple University Press.

Kuspit, D. (1990) The contradictory character of postmodernism. In H. J. Silverman (ed.), *Postmodernism – Philosophy and the Arts*. New York: Routledge.

Kvale, S. (1996) *InterViews: An Introduction to Qualitative Research Interviewing*. Thousand Oaks, CA: Sage.

Labovitz, L. (1972) 'Statistical usage in sociology: sacred cows and ritual', *Sociological Methods and Research*, 1: 13–37.

Labovitz, S. and Hagedorn, R. (1971) *Introduction to Social Research*. New York: McGraw Hill.

LaCapra, D. (1987) *History, Politics, and the Novel*. Ithaca: NY: Cornell University Press.

Lakatos, I. (1970) Falsification and the methodology of scientific research programmes. In I. Lakatos and A. Musgrave (eds), *Criticism and the Growth of Knowledge*, pp. 91–196. New York: Cambridge University Press.

Latour, B. (1987) *Science in Action: How to Follow Scientists and Engineers through Society*. Milton Keynes: Open University Press.

Latour, B. (1996) 'The trouble with actor-network theory', *Philosophia*, 25 (93–4): 47–64.

Lawrence, T. B. and Hardy, C. (1999) 'Building bridges for refugees: toward a typology of bridging organizations', *Journal of Applied Behavioral Science*, 35 (1): 48–70.

Lawson, T. (1999) 'Feminism, realism and universalism', *Feminist Economics*, 5 (20): 25–59.

Learmonth, M. (1999) 'The NHS manager: engineer and father? A deconstruction', *Journal of Management Studies*, 36 (7): 999–1012.

LeClere, F. B., Rogers, R. G. and Peters, K. (1998) 'Neighborhood social context and racial differences in women's heart disease mortality', *Journal of Health and Social Behavior*, 39: 91–107.

Lee, H. (2004) The public and the private manager: queer(y)ing health management. In M. Learmonth and N. Harding (eds) *Unmasking Health Management: A Critical Text,* pp. 129–142. New York: Nova Science.

Legge, K. (1995) *Human Resource Management: Rhetorics and Realities*. Basingstoke: Macmillan.

Legge, K. (1998) Is HRM ethical? Can HRM be ethical? In M. Parker (ed.), *Ethics and Organizations*, pp. 53–75. London: Sage.

Legge, K. (2001) Silver bullet or spent round? Assessing the meaning of the 'high commitment management/performance relationship'. In J. Storey (ed.), *Human Resource Management: A Critical Text*, pp. 21–36. Padstow, Cornwall: Thomson Learning.

Legge, K. (2005) *Human Resource Management: Rhetorics and Realities* (2nd edition). Basingstoke: Palgrave/Macmillan.

Leonard, P. (2003) 'Playing doctors and nurses? Competing discourses of gender, power and identity in the British National Health Service', *The Sociological Review*, 51 (2): 218–237.

Letherby, G. (2003) *Feminist Research in Theory and Practice*. Buckingham: Open University Press.

Letherby, G. (2004) 'Quoting and counting: an autobiographical response to Oakley', *Sociology*, 38 (1): 175–189.

Lewis, M. W. and Grimes, A. J. (1999) 'Metatriangulation: building theory from multiple paradigms', *Academy of Management Review*, 24 (4): 672–690.

Lewis, M. W. and Kelemen, M. L. (2002) 'Multiparadigm inquiry: exploring organizational pluralism and paradox', *Human Relations*, 55 (2): 251–275.

Lilley, S. (2001) Conspiracy, what conspiracy?: social science, funding and the politics of accusation. In J. Parish and M. Parker (eds), *Conspiracy Theory*. Oxford: Blackwell.

Lincoln, Y. S and Cuba, E. G. (1985) *Naturalistic Inquiry*. Newbury Park, CA: Sage.

Lincoln, Y. S and Denzin, N. K. (1998) The fifth moment. In N. K. Denzin and Y. S. Lincoln (eds), *The Landscape of Qualitative Research: The Theories and Issues*, pp. 407–430. London: Sage.

Linstead, A. and R. Thomas (2002) 'What do you want from me? A post-structuralist feminist reading of middle managers' identities', *Culture and Organization*, 8 (1): 1–21.

Linstead, S.A. (2000) Ashes and madness: the play of negativity and the poetics of organization. In S. A. Linstead and H. J. Höpfl (2000) *The Aesthetics of Organization*, pp. 61–92. London: Sage.

Linstead, S. A. (ed) (2004) *Organization Theory and Postmodern Thought*. London: Sage.

Lloyd, G. (1984) *The Man of Reason: 'Male' and 'Female' in Western Philosophy*. London: Routledge.

Luker, B., Luker, B. Jr., Cobb, S. L. and Brown, R. (1998) 'Postmodernism, institutionalism, and statistics: considerations for an institutionalist statistical method', *Journal of Economic Issues*, 32 (2): 449–456.

Lynch, M. (2000) 'Against reflexivity as an academic virtue and source of privileged knowledge', *Theory, Culture and Society*, 17 (3): 26–54.

Lyotard, J. F. (1984) *The Postmodern Condition: A Report on Knowledge* (trans. Geoffrey Bennington and Brian Massumi). Minneapolis: University of Minnesota Press.

Mabey, C., Skinner, D. and Clark, T. (1998) *Experiencing Human Resource Management*. London: Sage.

Malinowski, B. (1922) *Argonauts of the Western Pacific*. London: Routledge and Kegan Paul.

Mannheim, K. (1936) *Ideology and Utopia*. London: Routledge and Kegan Paul.

Manzo, K. (1991) 'Modernist discourse and the crisis of development theory', *Studies in Comparative International Development*, 26 (2): 3–36.

March, J. G. and Simon, H. (1958) *Organizations*. New York: Wiley.

Marquardt, M. (2000) 'Action learning and leadership', *The Learning Organization*, 7 (5): 233–240.

Marquardt, M. (2004) *Optimising the Power of Action Learning*. Palo Alto, CA: Davies-Black.

Marquardt, M. and Waddill, D. (2004) 'The power of learning in action learning: a conceptual analysis of how the five schools of adult learning theories are incorporated within the practice of action learning', *Action Learning: Research and Practice*, 1 (2): 185–202.

Marsden, P. V. and Podolny, J. (1990) Dynamic analysis of network diffusion processes. In H. Flap and J. Wessie (eds), *Social Networks Through Time*, pp. 197–214. Utrecht: ISOR.

Martin, J. (1990) 'Deconstructing organizational taboos: the suppression of gender conflict in organizations', *Organization Science*, 1 (4): 339–359.

Martin, J. (1992) *Cultures in Organizations: Three Perspectives*. New York: Oxford University Press.

Mauthner, M., Birch, M., Jessop, J. and Miller, T. (eds) (2002) *Ethics in Qualitative Research*. London: Sage.

McCloskey, D. N. (1994) *Knowledge and Persuasion in Economics*. Cambridge: Cambridge University Press.

McGill, I. and Beaty, L. (1995) *Action Learning: A Guide for Professional Management and Educational Development*. London: Kogan Page.

McGregor, J. and Tweed, D. (2002) 'Female small business owners in New Zealand', *Gender, Work and Organization*, 9 (4): 420–438.

McKinley, W. (1995) Commentary: towards a reconciliation of the theory-pluralism in strategic management – incommensurability and the constructivist approach of the Erlangen School. In P. Shrivastava and C. Stubbart (eds), *Advances in Strategic Management 12A*, pp. 249–260. Greenwich, CT: Jay Press.

McNay, L. (1992) *Foucault and Feminism: Power, Gender and the Self*. Cambridge: Polity.

McNay, L. (2000) *Gender and Agency: Reconfiguring the Subject in Feminist and Social Theory*. Cambridge: Polity.

McRuer, R. (2003) 'AS GOOD AS IT GETS: queer theory and critical disability', *GLQ: A Journal of Lesbian and Gay Studies*, 9 (1–2): 79–105.

McWhorter, L. (1999) *Bodies and Pleasure: Foucault and the Politics of Sexual Normalization*. Bloomington: Indiana University Press.

Meezan, W. and Martin, J. I. (eds) (2003) *Research Methods with Gay, Lesbian, Bisexual, and Transgender Populations*. New York: Harrington Park.

Merton, R. K., Fiske, M. and Kendall, P. (1956) *The Focused Interview: A Manual of Problems and Procedures*. Glencoe, IL: Free Press.

Mingers, J. (1997) Multi-paradigm methodology. In J. Mingers and A. Gills (eds), *Multimethodology*, pp. 1–22. New York: Wiley.

Mintzberg, H. (1973) *The Nature of Managerial Work*. New York: Harper and Row.

Morgan, G. (1983) *Beyond Method*. Newbury Park, CA: Sage.

Morgan, G. and Smircich, L. (1980) 'The case for qualitative research', *The Academy of Management Review*, 5 (4): 491–500.

Mottier, V. (2007) 'Pragmatism and feminist theory', *European Journal of Social Theory*, 7 (3): 323–335.

Munro, R. (1995) 'Managing by ambiguity: an archaeology of the social in the absence of management accounting', *Critical Perspectives on Accounting*, 6 (4): 433–448.

Namaste, K. (1996) The politics of inside/out: queer theory, poststructuralism, and a sociological approach to sexuality. In S. Seidman (ed.), *Queer Theory/Sociology*, pp. 194–212. Oxford: Blackwell.

Namaste, V. (2000) *Invisible Lives: The Erasure of Transsexual and Transgender People*. Chicago: University of Chicago Press.

Neal, R. and Gordon, J. (2001) 'Fieldwork among friends', *Resources for Feminist Research*, 28 (3–4): 99–113.

Newton, T. and Findlay, P. (1996) 'Playing God? The performance of appraisal', *Human Resource Management Journal*, 6 (3): 42–58.

Noddings, N. (1984) *Caring: A Feminine Approach to Ethics and Moral Education*. Berkeley and Los Angeles: University of California Press.

Nord, W. and Jermier, J. (1992) Critical social sciences for managers? Promising and perverse possibilities. In M. Alvesson and H. Willmott (eds), *Critical Management Studies*, pp. 202–222. London: Sage.

Nordenmark, M. (2002) 'Multiple social roles – a resource or a burden: is it possible for men and women to combine paid work with family life in a satisfactory way?', *Gender, Work and Organization*, 9 (2): 125–145.

Norris, C. (2002) *Deconstruction*. London: Routledge.

Nussbaum, M. (1992) 'Human functioning and social justice: in defense of Aristotelian essentialism', *Political Theory*, 20 (2): 202–246.

Nussbaum, M. (1999) *Sex and Social Justice*. Oxford: Oxford University Press.

Nussbaum, M. (2000) *Women and Human Development: The Capabilities Approach*. Cambridge: Cambridge University Press.

Oakley, A. (1981) Interviewing women: a contradiction in terms. In H. Roberts (ed.), *Doing Feminist Research*, pp. 30–61. London: Routledge and Kegan Paul.

Oakley, A. (1998) 'Gender, methodology and people's ways of knowing: some problems with feminism and the paradigm debate in social science', *Sociology*, 32 (4): 707–731.

Oakley, A. (2000) *Experiments in Knowing: Gender and Method in the Social Sciences*. Cambridge: Polity.

Orlikowski, W. J. (1992). 'The duality of technology: rethinking the concept of technology in organizations', *Organization Science*, 3 (3): 398–427.

Osborne, P. and Segal, L. (1994) 'Gender as performance: an interview with Judith Butler', *Radical Philosophy*, 67, Summer Issue.

Oultram, T. (2007) *Action Learning in the Micro Firm: A Critical Review*. Unpublished MRes thesis, Keele University.

Parker, M. (1992) 'Post-modern organizations or postmodern organization theory?', *Organization Studies*, 13 (1): 1–17.

Parker, M. (1995) 'Critique in the name of what? Postmodernism and critical approaches to organization', *Organization Studies*, 16 (4): 553–565.

Parker, M. (ed.) (1998) *Ethics and Organizations*. London: Sage.

Parker, M. (2000) *Organizational Culture and Identity*. London: Sage.

Parker, M. (2001) 'Fucking management: queer, theory and reflexivity', *Ephemera: Critical Dialogues on Organization*, 1 (1): 36–53.

Parker, M. (2002a) *Against Management: Organization in the Age of Managerialism*. Cambridge: Polity.

Parker, M. (2002b) 'Queering management and organization', *Gender, Work and Organization*, 9 (2): 146–166.

Parker, M. (2006) 'Stockholm syndrome', *Management Learning*, 37 (1): 39–41.

Parker, M. and McHugh, G. (1991) 'Five texts in search of an author: a response to John Hassard's multiple paradigms and organizational analysis', *Organization Studies*, 12 (3): 451–456.

Parkhe, A. (1993) '"Messy" research, methodological predispositions, and theory development in international joint ventures', *The Academy of Management Review*, 18 (2): 227–268.

Pearson, G. (1995) *Integrity in Organizations: An Alternative Business Ethics*. London: McGraw-Hill International.

Petersen, A. (1998) *Unmasking the Masculine: 'Men' and 'Identity' in a Sceptical Age*. Thousand Oaks, CA: Sage.

Pfeffer, J. (1993) 'Barriers to the advance of organizational science: paradigm development as a dependent variable', *Academy of Management Review*, 18 (4): 599–620.

Pfeffer, J. (1997) 'Mortality, reproducibility, and the persistence of styles of theory', *Organization Science*, 6 (4): 681–686.

Pollner, M. (1991) 'Left of ethnomethodology: the rise and decline of radical reflexivity', *American Sociological Review*, 56 (3): 370–380.

Prasad, A. and Prasad, P. (2002) Otherness at large: identity and difference in the new globalized organizational landscape. In I. Aaltio and A. J. Mills (eds), *Gender, Identity and the Culture of Organizations*, pp. 57–71. London: Routledge.

Pugh, A. (1990) My statistics and feminism – a true story. In L. Stanley (ed.), *Feminist Praxis*, pp. 103–113. London: Routledge

Pullen, A. (2006) 'Gendering the research self: social practice and corporeal multiplicity in the writing of organizational research', *Gender, Work & Organization,* 13(3): 277–98.

Puwar, N. (1997) 'Reflections on interviewing women MPs', *Sociological Research Online*, 2(1), at http://www.socresonline.org.uk/socresonline/2/1/4.html

Raelin, J. A. and Schermerhorn, J. (1994) 'A new paradigm for advanced management education – how knowledge merges with experience', *Management Learning*, 25 (2): 195–200.

Ramazanoglu, C. and Holland, J. (2002) *Feminist Methodology: Challenges and Choices*. London: Sage.

Raymond, J. (1986) *A Passion for Friends: Toward a Philosophy of Female Affection*. Boston, MA: Beacon.

Reed, M. (1985) *Redirections in Organizational Analysis*. London: Tavistock.

Reed, M. (1997) 'In praise of duality and dualism: rethinking agency and structure in organizational analysis', *Organization Studies*, 18 (1): 21–42.

Reinharz, S. (1979) *On Becoming a Social Scientist: From Survey Research and Participant Observation to Experiential Analysis*. San Francisco, CA: Jossey-Bass.

Reinharz, S. (1984) *On Becoming a Social Scientist*. New Brunswick, NJ: Transaction.

Reinharz, S. (1992) *Feminist Methods in Social Research*. New York: Oxford University Press.

Reinharz, S. and Chase, S. E. (2003) Interviewing women. In J. A. Holstein and J. F. Gubrium, (eds), *Inside Interviewing: New Lenses, New Concerns*, pp. 73–90. London: Sage.

Revans, R. (1980) *Action Learning: New Techniques for Action Learning*. London: Blond & Briggs.

Rhodes, C. (2000) 'Reading and writing organizational lives', *Organization*, 7 (1): 7–29.

Ridgeway, C. (1982) 'Status in groups: the importance of motivation', *American Sociological Review*, 47 (1): 76–88.

Roper, M. (1994) *Masculinity and the British Organizational Man since 1945*. Oxford: Oxford University Press.

Roseneil, S. (2000) 'Queer frameworks and queer tendencies: towards an undersatnding of postmodern transformations of sexuality', *Sociological Research Online*, 5(3), at http://www.socresonline.org.uk/5/3/roseneil.html

Rottmann, C. (2006) 'Queering educational leadership from the inside out', *International Journal of Leadership in Education*, 9 (1): 1–20.

Ruddick, S. (1980) 'Maternal thinking', *Feminist Studies*, 6: 342–364.

Rudy, K. (2000) 'Queer studies and feminism', *Women's Studies*, 29 (2): 195–217.

Rumens, N. (2005) Acting like a professional: identity dilemmas for gay men. In M. S. Breen and F. Peters (eds), *Genealogies of Identity: Interdisciplinary Readings on Sex and Sexuality*, pp. 221–236. Amsterdam: Rodopi.

Rumens, N. (2007) In the company of friends: insights into gay men's friendships at work. In N. Rumens and A. Cervantes-Carson (eds), *Sexual Politics of Desire and Belonging*, pp. 100–123. Amsterdam: Rodopi.

Rumens, N. (2008a) 'Working at intimacy: gay men's workplace friendships', *Gender, Work and Organization*, 15 (1): 9–30.

Rumens, N. (2008b) 'The complexities of friendship: exploring how gay men make sense of their workplace friendships with straight women', *Culture and Organization*, 14 (1): 79–95.

Russell, S.T. (2003) 'Sexual minority youth and suicide risk', *American Behavioral Scientist*, 46: 1241–1257.

Salzinger, L. (2000) 'Manufacturing sexual objects: "harassment", desire and discipline on a Maquiladora shopfloor', *Ethnography*, 1 (1): 67–92.

Sarbin, T. R. and Kitsuse, J. I. (1994) *Constructing the Social*. London: Sage.

Sawicki, J. (1991) *Disciplining Foucault: Feminism, Power and the Body*. New York: Routledge.

Schatzki, T. R. (2001) Introduction: practice theory. In T. R. Schatzki, K. Knorr Cetina and E. von Savigny (eds), *The Practice Turn in Contemporary Theory*, pp. 1–14. London: Routledge.

Scherer, A.G. (1998) 'Pluralism and incommensurability in strategic management and organization theory: a problem in search of a solution', *Organization*, 5 (2): 147–168.

Schultz, M. and Hatch, M. J. (1996) 'Living within multiple paradigms: the case of paradigm interplay in organizational culture studies', *Academy of Management Review*, 1 (2): 529–557.

Schutz, A. (1967) *The Phenomenology of the Social World*. Evanston: Northwestern University Press.

Schwalbe, M. and Wolkomir, M. (2001) 'The masculine self as problem and resource in interview studies of men', *Men and Masculinities*, 4 (1): 90–103.

Scott, W. G. (1992) *Chester I. Barnard and the Guardians of the Managerial State*. Lawrence: University of Kansas Press.

Sedgwick, E. K. (1990) *The Epistemology of the Closet*. Berkeley: University of California Press.

Segal, L. (1990) *Slow Motion: Changing Masculinities, Changing Men*. London: Virago.

Seidman, S. (1993) Identity and politics in a 'postmodern' gay culture: some historical and conceptual notes. In M. Warner (ed.), *Fear of a Queer Planet: Queer Politics and Social Theory*, pp. 105–142. Minneapolis: University of Minnesota.

Seidman, S. (1996) Introduction. In S. Seidman (ed.), *Queer Theory/Sociology*, pp. 1–29. Oxford: Blackwell.

Seidman, S. (1997) *Difference Troubles*. Cambridge: Cambridge University Press.

Seidman, S. (2002) *Beyond the Closet: The Transformation of Gay and Lesbian Life*. New York: Routledge.

Seigfried, C. H. (1996) *Pragmatism and Feminism: Reweaving the Social Fabric*. Chicago: Chicago University Press.

Seigfried, C. H. (ed.) (2001) *Feminist Interpretations of John Dewey*. University Park: Pennsylvania State University Press.

Senge, P. (1990) *The Fifth Discipline: The Art and Practice of the Learning Organization*. New York: Doubleday.

Sevenhuijsen, S. (1998) *Citizenship and the Ethics of Care: Feminist Considerations on Justice, Morality and Politics*. London: Routledge.

Sewell, W. H. (1992) 'A theory of structure: duality, agency and transformation', *American Journal of Sociology*, 98 (1): 1–29.

Shalin, D. N. (1992) 'Critical theory and the pragmatist challenge', *American Journal of Sociology*, 98 (2): 237–279.

Sherry, M. (2004) 'Overlaps and contradictions between queer theory and disability studies', *Disability and Society*, 19 (7): 769–783.

Shield, P. (2003) 'The community of inquiry: classical pragmatism and public administration', *Administration and Society*, 35 (5): 510–538.

Simon, H. A. (1962) 'New developments in the theory of the firm', *American Economic Review*, 52: 1–15.

Simmel, G., Frisby, D. and Featherstone, M. (1997) *Simmel on Culture: Selected Writings*. Thousand Oaks, CA: Sage.

Skeggs, B. (2001) Feminist ethnography. In P. Atkinson, A. Coffey, S. Delamont, J. Lofland and L. Lofland (eds), *Handbook of Ethnography*. London: Sage.

Smedes, L. B. (1991) *Choices: Making Right Decisions in a Complex World*. New York: HarperCollins.

Smircich, L. (1983) 'Concepts of culture and organizational analysis', *Administrative Science Quarterly*, 28: 339–358.

Smith, W., Higgins, M., Parker, M. and Lightfoot, G. (eds) (2001) *Science Fiction and Organization*. London: Routledge.

Sotirin, P. and Tyrell, M. (1998) 'Wondering about critical management studies', *Management Communication Quarterly*, 12 (2): 303–336.

Spender, J. C. (1998) 'Pluralist epistemology and the knowledge-based theory of the firm', *Organization*, 5 (2): 233–256.

Sprague, J. (2005) *Feminist Methodologies for Critical Researchers: Bridging Differences*. Lanham, MD: AltaMira/Rowman & Littlefield.

Spurlin, W. J. (2006) *Imperialism Within the Margins: Queer Representation and the Politics of Culture in Southern Africa*. Basingstoke: Palgrave/Macmillan.

Stanley, L. and Wise, S. (1983) *Breaking Out: Feminist Consciousness and Feminist Research*. London: Routledge and Kegan Paul.

Stanley, L. and Wise, S. (1990) Method, methodology and epistemology in feminist research processes. In L. Stanley (ed.), *Feminist Praxis*, pp. 20–60. London: Routledge.

Stanley, L. and Wise, S. (1993) *Breaking Out Again: Feminist Ontology and Epistemology*. Abingdon: Routledge.

Stanley, L. and Wise, S. (2000) 'But the empress has no clothes: some awkward questions about the "missing revolution" in feminist theory', *Feminist Theory*, 1 (3): 261–288.

Stewart, R. (1989) 'Studies of managerial jobs and behaviour: the ways forward', *Journal of Management Studies*, 26 (1): 71–93.

Stoltenberg, J. (1990) *Refusing to be a Man: Essays in Sex and Justice*. California and Suffolk: Fontana/Collins.

Strang, D. and Tuma, N. B. (1993) 'Spatial and temporal heterogeneity in diffusion', *American Journal of Sociology*, 99: 614–639.

Strinati, D. (1993) 'The big nothing? Contemporary culture and the emergence of postmodernism', *The European Journal of Social Sciences*, 6 (3): 359–375.

Suchman, L. (2000) 'Organizing alignment: a case of bridge building', *Organization*, 7 (2): 311–327.

Sullivan, A. (1995) *Virtually Normal: An Argument about Homosexuality*. London: Picador.

Symon, G. (2004) Qualitative research diaries. In C. Cassell and G. Symon (eds), *Essential Guide to Qualitative Methods in Organizational Research*, pp. 98–113. London: Sage.

Talburt, S. (1999) 'Open secrets and problems of queer ethnography: readings from a religious studies classroom', *International Journal of Qualitative Studies in Education*, 12 (5): 525–539.

Talburt, S. (2000) *Subject to Identity: Knowledge, Sexuality, and Academic Practices in Higher Education*. Albany, NY: State University of New York Press.

Taylor, P. and Bain, P. (1999) 'An assembly line in the head: work and employee relations in the call centre', *Industrial Relations Journal*, 30 (2): 101–117.

Tester, K. (1993) *The Life and Times of Post-modernity*. London: Routledge.

Thanem, T. (2006) 'Living on the edge: towards a monstrous organization theory', *Organization*, 13 (2): 163–193.

Thayer, H. S. (1981) *Meaning and Action: A Critical History of Pragmatism*, 2nd edition. Indianapolis: Hackett.

Thayer-Bacon, B. (2003) 'Pragmatism and feminism as qualified relativism', *Studies in Philosophy and Education*, 22 (6): 417–438.

Thomas, C. (2000) Introduction: identification, appropriation, proliferation. In C. Thomas (ed.), *Straight with a Twist: Queer Theory and the Subject of Heterosexuality*, pp. 1–10. Urbana and Chicago: University of Illinois Press.

Thomas, R. and Davies, A. (2005) 'What have feminists done for Us? Feminist theory and organizational resistance', *Organization*, 12 (5): 711–740.

Tierney, W. G. (1997) *Academic Outlaws: Queer Theory and Cultural Studies in the Academy*. Thousand Oaks, CA: Sage.

Tierney, W. G. (2000) Undaunted courage: life history and the postmodern challenge. In N. K. Denzin and Y. S. Lincoln (eds), *The SAGE Handbook of Qualitative Research*, pp. 537–554. London: Sage.

Tobin, R. D. (2005) Kertbeny's 'homosexuality' and the language of nationalism. In M. S. Breen and F. Peters (eds), *Genealogies of Identity: Interdisciplinary Readings on Sex and Sexuality*, pp. 3–18. Amsterdam: Rodopi.

Townley, B. (1992) In the eye of the gaze: the constitutive role of performance appraisal. In P. Barrar and C. Cooper (eds), *Managing Organizations in 1992: Strategic Responses*, pp. 185–202. London: Routledge.

Townley, B. (1993a) 'Foucault, power/knowledge, and its relevance for human resource management', *Academy of Management Review*, 18 (3): 518–545.

Townley, B. (1993b) 'Performance appraisal and the emergence of management', *Journal of Management Studies*, 30 (2): 221–238.

Trevino, L. K. (1986) 'Ethical decision making in organizations: a person-situation interactionist model', *Academy of Management Review*, 11 (3): 601–617.

Trinh, M. (1989) *Native, Woman, Other.* Bloomington: Indiana University Press.

Van den Bulte, C. and Lilien, G. L. (2001) 'Medical innovation revisited: social contagion versus marketing effort', *American Journal of Sociology*, 106: 1409–1435.

Vincke, J. and Bolton, R. (1994) 'Social support, depression and self-acceptance among gay men', *Human Relations*, 47 (9): 1049–1062.

Wajcman, J. (1998) *Managing like a Man: Women and Men in Corporate Management.* Cambridge: Polity.

Walby, S. (1990) *Theorizing Patriarchy.* Oxford: Blackwell.

Walker, M. U. (1992) 'Feminism, Ethics, and the Question of Theory', *Hypatia*, 7 (3): 23–28.

Wallace, M. (1990) 'Can action learning live up to its reputation?', *Management Education and Development*, 21 (2): 89–103.

Ward, J. and Winstanley, D. (2003) 'The absent present: negative space within discourse and the construction of minority sexual identity in the workplace', *Human Relations*, 56 (10): 1255–1280.

Ward, J. and Winstanley, D. (2004) 'Sexuality and the city: exploring the experience of minority sexual identity through storytelling', *Culture and Organization*, 10 (3): 219–236.

Ward, J. and Winstanley, D. (2005) 'Coming out at work: performativity and the recognition and renegotiation of identity', *The Sociological Review*, 53 (3): 447–475.

Ward, J. and Winstanley, D. (2006) 'Watching the watch: the UK Fire Service and its impact on sexual minorities in the workplace', *Gender, Work and Organization*, 13 (2): 193–219.

Warner, D. M. (2004) 'Towards a queer research methodology', *Qualitative Research in Psychology*, 1 (4): 321–337.

Warner, M. (1993) *Fear of a Queer Planet: Queer Politics and Social Theory.* Minneapolis: University of Minnesota.

Warner, M. (1999) *The Trouble with Normal: Sex, Politics, and the Ethics of Queer Life.* New York: Free Press.

Warren, S. (2002) 'Show me how it feels to work here: using photography to research organizational aesthetics', *Ephemera: Theory and Politics in Organization*, 2 (3): 224–245.

Warren, S. (2005) 'Photography and voice in critical qualitative management research', *Accounting, Auditing & Accountability Journal*, 18 (6): 861–882.

Watson, T. (1994) *In Search of Management: Culture, Chaos and Control in Managerial Work.* London: Routledge.

Watson, T. (2001) 'Beyond managism: negotiated narratives and critical management education in practice', *British Journal of Management*, 12 (4): 385–396.

Weber, M. (1930/1992) *The Protestant Ethic and the Spirit of Capitalism* (translated by T. Parsons). London and New York: Routledge.

Weedon, C. (1987/1997) *Feminist Practice and Poststructuralist Theory*. Oxford: Blackwell.

Weeks, J. (1985) *Sexuality and its Discontents: Myths, Meanings and Modern Sexualities*. London: Routledge and Kegan Paul.

Weeks, J. (1995) *Invented Moralities: Sexual Values in an Age of Uncertainty*. Cambridge: Polity.

Weeks, J., Heaphy, B. and Donovan, C. (2001) *Same-Sex Intimacies: Families of Choice and Other Life Experiments*, London: Routledge.

Weick, K. E. (1969) *The Social Psychology of Organizing*. New York: Addison-Wesley.

Weick, K. E. (1976) 'Educational organisations as loosely coupled systems', *Administrative Science Quarterly*, 21: 1–19.

Weick, K. E. (1988) 'Enacted sensemaking in crises situations', *Journal of Management Studies*, 25: 305–317.

Weick, K. E. (1999) 'Theory construction as disciplined reflexivity: tradeoffs of the 90s', *Academy of Management Review*, 24 (4): 797–807.

Weick, K. (2002) 'Essai: real-time reflexivity: prods to reflection', *Organization Studies*, 23 (6): 893–898.

Weinstein, K. (1995) *Action Learning: A Journey in Discovery and Development*. London: Harper-Collins.

Weitzner, D. (2007) 'Deconstruction revisited: implications of theory over methodology', *Journal of Management Inquiry*, 16 (1): 43–54.

Whitbeck, C. (1983) A different reality: feminist ontology. In C. C. Gould (ed.), *Beyond Domination*. Totowa, NJ: Rowman and Allanheld.

White, J. (1999) 'Ethical comportment in organizations: a synthesis of the feminist ethic of care and the Buddhist ethic of compassion', *International Journal of Value-Based Management*, 12 (2): 109–128.

Whitehead, S. (1998) 'Disrupted selves: resistance and identity work in the managerial area', *Gender and Education*, 10 (2): 199–216.

Whitehead, S. (2001) 'The invisible gendered subject: men in education management', *Journal of Gender Studies*, 10 (1): 67–82.

Whitehead, S. (2002) *Men and Masculinities*. Cambridge: Polity.

Whyte, W. F. (1943) *Street Corner Society: The Social Structure of an Italian Slum*. Chicago: Chicago University Press.

Wicks, A. C. and Freeman, E. (1998) 'Organization studies and the new pragmatism: positivism, anti-positivism, and the search for ethics', *Organization Science*, 9 (2): 123–140.

Willmott, H. (1994) 'Management education: provocations to a debate', *Management Learning*, 25 (1): 105–136.

Willmott, H. (1995) 'The odd couple?: Re-engineering business processes: managing human relations', *New Technology, Work and Employment*, 10 (2): 89–98.

Willmott, H. (1998) Towards a new ethics? The contributions of poststructuralism and posthumanism. In M. Parker (ed.), *Ethics and Organizations*, pp. 76–121. London: Sage.

Willmott, H. (2006) 'Pushing at an open door: Mystifying the CMS manifesto', *Management Learning*, 37 (1): 33–37.

Wolf, W. B. (1994) 'Understanding Chester Barnard', *International Journal of Public Administration*, 17 (6): 1035–1069.

Woodall, J. and Winstanley, D. (2001) The place of ethics in HRM. In J. Storey (ed.), *Human Resource Management: A Critical Text*, pp. 37–56. Padstow, Cornwall: Thomson Learning.

Woods, J. D. and Lucas, J. H. (1993) *The Corporate Closet: The Professional Lives of Gay Men in America*. New York: Free Press.

Woolgar, S. (ed.) (1988) *Knowledge and Reflexivity: New Frontiers in the Sociology of Knowledge*. London: Sage.

Wray-Bliss, E. (2002) 'Interpretation-appropriation: (making) an example of labor process theory', *Organizational Research Methods*, 5 (1): 81–104.

Wray-Bliss, E. (2003) 'Research subjects/research subjections: exploring the ethics and politics of critical research', *Organization*, 10 (2): 307–325.

Young, I. M. (1997) *Intersecting Voices: Dilemmas of Gender, Political Philosophy and Policy*. Princeton: Princeton University Press.

Index

Note: the letter 'f' after a page number indicates a figure and the letter 't' a table